The Production

of

Medieval Church

Music-Drama

THE PRODUCTION OF MEDIEVAL CHURCH MUSIC-DRAMA

FLETCHER COLLINS, JR.

THE UNIVERSITY PRESS OF VIRGINIA
CHARLOTTESVILLE

Contents

Illustrations

Preface

MORE than a century has passed since Edmond de Coussemaker published the first collected edition of music-dramas from the repertory of the medieval church. Though unable in those times to transcribe the mensural music into modern notation and so make these plays available for performance, he nevertheless established a canon of plays, the latest and most mature works of the period. Since Coussemaker's there has not been another collected edition of the plays with their music, and the roster of produceable plays has not been much expanded from his, despite more than a hundred years of dedicated scholarship by a number of first-rate investigators.

There are several explanations for this failure to follow up Coussemaker's ardent plea for interpretation of the plays as music-drama, not merely as literary texts. For one thing, musicologists have been able only in the twentieth century to risk a realization of the notation, and much of their work is still unpublished. Meanwhile the literary scholars have settled for what they could practically undertake, a study of the liturgical origins and literary development of the plays from the hundreds of literary texts available. One noteworthy example of their copious work is E. K. Chambers's *The Medieval Stage* (1903). Karl Young's literarily definitive work, *The Drama of the Medieval Church* (1933), contains nearly 1300 pages of texts, documents, analyses, and appraisals. Unfortunately not one of the 1300 pages has a single note of modern musical notation, and most professionals in theater and opera today value Young's work only for its historical contribution. General histories of the theater do not reflect his work.

Young himself was not happy about the limitations of his book. He recognized that his most highly artistic texts were mainly those that had already been published by Coussemaker, and that they could not be fully known or interpreted without their music. While the preface to his work stressed this need, not for another quarter of a century did the void begin to be filled by the public performance of musical scores for nine of the plays: *The Play of Daniel, The Visit to the Sepulcher, The Play of Herod with The*

Slaughter of the Innocents, The Lament of Mary, The Pilgrim, The Shepherds, The Wise and Foolish Maidens, The Three Daughters, and *The Raising of Lazarus.*[1] All of these scores have been tested by public performance in England and America by Noah Greenberg, E. Martin Browne, and the author. At the present writing only seven plays remain to be revived: three slight dramas (*The Three Clerks, The Annunciation,* and *The Purification*), one theatrically awkward play (*The Conversion of St. Paul*), and three major works (*The Image of St. Nicholas, The Son of Getron,* and *The Procession of the Prophets*).

As a practical repertory becomes available, there emerges a need, recognized by current or potential producers of the nine plays now available, for a detailed study of the production elements of all the plays. Without comprehensive and reasonably accurate information, the productions will fail to realize the intentions of their authors and editors. The visualization of the plays is probably as crucial as the realization of their music, both for the producer and for students of this major segment of medieval art. Young was aware also of this need in candidly recounting the shortcomings of his work. "Among the ungrasped opportunities suggested by the present study I would mention, finally, those associated with the physical background of the performances. . . . The final comprehensive study of *mise en scène* in liturgical drama, indeed, has not yet been made."

The present investigation of this matter is not put forward as "the final comprehensive study," but at least it makes an extensive beginning. It utilizes a large body of highly relevant material from the visual arts, a rich source of information not hitherto systematically mined by scholars in this field, and mates this information with the often reticent stage directions in the texts of the plays. The concept of the plays as music-drama is primary, and their full interpretation is regarded as requiring coordinate attention to three aspects: literary text, musical score, and theatrical visualization.

Some literary scholars in the field of medieval drama still insist that we do not really need to know about the nonliterary elements of a play in order to understand and interpret it. There can be no doubt, however, that artists who write in theatrical form have always included a concept of staging in their compositions, and that these practical considerations cooperate with the dialogue to determine the shape and even the action of the play. The medieval playwright-poet-composer also directed the production of his work, as in all great periods of drama. In the scripts of

[1] Six of these plays have been published by the Oxford University Press. A practical repertory is projected in the appendix.

such a playwright the paucity of stage directions is inversely proportional to his concern and responsibility for production patterns, the laconic directions indicating that the playwright staged his own work and communicated in person the fullness of his concept, without having to record it in all its richly functioning detail. For him there was only one way to produce his work: the way he himself composed it and visualized it.

My method of study has been to consider in relation to the musical scores some ten basic production elements: tone and quality, determination of major episodes, characterization, movement and gesture, costumes, properties and furnishings, staging and the definition of acting areas, makeup, lighting, and sound effects. A general introduction in terms of these ten elements is followed by critical analyses of the sixteen plays of the repertory, and by notes on production. Confident appraisal of the plays and full recognition of their individual production requirements are patently impossible for the seven plays of the repertory that remain untried in modern times. Without in any way presuming to dictate to other producers, however, I have attempted to anticipate their requirements in the light of my experience as producer of eight other plays of the repertory. I have tentatively transcribed the scores of all unproduced plays from the original manuscripts as a preliminary to their proper study as music dramas, and several samples of these have been included in order to help suggest the particular tone and quality of a play.

Evidence is presented from the visual arts of many localities; it is usually of the twelfth century or the first half of the thirteenth, a period during which the arts of painting, sculpture, architecture, and drama reached their highest Romanesque or pre-Gothic form. The abstraction of period, as always, somewhat obscures particularities, and is therefore defensible only because this study has as its main purpose not a contribution to the history of late Romanesque art but rather an accurate visualization and interpretation of the neglected art form of medieval music-drama.

Except in the case of the architecture at Padua and Cividale, there is little hope of establishing a direct relationship between the extant works of art of any locality and the music dramas it produced. For the most part we must be content with those representations, wherever made, that bring into focus some facet of the theatrical image. Medieval single-mindedness in visual expression encourages us to correlate almost any artist's image, in whatever medium, with that of playwrights and audiences of the same period. Further, because the shape and style of such objects as the thurible, the pyx, the crosier, and the crown light are traditional, we may assume that these shapes and styles were used in the plays, when these objects are either called for in the rubrics or implicitly required for an appropriate and adequate performance.

The representational evidence has been documented with a comparatively small quantity of plates in this publication. From the 125,000 photographs in the Index of Christian Art, and from those I have examined in other collections, many more of equal import could be selected. What cannot be documented, but is a large part of the evidence, is my extensive survey of the Index. Statements qualified by "usually," "frequently," or "most," signify that I have surveyed the Index file and found a preponderance of supporting examples. Because the Index is available not only at its home in Princeton University but also in two other centers in the United States and two in Europe, the accuracy of the surveys can easily be tested. The photographic illustrations included in this publication have been secured mainly from the present custodians of the objects.

As a by-product of what was originally undertaken as a practical study, the materials here presented may suggest to theater historians a need to revise their accounts and appraisals of European theater in the twelfth and thirteenth centuries. The extent of ignorance and misinterpretation in this area is considerable.

I would like to acknowledge my gratitude to The Clarendon Press for permission to quote from Karl Young, *The Drama of the Medieval Church;* to Oxford University Press for permission to quote from Noah Greenberg and W. H. Auden, eds., *The Play of Daniel: A Thirteenth-Century Musical Drama;* and to Professor Otto Pächt for permission to quote from *The St. Albans Psalter,* Studies of the Warburg Institute, XXV.

My indebtedness is large to scholars who have cultivated "these old fields," especially to the following who have been abundantly generous with encouragement and aid: E. Martin Browne, Père Lin Donnat, William H. Forsyth, Margaret B. Freeman, Rosalie B. Green, Noah Greenberg, O. B. Hardison, Jr., Rensselaer W. Lee, William L. Smoldon, and Hanns Swarzenski. In my own backyard Ulysse Desportes, Kurt Kehr, and Gordon C. Page —colleagues at Mary Baldwin College—have been of repeated assistance. No one but myself is, however, responsible for errors of fact or interpretation.

For the typing of major portions of the text I am grateful to my son Francis, and to Janet C. Collins and Jan Triplett. The many courtesies of libraries and museums on both sides of the Atlantic are only faintly suggested by credit lines for the illustrations. Frequent mention of the Index of Christian Art at Princeton University is an indication of the extent of my gratitude to it.

Three debts are of such magnitude that their acknowledgment here should be considered a kind of dedication:

To Mary Baldwin College for its repeated financial aid to this project,

To the memory of Karl Young for his encouragement in the beginning, and for the legacy of his photographs of medieval playscripts,

And to my wife Margaret for her belief and love.

Mary Baldwin College   FLETCHER COLLINS, JR.
May, 1971

The Production

of

Medieval Church

Music-Drama

Introduction

General Considerations

THE composition and performance of the plays of the repertory with which this study is concerned took place over a period of less than two centuries, the eldest dating from shortly before the beginning of the twelfth century, the youngest being recorded in a manuscript of the fourteenth. Since extant playscripts are sometimes copies of earlier manuscripts, the great period of medieval music-drama may be further defined as extending from 1100 to about 1275, after which a cultural and political upheaval retired the plays and the society which nourished them. This era of the plays has been termed Pre-Gothic, Romanesque, or Twelfth-Century Renaissance; no one has yet found a satisfactory name for it. The current obsession with modernism has tended to fade this period into the later Gothic and the Italian renaissance, with the belief that everything improved as the Middle Ages receded and the Renaissance and "Man" triumphed. One of the by-products of the present study is the discovery that the theater of this high period was aware of man's eternal condition and spoke to it through its playwrights more eloquently and beautifully than did the vernacular craft-cycle or "mystery" plays which succeeded the music-dramas.

The plays under consideration were composed in cultural centers throughout Western Europe, from Rouen in France to Cividale in northeastern Italy. Unfortunately no playscripts of this kind survived the fury of the English reformation, and those which have remained from Germany usually lack decipherable music.

The occasions which motivated their composition and performance were ecclesiastical and festive, chiefly during the Christmas and Easter seasons, when the liturgy in which they were begotten and imbedded encouraged their elaboration from semi-dramatic ritual to full-fledged music-dramas of up to an hour in length. This development within the churches, as a liturgical "special event," ran parallel to maturations in painting, sculpture, and architecture during the same period. The plays were sung,

mostly in Latin, because the liturgy was so performed; the manuscripts of
the plays are therefore generally found in service books, the stage directions being literally rubrics.

TONE AND QUALITY

Medieval playwrights, like the visual artists who illustrated the stories
they dramatized, saw the world whole, if not steadily. They saw it as
God's work of art, and saw man's art as a mirror of that world. They saw
it peopled with men and women who are at once tragic and comic, pitiful
and ridiculous, and who are never monolithic, mere *tableaux vivants* of
vices or virtues. This kind of specialization did not occur until the late
fourteenth and fifteenth centuries, when the morality plays came into
fashion. There are few moral tags on the twelfth- and thirteenth-century
religious plays, for their purpose was not so much didactic as artistic and
devotional.

All earthliness was to be accepted if it could be transformed through
the spirit. *The Shepherds Play* from Rouen, for example, has a devout line
in which the Virgin Mary is implored "a peccati purga faece." The Vulgate
Latin of a famous passage, from 1 Corinthians 13:8–11, similarly, has
forms of the verb "evacuare" (to defecate) three times in four lines,
Paul's metaphor being entirely clear. The King James Version, however,
translates the Latin verb prudishly as "fail," "done away," and "put away,"
and most modern translations come no closer to the reality which Paul
and the medieval shepherds knew and faced.

The intent of the medieval playwright, and the corresponding effects
upon, or expectations of, his audience, are matters which have been
considerably misrepresented by scholarly appraisers of the church plays.
Karl Young, whose interpretation has been widely followed and never
challenged, concluded that the plays were created "in a manifest desire to
convey edifying instruction." [1] He quotes perhaps ten medieval and
Reformation statements as to what was then considered the purpose or the
effect of the church music-dramas, and is careful to exclude statements
which apply only to vernacular plays or to the feast of fools.[2] What probably led to his misinterpretation was a willingness to accept statements
from outside the high period of composition of these plays as indications of

---

[1] Karl Young, *The Drama of the Medieval Church* (Oxford, 1933), II, 410. Hereafter referred to as Young.

[2] Young, II, 411–17.

their intent, and to be somewhat indiscriminate in his evaluation of witnesses within the period.

The valid evidence from the period 1100–1275 turns out to be scarce, possibly because there were few objectors to the church drama and therefore little need for its supporters to state their purposes and justify their results. Assuming, as we must, that Young has presented all the extant records on this subject, we find that there are only three relevant documents. Each of these must be scrutinized for its real import. The earliest, excluding the *Regularis Concordia* as being about 130 years out of date when our period began with *The Wise and Foolish Maidens* at Limoges (ca. 1100), is the diatribe by Gerhoh of Reichersberg (1093–1169), based on his unhappy experience as master of scholars in the Augsburg monastery about 1122. Gerhoh complained that some of the brothers used the Augsburg refectory for meetings only when there was to be a play about Herod or the slaughter of the Innocents, or other spectacles or dramatic exhibitions, and that these gatherings (in Young's translation) "provided an incentive to conviviality." Gerhoh's objection to the plays is that their effect was convivial, and that the intent was *not* instructional. If it was not didactic, it could only have been artistic, and the art of the theater is necessarily social, convivial. Gerhoh was disturbed that the audience enjoyed the plays together, rather than studying in ascetic solitude or being lectured on Church doctrine (by Gerhoh). This bent of mind would not, and probably could not, compose a play. Gerhoh's attitude contrasts too sharply with that of the playwrights for his statements to be representative of the playwrights' purpose or of the effect of their plays on an audience.

Herrad of Landsberg, abbess of a monastery at Hohenberg from 1167 to 1195, stated that the purpose of the plays should be instructional, as she declared it was in the old days, but that the plays had become in her time the occasion for scurrilous and lascivious behavior and should therefore be abolished.[3] Herrad was of course speaking of what happened with her Hohenberg nuns, who may very well have been transported by the dramatic impulse, particularly when acting the roles of men—Herod, for instance. She would not have thought it seemly for her girls to strut around like men; to her such conduct would indeed have seemed lascivious, scurrilous, and irreligious (her words), and the better the girls acted the worse their conduct would have appeared. She could hardly speak for the monastic and cathedral world of the twelfth century her problems and

---

[3] Paraphrased from her *Hortus Deliciarum,* as excerpted by Young, II, 412–14.

her point of view being too special. But, like Gerhoh, she does testify that in her experience the effect of the plays was *not* instructional, and thus a second piece of supposed evidence for the didactic purpose of the plays really tends to deny the existence of such a purpose in the period of their most artistic composition.

The third witness is Pope Innocent III (1198–1216), whose ruling in 1207 prohibited vulgar theatrical spectacles in churches. Some years later Pope Gregory IX (1227–41) clarified the intent of Innocent's ruling by specifying that it did not apply to the admirable plays of the church repertory. "Nam tamen hoc prohibetur representare *Praesepe Domini, Herodem, Magos,* et qualiter *Rachel Plorant Filios Suos,* et cetera, quae tangunt festivitates illas de quibus hic fit mentio, cum talia potius inducant homines ad compunctionem quam ad lasciviam vel voluptatem, sicut in Pascha *Sepulchrum Domini* et alia representantur ad devotionem excitandam." (It is not, however, prohibited to play *The Manger of the Lord, The Herod, The Magi,* and of course *Rachel Crying for Her Sons* and other plays which pertain to those festivities of which mention is here made, with such kind as lead men rather to conscience than to lasciviousness or sensuality, just as at Easter *The Sepulcher of the Lord* and other such plays are performed to excite devotion.) [4] Gregory mentioned versions of three of the plays of the repertory—*The Shepherds, The Herod and The Slaughter of the Innocents,* and *The Visit to the Sepulcher,* and probably alluded (under "such plays") to *The Pilgrim, The Procession of Prophets, The Wise and Foolish Maidens, The Lament of Mary, The Annunciation,* and *The Purification*—more than half the extant produceable repertory.

Gregory's phrase, "ad devotionem excitandam," certainly means what it says, that the plays were exciting in the best way, to the devout and not to the lascivious, and that they were an emotional experience, and not merely instruction. His statement, which is at once general and specific —apparently from personal experience of the plays as well as the reports from many of his prelates—must surely be accepted as reflecting the intent and the effect of the plays more accurately than Young's "we may assume that a . . . didactic purpose was general among the playwrights." [5]

The plays were no more instructional than their antecedent Gospels, antiphons, and hymns, the major purpose of which in the church may also be described as devotional and celebrational. The visual artists reflect

---

[4] Quoted by Young, II, 416–17, from *Compilatio Decretalium Domini Gregorii Pape Noni* (1482). The compilation is later than this portion of its contents; see Young, II, 416. The translation is mine.

[5] Young, II, 411.

the same intent in their best work, directly connected as much of it is with the liturgy. This purpose was more precisely the evocation of a religious euphoria, an ecstasy, and the effect was only by coincidence educational. Had the playwrights begun with a strictly didactic purpose, there is small likelihood that they would have created such masterworks as those of the surviving repertory.

Like artists in any period, the playwright and the visual artist of the Middle Ages composed out of their experience. Monastic as they were, the sum of their experience included observation of the life around them as well as study in the Bible and other books and treatises in the monastery library. In their plays are many and varied reflections of their experience, which build into a kind of composite biography of the playwright, and so help us to understand the artist within the art.

The Christus in *The Pilgrim* is the good monastic teacher, whose character is developed beyond its gospel sources in such a line as "O cum sitis eius discipuli," the kind of spurring remark the Beauvais students had surely heard one of their masters make. It reflects something of the excitement and challenge of a good teacher, one who could attract such a student as the anonymous author of the Beauvais *Pilgrim*. Or was he himself the good teacher? Perhaps the playwright was hinting that what appeared to be rough treatment of students was ironically often the sign of a good teacher, even of the gentle Jesus? *The Three Clerks* reflects a medieval student bias against innkeepers. They are all rascals and their wives are witches, when entrusted with poor innocent goliards.

In this period military warfare—carrying with it the threat of destruction to any monastery that refused to yield up its treasures, or forcing abbeys to be used as fortresses and risk destruction by another attacker—was never far away. The Romanesque bell towers were built as monastic fortresses against the roving might of the Herods, the Belshazzars, the Dariuses, and the Marmorinuses of the twelfth century. The playwrights had seen them and their princes and counselors and Norman soldiers, and were pleased to give these potentates their due in the plays, as Anouilh did to the Nazis in his *Antigone,* safely but devastatingly. Satire on the potentates of church and state was fairly common in the twelfth century.[6]

Shepherds and their sheep were a commonplace of the northern European landscape, and monasteries raised sheep for food, clothing, and parchment. When the monks played *The Shepherds* they knew how a shepherd carried himself and his staff, how he hunkered down by his small fire on a

[6] Charles H. Haskins, *The Renaissance of the Twelfth Century* (Cleveland and New York, 1957), pp. 177–88.

cold winter's night, how he might react to the descent of an angel on such a night. They had a community of feeling with the biblical shepherds, and read or sang the pastoral passages of Luke as if the shepherds were in the pasture just beyond the monastery walls.

Few of the playwrights, or their audiences, had been born of Latin-speaking parents, but those who lived in the monasteries and cathedral schools heard and spoke Latin almost exclusively. The playwrights composed their versified dialogue in Latin, often imitating the hexameters of Virgil with which they were as well acquainted as is a modern poet with the pentameters of Shakespeare.

Singing in Latin was a large part of their daily activity, whether they were audience, actors, or playwrights; and so the natural medium for the plays in the church was sung Latin, which was as easily understood by singers and audience as the lyrics of a modern musical comedy to today's playgoers. The playwright as composer was steeped in the hundreds of traditional melodies of the liturgy, and from them, as well as from visiting trouvères, he learned how to adapt a liturgical melody and to shape his measured compositions, which took their rhythms from the metrics of the new poetry. The playwright was presumably the choirmaster of his monastery or cathedral school, and was therefore the most accomplished musician in the community. He trained his choir of boys and men to sing the extensive contents of the antiphonary and of the gradual of the Mass. The plays were in this context a welcome diversion for him and his choir from the routine of the canonical services, and were in this sense the only fresh pieces the choir had to work on. Though they were new only the first time they were performed, they were never performed more than once a year, as special features of important feast days. They were rehearsed as a modern church choir rehearses special pieces for Christmas or Easter, usually in connection with a service.[7]

The lack of extant part-scores for the individual actor of a church play suggests that they never existed in this period—parchment was too expensive—and that the actor had to learn his role from the choirmaster's score. Even though the actor could read musical notation fluently, he must have had to be "quick-study" to memorize a leading role in a play in time to rehearse the acting of it with the choirmaster and fellow choristers. After the first performance the finished script was inserted in a service book,

---

[7] Gustave Cohen, *Histoire de la Mise en Scène dans le Théâtre Réligieux du Moyen Age* (Paris, 1951), p. 33, surmises that the director of a liturgical play was usually "the choirmaster, who, book in hand, followed and directed the movement of the play" (my translation). Cohen does not consider the possibility that this choirmaster-director was often the playwright as well.

which was not kept in the possession of the choir, but was available from the librarian for refreshing one's memory before performance the following year. This finished script was probably prepared by monastic scribes only after the first performance, for none of the extant manuscripts shows signs of having been handled and marked up as a rehearsal score inevitably is. The working draft of the play, in the handwriting of the choirmaster-playwright, was undoubtedly rather messy and would have been erased after the scribes had prepared the permanent copy for the service book.

When the script had been brought to the monastery from another church, the manuscript must have been regarded as a working copy and have been marked up and revised by the choirmaster. This process would explain the fact that many of the lines in the extant versions are identical. Even in very similar versions the stage directions are seldom as similar as the verbal dialogue, and sometimes the melodies are not the same, the choirmaster having been perhaps more free to adapt the composed music and the staging to local conditions and his preferences than to change the versification, which was the narrative and metrical foundation of the imported composition.

The inclusion of any stage directions was surely the sole province of the choirmaster, and one may generalize that the directions as we have them represent only whatever essential data the choirmaster thought he might forget in a year's time. Of course these would automatically be transferred to a copy made to be taken home by a visitor, whose own choirmaster might retain some of the original staging information and revise or omit other production data. This process would explain, for example, the use of the word *pedetemtim* in the stage directions of five versions of *The Visit to the Sepulcher,* and apparently not elsewhere in medieval writings.[8]

The choirmaster and his choir, who were certainly happy enough to perform these plays, were no doubt aware that the sudden introduction of secular material or characters, as with costumes or comic actions, might put the play in jeopardy with the local authorities, who were aware of such objections as Innocent III's against vulgar theatrical exhibitions. This situation may explain why in many manuscripts the description of costumes in the heading is extremely conservative, all costumes being referred to as dalmatics when they must at the very least have been greatly modified to be appropriate as, for example, the Midwives' dresses in *The Shepherds* at Rouen. The choirmaster knew that the monastic authorities, in glancing through a script, would be pleased to note the use of official, consecrated

---

[8] See below, pp. 71–72.

vestments, and would prefer not to see what a Fleury heading contained, that Mary Magdalene was to be "in habitu meretricio" (in the costume of a whore). We should not, therefore, be overimpressed by references to ecclesiastical vestments in the more advanced plays of the repertory.

The choirmaster's authorship of the stage directions is also suggested by the common direction to let the play begin as soon as certain actors are ready ("parati"). This direction is certainly not for the choirmaster's benefit; he would not think of starting off the play without being sure the actors were ready. It is more plausible that he wrote the direction for the officiating priest to see in the service book, as a reminder to check with the director about the actors' readiness before launching into the opening antiphon of the play.

The ideal medieval playwright was thus required to be a man of parts: a composer and adapter of verse, melody, and drama; a hard-driving choirmaster, who could drill his choir in the learning and proper singing of his dialogue; a producer-director, responsible not only for staging and acting but also for the preservation of peace with the dean, abbot, or prior; and finally an editor, who had to prepare his script for the scribes. In all this activity his purpose was to mirror the world that God made, and to express his own devout excitement—the words are Gregory's—in religious music drama.

DETERMINATION OF MAJOR EPISODES

Visual representations of the stories of the plays tend to define the medieval concept of crucial episodes, essential scenes. A simple example is found in the two major episodes of *The Shepherds:* the annunciation scene in the fields, and the manger scene at Bethlehem. These two episodes are frequently portrayed in the art of the period (e.g., plates 26–28), while other actions—such as the travel of the shepherds from the fields to Bethlehem—are seldom illustrated, although in the play such an episode is sung in dialogue and necessitates movement from one stage location to another. Conversely, no moment outside the play—such as the return of the shepherds from Bethlehem—is likely to be portrayed in art works. One concludes that there was tacit agreement among graphic artists and playwrights as to major episodes of a story.

Other plays of the repertory have corresponding and defining illustrations in stone, metal, and paint; relevant works of visual art are dealt with in detail in the analysis of each play. A consequence of this concordance is that art works from the same period as the plays provide a reliable indication of which scenes the playwright regarded as climactic, scenes to be built to, and which episodes were interscenic. With only one exception in the repertory, travel scenes were not regarded as major ones by the playwright or artist, and were not to be emphasized by complete spatial realization.

There was often a practical reason, moreover, for not emphasizing a travel scene. In multi-scene plays, which are the norm in the repertory, a cathedral audience on some occasions may have been accustomed to move to the location of each scene. There were no pews in a medieval cathedral, and the audience usually stood throughout the play and the service. While the spectators trailed the actors across the stone floor to a new scenic location, important and detailed dramatic incident was clearly impractical. In the somewhat smaller, monastic abbeys the multiple locations may have been within sight and hearing of a stationary audience, but in such instances the travel of actors from one stage to another was probably seldom regarded as an opportunity for dramatic excitement.

Another practical consideration was that the province of the choir in cathedral or abbey was primarily the area named for that group. Unless there were compelling theatrical reasons to move the scene out of the choir and into the nave—as sometimes happened—the major scenes of the play were mounted in the usually large choir area of the Romanesque church. As we shall see in detailed discussions of the staging of each play, the most usual arrangement was two *sedes* or platforms, at left and right in the choir, with a *platea* or open area between them to represent such travel scenes as street or fields.[9] It is remarkable how consistently the visual artists' definition of the *sedes* scenes corresponds to internal evidence, including stage directions, as to what and how many such scenes are actually required by the play.

CHARACTERIZATION

Modern actors, eager to study in depth the personalities of their characters, are often frustrated by the slight and even ambiguous indications of character and its motivation in the medieval plays. This difficulty derives, as do the plays and the art works, from the Bible itself, the narrative style of which is essentially direct, with little attention to analysis of motives.

[9] See below, p. 30, for comment on the similarity of these arrangements to those of classical Roman stages.

This approach is in severe contrast to that of the modern novel or play, in which motivations are copiously and even tediously uncovered and displayed. Curiously enough, the direct narrative approach of the ballad and the folk story, secular or religious, may be just as moving in all its brevity as that of the five hundred-page novel or the two-hour play.

Traditional characters, whether in Bible or ballad, generally know who they are, and feel no need to explain themselves. They have little interest in introspection, which seems to have been a Renaissance invention in Western art, for the corresponding portraits in the art of the twelfth and thirteenth centuries also depict traditional characters rather than individuals. The medieval artist had no more interest in psychologizing his subjects than did the playwrights and actors. Often the face of a character in a medieval portrait is contained and almost expressionless, not because the artist was unable to render nuances of feeling but because he felt no need to analyze characters who obviously and traditionally were what they were. His audience, moreover, like that of the playwright, would feel uneasy if presented with clinical studies of familiar Biblical and legendary characters.

Another reason for the lack of psychological depth in medieval characterizations involves the degree of idealization, even abstraction, in the characters of a music drama, whether it be Japanese *nō* or classical Greek, music itself being a formal, nonpsychological medium. The difficulty with most Renaissance opera is that the medium requires the use of legendary characters but the audience has not lived the legends. Like the *nō* and the Greek, the medieval music-drama represents a universality and stature in its characters because they were not created out of whole cloth by the playwright.

Medieval portraiture seems to have proceeded on the same basis. Art historians, who are generally also astute interpreters, have often pointed out that medieval religious figures seem to be souls clothed in flesh, and that the soul is more interesting to the artist than the flesh. In medieval music drama and visual portraiture behavioristic elements seldom show. Except for the past of Mary Magdalene and the plan for the eldest daughter to emulate her in *The Three Daughters,* one would hardly know that sexuality exists. In fact, the sex of the characters in artistic representations is often difficult to determine. In part this is a consequence of the monastic circumstances of the artists and playwrights; more importantly it is their admirable inclination to spiritualize the earthly.

Considerable help in interpreting the characters of a medieval music-drama may nevertheless be had from contemporary art, so long as one looks for what is there rather than for what intentionally is not. The age of the characters is suggested rather clearly. Herod is always depicted in the full vigor of his imperious manhood—never sick, old, or neurotic. The manly compassion of the Christus is apparent in whatever scene of his life is portrayed. The father in *The Three Daughters* is, on the other hand, feeble and broken in spirit, a fact of which we could not be sure from the play. The attitude of Mary in the nativity scene with the shepherds is, as Mâle pointed out, quite unexpected: she is austere, remote, and meditative, not at all the radiant young mother with her first-born.

While most of the characters are traditional and legendary, many of the secular characters—kings, princes, soldiers, students, robbers, and innkeepers—owe much to the playwright's observation of life around him, and are thus more immediately available to us as realistic human beings. Deliberate anachronism in behavior and costume, which, as O. B. Hardison points out was "a form of verisimilitude in medieval drama and remains so in the drama of Shakespeare," [10] permitted the playwright, like the artist, to show Roman soldiers wearing the chain mail of contemporary soldiers, and ancient kings and princes behaving like the European potentates the playwright observed at the abbey or cathedral. St. Nicholas, actually a legendary character, appears in medieval portraits dressed as a twelfth-century bishop, not as a historical personage of the fourth century. The non-legendary characters in the St. Nicholas miracle plays are much more homespun: the students could be from the playwright's school and the spice and oil merchants from the square outside the cathedral or abbey; the innkeeper and his wife are contemporary caricatures.

Four characters, all traditional Gospel figures, have leading roles in more than one of the sixteen plays of the practical repertory. The Christus, as one might expect, is the most frequent major character, appearing in eight of the plays, and mentioned in others. While the idealization of his character must have threatened to stereotype it in the eight plays, we find that in those in which he is represented as a mature man his character has considerable variety. The Jesus of the *Lazarus,* for example, is not quite the same person as the Christus of the two Resurrection plays, and the Lord Christ of *The Wise and Foolish Maidens* shows a very different aspect of his character.

The Virgin Mary has leading roles in four of the plays, but is intentionally missing from *The Visit to the Sepulcher.* Had the cult of the Virgin been more influential in the making of medieval music-drama, she

[10] O. B. Hardison, Jr., *Christian Rite and Christian Drama in the Middle Ages* (Baltimore: Johns Hopkins, 1965), p. 246. Hereafter referred to as Hardison.

might have appeared in more of the repertory. As things fortunately worked out, she is shown in action, not on a pedestal, at the four most important moments of her life—in *The Annunciation, The Purification, The Shepherds* (depicting the Nativity), and *The Lament of Mary.* In these four we have a Marian cycle, with some emotional variety in each play, as occasioned by its circumstances.

Mary Magdalene, in accordance with her medieval popularity, appears in only one fewer play than the Virgin, who is sometimes called Mary Major.[11] In *The Visit to the Sepulcher* and the *Lazarus* she has the leading roles, and is second only to the Virgin Mary in *The Lament of Mary.* In all three she is a good example of the medieval ability to accept and transform the earthly. Although she appears in her whore's dress of red, she is the most warmly spiritual character in the entire repertory, on a much more substantial basis than the modern, sentimentalized whore-with-the-heart-of-gold.

The only other biblical character with more than one role in the repertory is John. The art of the period confirms the popularity of the four leading characters in the plays. Frequently only the two figures of Mary and John are portrayed in the postcrucifixion scene, as in the two statues from Cividale (the original location of *The Lament of Mary*) and the two from The Cloisters (plates 15, 16). This fact should restrain us from assuming that the playwrights cared less for John than for the women. In his typical monastic costume he may well have been considered by medieval playwrights and artists the prime representative of their own monastic life, much more than Peter or Paul.

Angels or archangels, notably Gabriel, appear in several of the plays; they are agents of God the Father, who never appears in the plays, and of the Holy Ghost, who appears only as a dove in *The Annunciation.* The visual artists of the period confirm this protocol as medieval. What cannot be confirmed by them, and was of some concern to the producer of medieval plays, was whether the angelic roles were to be assigned to men or to boys. Medieval practice was not uniform in this matter, or in whether there were one or two angels in *The Visit to the Sepulcher.* From a survey of the stage directions of all relevant scripts in Young's extensive work, a number of indications of customary practice may be derived.

Of thirteen versions of *The Shepherds* and the *Herod,* five[12] specify a boy as the angel or archangel, and the other eight are noncommittal. One

---

[11] See below, p. 92, for the authenticity of this epithet for the Virgin Mary.
[12] Young, II, 12, 14, 34, 71, 100.

may conclude that generally the Angel in these two plays was acted by a choirboy.

The choice is substantially the same for *The Annunciation.* Of four actual plays, dating from the fourteenth to the sixteenth century, three specify that Gabriel is a boy, and the fourth is silent.[13] Although the Annunciation theme seems to have come to the plays much later than to the visual arts, we are usually unable in the latter to distinguish between man and boy. In this instance, the plays seem to reflect at least a dramatic tradition for a boy to play Gabriel. The only corroboration from art is that Gabriel is never given a beard, either in the Annunciation scene or elsewhere. One may even speculate that the annunciatory angel, whether in *The Shepherds,* the *Herod,* or *The Annunciation,* was played by a choirboy.

Quite different is the physical aspect of the angels in *The Visit to the Sepulcher.* A survey of sixty versions in Young reveals that men (either one or two) were much preferred to boys. The roles were played in twenty-six versions by two men, in fifteen by one man, in sixteen by two boys, and in only three by one boy.[14] One may conclude that a majority of dramatic groups felt that men were needed in *The Visit to the Sepulcher* to lend greater authority to the fact of the Resurrection than could boys. On the other hand, the basis of choice may have been primarily aesthetic: in a play dominated by women the mixing in of the angels' deeper voices gave a better tessitural pattern to the total composition. These two explanations are of course entirely compatible, and are likely to have combined in a playwright's conception of the play.

Since with only a few exceptions the plays of the repertory were acted entirely by men and boys of the choir, one would expect that the dramatis personae would have leaned heavily toward masculine roles as did those of the Elizabethans, also confronted with an exclusively male acting company. In the plays of the practical medieval repertory there is a total of only thirty-eight female roles, an average of only about two per play.[15] Only *The Wise and Foolish Maidens* has a large number of female roles. *The Image of St. Nicholas, The Pilgrim,* and *The Conversion of St. Paul* have all-male casts, and *The Procession of the Prophets, The Three Clerks,* and the *Daniel* have only one female role apiece. Nevertheless, the

---

[13] Young, II, 246, 248, 482, 484.

[14] Two-thirds of the versions assessed on this point are from the beginning through the fourteenth century, the others later.

[15] I exclude the St. Quentin *Visitatio* as atypical in this regard. For the rare productions by nuns, see below, p. 65n.

number of excellent female roles in the drama of both periods is remarkable, and speaks as well for the talent of the boy actor in the medieval theater as it does for his Elizabethan descendant. The task of the medieval boy actor may have been somewhat easier than that of the Elizabethan, inasmuch as the medieval music-drama was a more formal, less representational medium than the blank verse plays of the Elizabethans, and there is no extended portrayal of romantic love in any of the medieval plays. The only exception is the Suitor-Daughter couples in *The Three Daughters,* who are hardly Romeos and Juliets. The monastic church stage, unfortunately, had no place for such characters. The goliard songwriter could get away with ribald and romantic lyrics about women, but the chancel could hardly tolerate such women on the stage, even if the boys, given the opportunity, might have acted as competently as the Elizabethan boys did in the roles of Cleopatra, Miranda, and Doll Tearsheet.

MOVEMENT AND GESTURE

Many works of pictorial art from the period of the plays are tableaux, revealing the characters at a crucial moment of the story. Some seem posed, as if the subjects were holding their positions for a time exposure and the effect is as still and undramatic as posed photographs of a modern play. In many portrayals, however, there is some indication of dramatic movement and gesture. In spite of the rather fully draped medieval figure, with articulation of legs, torso, and shoulders perceived only through the drapery, there remains visible such significant movements as the tilt of the head and the gestures of arms, hands, and fingers. Thus the works of medieval visual artists provide for us an index to the kind of movement and gesture the medieval actors would have used.

I have searched in visual representations of the Passion scene for movements and gestures that would adequately illustrate the stage directions in *The Lament of Mary,* of which there is an unusually high number, some seventy-nine. Many of these directions call for Mary to beat her breast. Only a few illustrations of the Passion depict her doing so, but grief, anger, despair, and joy are represented by movement and gesture in many medieval pictures of unrelated subjects. Because a play is an unbroken, dynamic succession of movements and gestures evoked by dramatic feeling or evoking that feeling, one can hardly hope for a cinematic demonstration in the art works. Just as the visual arts help one determine the major episodes in story or play, they lend considerable assistance in establishing certain details of motion and gesture, which may be complemented with improvisation in the same style.

To judge from the visual arts and from the quality of the plays themselves, the style of movement and gesture was formal and sustained, much as we find it in the Japanese *nō* dramas and in the vase illustrations of Greek plays. Modern efforts to perform plays of the medieval repertory suggest that a style of acting that avoids the stilted and has strong theatrical interest is best produced by patient study of the relevant art works, combined with choreographic directions from the rich rhythms of the music, even to performing the gesture with the musical phrase. From these attempts at the re-creation of medieval acting, one readily infers that in order to be effective, the actors of these plays must have been far from amateurish.

The performers of the earliest medieval church plays were not professional singer-actors, and so did not bring to the plays a developed style of acting. The lack of a traditional style, apart from the customary verve and elegance of monastic performances of the Mass and the canonical offices, may partially explain why the ceremonial improvisations took so long to develop into full scale dramas.[16] If the dramatic potential of the liturgy in the tenth century had been in the hands of professional acting companies and playwrights, theatrical changes would have occurred more rapidly. In the medieval scheme of things there was small place for secular theater and consequently evidences of dramatic activity by the amateurs of folk drama or by the professional jongleurs and mimes are few and uncertain.[17] Furthermore, the official church position was hostile to secular theatrical activity, as we have seen in Innocent III's ruling.

The actors of the great plays of the repertory must have been highly-trained singers. Such roles as those of the Christus in *The Pilgrim,* the Jew in *The Image of St. Nicholas,* and the Virgin Mary in *The Lament of Mary* require considerable talent and training in the art of singing dramatic dialogue. The difficulty of such roles suggests that because the plays are genuine music-dramas, not merely oratorios, their performers may well have been as skilled in acting as in singing. Had the singers merely stood and sung, they would have been false to the intent of the

[16] Something of this can still be observed today in the ceremonial practices of the Benedictines in France.

[17] See E. K. Chambers, *The Medieval Stage* (Oxford, 1903), I, 68–70, and Allardyce Nicoll, *Masks, Mimes, and Miracles* (New York, 1963). These two works are hereafter referred to by the names of their authors.

composer, who was also their director. What seems most probable is that, as the plays improved and blossomed into great drama by the twelfth century, the art of acting them necessarily kept pace. This kind of corollary is more than mere speculation; it is generally posited for Greek and Elizabethan acting, and evident in modern performances of the *nō* dramas.

Acting as he did in a singing environment, but performing daily in dramatic liturgical ceremonies that were almost entirely sung, the medieval actor was not a specialist. The profession of actor was not then discrete, because the music-dramas could not have used an actor who could not sing. No doubt some members of the choir had more dramatic talent than others, and were regularly assigned the best roles in the plays, but all the choristers, good actors or bad, performed for the glory of God, not for money or personal fame. One suspects that careless acting was considered a sin, which would have been a powerful stimulus to learning the discipline of acting.

The repertory of popular gestures, as expressed in Christian art from the third century, and still used among conservative peoples in Mediterranean countries, is a fertile ground for the discovery of gestures for the medieval plays. Walter Lowrie has pertinent remarks on this largely unexplored subject:

It is often said that Italians speak with their hands. This is more nearly true than most people recognize. To the Sicilians a play without words is perfectly intelligible. It is a popular theatrical diversion. But this was once true of the whole Mediterranean basin where Christian art was developed. Even now in Italy one who would get rid of a beggar has only to shake indolently two fingers of the right hand which hangs limply by his side. The beggar is sure to see this almost invisible gesture, and likely he will depart. Frenchmen and Spaniards also talk with their hands; but they talk thus in vain to people who are not accustomed to listen with their eyes. . . . Even archaeologists often fail to discriminate between the woman who mutely touched Christ's garment, the Canaanitish woman who knelt at Christ's feet loudly imploring that He heal her daughter, and Mary [Magdalene] who prostrated herself at His feet as an expression of gratitude for the raising of her brother Lazarus.[18]

Lowrie also calls attention to the traditional Roman thumbs-down gesture, "whereby an emperor denied clemency to a defeated gladiator." The import of this gesture is still what the Romans saw in it, and one imagines that the medieval actor used it on occasion.

[18] Walter Lowrie, *Art in the Early Church* (New York, 1965), p. 177. Hereafter referred to as Lowrie.

If anatomies of gesture were compiled during the Middle Ages I have not encountered them. There is, however, a recent monograph on Elizabethan acting, in which 121 illustrations from two pre-Restoration anatomies of gesture are reproduced and demonstrated to be relevant both to life and to Elizabethan stage gestures.[19] Although the Elizabethan style of acting was obviously different from that of the twelfth century, most of the hand gestures are in the popular category and presumably antedate the Elizabethan stage. There is some likelihood that many of them were used by medieval actors.

COSTUMES

In relation to characterization, I have noted Hardison's insight that "anachronism is a form of verisimilitude." This is also true in the graphic arts of the Middle Ages. Except when merely copying the illuminations of an earlier period, the medieval artist never tried for historicity, but clothed Darius or David or Christ in the costumes of his own day. One would suppose that the play-producing choirmaster would have had the same feeling about costuming his play, but unfortunately for neat historical patterns this would be an oversimplification of what seems to have happened.

Actually the visual artists had been clothing their characters in contemporary dress for centuries, for so long that fourth-century illustrations depict contemporary ecclesiastical vestments as identical with the clothing of upperclass citizens of that era. Apparently the same impulse that prompted early Christian leaders to adopt the secular fashions of their times as vestments also motivated the artists. The playwrights began within the dramatic rites of the church, by improvising costumes from the vestments in the wardrobe. The desire for verisimilitude grew very slowly. To illustrate, let us compare the costume requirements of a two-minute playlet from the tenth-century *Regularis Concordia* with those about two hundred years later in the related Fleury version of the same play,[20] now

---

[19] Bertram L. Joseph, *Elizabethan Acting* (Oxford, 1964). The anatomies are by John Bulwer.

[20] The extent of the indebtedness of *Regularis Concordia* to tenth-century Fleury rituals is revealed by Père Lin Donnat, "Recherches sur l'influence de Fleury au Xe et XIe siècles," in *Actes de la Semaine mediévale de Saint-Benoît-sur-Loire, 1969,* ed. René Louis (forthcoming from Paris-Tours: Presses Universitaires de France). Père Lin présents documentary evidence that Fleury customs were the detailed source of most of *Regularis Concordia.*

twenty-five minutes long and one of the finest achievements of medieval church drama.

The first rubric of the early *Visit to the Sepulcher* reads:

Dum tertia recitatur lectio, quatuor fratres induant se quorum unus, alba indutus, acsi ad aliud agendum ingrediatur atque latenter Sepulchri locum adeat, ibique, manu tenens palmam, quietus sedeat. Dumque tertium percelebratur responsorium, residui tres succedant, omnes quidem cappis induti, turribula cum incensu manibus gestantes ac pedetemptim ad similitudinem quaerentium quid, veniant ante locum Sepulchri.[21]

(While the Third Lesson is being read, let four of the brothers vest themselves. But let one of them, clothed in an alb, go privately by another way to the place of the Sepulcher, and there, holding a palm-frond in his hand, let him quietly sit. And while the Third Responsory [to the Lesson] is being celebrated, let the other three brothers follow, all of them vested in copes and carrying in their hands thuribles with incense, but feeling their way with their feet in the manner of searchers, and let these come before the place of the Sepulcher.)

The costumes are common ecclesiastical vestments. The alb is a long white linen garment with tight sleeves and a belt at the waist; the copes, long heavy capes for outdoor wear, have hoods which when pulled over the heads of the brothers may have imparted a slightly feminine look, by covering their tonsures. From the dialogue which follows we gather that the monk in the alb is the Archangel who will ask the famous question, "Quem quaeritis in Sepulchro, Christicolae?" and that the other three monks are the Marys. There is no call here for such elaborate apparatus as wings for the Archangel, though visual artists had already given him wings in tenth-century illustrations of the scene, such as those in Hartker's *Antiphonary,*[22] or in the Bernward sculptures at Hildesheim; they had done so as far back as the fifth century.[23]

The corresponding stage directions for the opening of the Fleury version of *The Visit to the Sepulcher* reads:

Ad faciendam similitudinem Dominici Sepulcri, primum procedant tres fratres preparati et vestiti in similitudinem trium Mariarum, pedetemtim et quasi tristes. . . . Angelus sedens foris ad caput Sepulcri, vestitus alba deaureata, mitra tectus caput etsi deinfulatus, palmam in sinistra, ramum candelarum plenum tenens in manu dextera . . .[24]

(A likeness of the Lord's Sepulcher having been constructed, first let three of the brothers, in the likeness of the three Marys, proceed [toward the Sepulcher], feeling their way with their feet and as if sad . . . The Archangel, sitting out-

---

[21] Quoted from Young, I, 249 (punctuation altered).

[22] Reproduced by Young, plate I, and by W. L. Smoldon, *Visitatio Sepulchri: A Twelfth-Century Easter Music-Drama* (London, 1963), p. ii.

[23] For the early use of angel wings, see Lowrie, p. 137.   [24] Young, I, 393–94.

side the tomb at the head of the Sepulcher, vested in a gilded alb, a tight coif around his head but without a fillet over the coif, holding a palm frond in his left hand, a flaming candelabra in his right . . .)

Apart from the much more elaborate costume for the Archangel—no wings are here specified, although they often are in twelfth- and thirteenth-century versions—the important difference from the earlier version is the insistence that the three monks be dressed "in similitudinem," in the likeness of the three Marys. This requirement calls, I believe, for contemporary women's dresses and veils for the heads, as the artists had long been showing them. Only when the scale of dramatic effort is increased do we find that costuming ceases to be entirely improvised from the ecclesiastical wardrobe, as in a charade, and begins to require special costumes that would have had to be borrowed, or else made, for the play. Copes would no longer do; their hoods were nothing like women's veils or coifs. If the dresses could not be borrowed from the laity, they would have had to be produced by the robe makers of the monastic community.

One confusing matter in the stage directions for costumes, early and late, is that the monastic playwright knew very little about secular clothing, particularly women's, and was inclined to use the nomenclature for ecclesiastical vestments for all stage clothing needs. Perhaps for this reason there is in the stage directions a mounting insistence upon similitude, even though the vestment terms might still be used to give a general idea of what was wanted. This ambiguity is considerably dispelled by observation of the frescoes, sculptures, and illuminations of the period, their artists being much more free to use contemporary dress. I have mentioned the ultimate freedom of the playwright to describe Mary Magdalene's dress in the *Lazarus* as "habitu meretricio" (the dress of a whore), and have suggested that the playwrights' earlier and general conservatism in describing the costumes of their characters was owing to fear of offending those church officials who were zealous to keep worldliness out of the monastery.

In opposition to this view of the gradual development of realistic costuming, which I believe had reached full contemporaneity by the time the great plays were produced, it is only fair to present the earlier conclusions of the leading modern authority on such matters, the late Karl Young: "For our facts, then, we must resort chiefly to the uncommonly generous rubrics in the many versions of the Easter play. In these, it would appear, the costumes were usually the ordinary vestments of the sacristy, often slightly rearranged and sometimes supplemented by realistic or symbolical objects, through an earnest effort toward accuracy of impersonation." [25]

[25] Young, II, 401.

I doubt that Young would have so concluded in 1933 if he had then been able to see the quantities of pertinent illustrations from the visual arts of the great period, and to recognize in them the strong demand for realistic costuming. Once the plays began to have an artistic integrity, the demand upon the playwrights for realism must have been comparable. It is likewise incredible, with the impressive developments in all other aspects of the dramatic art of the music-drama, that the costuming would or could have remained on the original plane of improvisation from sacristy vestments. Finally, the vestment theory cannot account for the costumes of such characters as the Soldiers in the *Herod,* the *Daniel,* and *The Visit to the Sepulcher,* or Mary Magdalene's dress in the *Lazarus,* let alone the lions' outfits in the *Daniel.*

Mention should be made of a revolution in secular dress at the end of the period in which the plays of the repertory were produced. At the end of the thirteenth century the age-old use of draped and belted cloth for both men's and women's dress was superseded by fitted and tailored bodices, tunics, sleeves, veils, and the like. The new fashion was soon reflected in the visual arts. For this reason, illustrations from the fourteenth and fifteenth centuries are unreliable guides to costuming in the plays. The new style in clothes was one symptom of the general revolution in social, political, and artistic matters, which was to result by the end of the fourteenth century in the transfer of religious drama from the chancel to the street, the innovation of speaking vernacular poetry rather than singing it, increased attention to polyphonic vocal and instrumental music for secular use, the late gothic style in architecture, and on a larger scale, the Peasants' Revolt, the Wycliffite heresies, and many other signs that the Middle Ages were passing.

Further general consideration of costuming seems inappropriate here. Descriptions of ecclesiastical vestments are easily available in any large modern dictionary, and detailed costume concerns are treated below in discussions of the costuming of each play.[26]

PROPERTIES AND FURNISHINGS

In properties and furnishings the relation between the ecclesiastical and the secular is much clearer than in costumes. Any ecclesiastical items

[26] Descriptions of these and secular costumes of the period are to be found in Joan Evans, *Dress in Medieval France* (Oxford, 1952), pp. 1–9 and 67–74; and in Mary G. Houston, *Medieval Costume in England and France* (London, 1939), pp. 2–7. These are full-length works but deal only summarily with the Romanesque period.

necessary for the play would be available from the sacristy or treasury, and could be used without fear of seeming unrealistic. Such articles as the thurible and the crosier are still used in Catholic churches, virtually unchanged in a thousand years. These traditional properties and others are also abundantly illustrated in the art works of the period. The spice boxes carried by the Marys and the Magi were quite uniform in size and shape, as hundreds of visual portrayals testify. These pyxes, as the stage directions usually call them, seem always to have been carried upright in the palm of the hand. They look heavy, but one of the most elaborate of them, the Malmesbury pyx (plate 7), weighs less than three pounds, and can be carried comfortably in one hand.

The thuribles, likewise, are the ordinary censers of the modern Roman church. They were made in several sizes, the smallest of which would have been what the Marys carried on the way to the sepulcher. The crosier, which is used in seven of the plays of the repertory, including the four St. Nicholas plays, is demonstrated in the art of the period to be the same bishop's crosier, more or less ornamented, that one finds in Catholic churches today (see plate 56).

One may also speculate that, whenever an ecclesiastical hand-property was used, it was regarded as having the utmost verisimilitude. When the crosier was brandished by the Christus, it was probably imagined by the actors and most of the audience to be a relic, the very staff he had carried.

Not all hand properties required by the plays share this traditional value. For those that do not, we can find information from the visual arts as to their use, size, and shape. Furnishings, more perishable, are also pictorially described. Thanks to the artists of the period we can see what a bed at an inn looked like, its dimensions and style of bolster, and we can thus visualize the cramped little beds for the Three Clerks in the St. Nicholas play. (plate 58). Other illustrations show the richer kind of bed the Magi would have slept on in the twelfth-century plays (plate 34). Mary's child-bed is sometimes of a very different style; in some Nativity pictures it is a curved pallet (plate 31), and elsewhere it is similar to that of the Father in *The Three Daughters* (cp. plate 28 with plate 54, and Young, II, plate XXI).

I find no evidence in any stage directions that a needed property or furnishing was to be merely imagined or pretended; those called for were certainly there, to the life. No property, however, was likely to be introduced purely for decoration or atmosphere; it was used or it was not provided. Table settings for *The Pilgrim, The Wise and Foolish Maidens,* and the *Lazarus* are no exception, since a dining table in use must be spread with food, whether to be eaten on scene or not.

STAGING AND THE DEFINITION OF ACTING AREAS

A Romanesque abbey or cathedral, like the liturgy performed in it, encouraged theatrical endeavor. A variety of related areas and levels gave ample scope for fluid and multiscene staging, and the floor space was wide and deep enough to accommodate sweeping patterns of dramatic movement. The possibilities of this stage area far exceed those of the picture stage that was our only theatrical provision from the seventeenth century until the second quarter of the twentieth, and the monks recognized them long before the first formal plays were created and staged there. As Hardison observes, "Religious ritual *was* the drama of the early Middle Ages and had been ever since the decline of the classical theater. . . . The Mass was consciously interpreted as drama during the ninth century, . . . and representational ceremonies were common in the Roman liturgy long before the earliest manuscripts of the 'Quem quaeritis' play." [27] The playwright-producer of the twelfth and thirteenth centuries inherited a dramatic tradition in a building fully capable of containing the most ambitious plays he wished to produce.

The demands of these plays seem to have augmented the existing facilities mainly by the use of platforms, which provided a more realistic definition of acting areas. Before this, several locations in the cathedral, including the nave and its bays, the transepts and their subsidiary altars, and above all the chancel, with its deep choir area and sometimes elevated sanctuary beyond, had been rather thoroughly explored as articulate dramatic areas. At this time the chancel was unencumbered by a rood screen at its entrance or a wall or screen behind the altar.[28] Processions in the nave, ceremonies at the crossing and in the transepts, and daily chancel rites that focussed on the high altar toward the rear of the sanctuary—all of these preceded the drama of the twelfth century by several hundred years, and paved the way for it. The church building and

[27] Hardison, p. viii.
[28] The vogue of the rood screen, fortunately for the production of the church plays, did not arise until the thirteenth century; see R. de Laysterie, *L'Architecture Réligieuse en France à l'Époque Gothique* (Paris, 1927), II, 486–87.

its ritual uses made the music-dramas possible and so deeply conditioned their form that modern productions of most of these plays seem somewhat dislocated when staged elsewhere than in the architecture for which they were composed.

The playwrights had ample precedent for staging their plays in whatever areas of the building were felt to be, or traditionally had been, liturgically and dramatically appropriate. For example, Young noted that a wide variety of locations for the sepulcher were specified in a dozen or more versions of *The Visit to the Sepulcher,* an indication both of the large amount of local variation in using the same type of building for the same rite, and of the latitude permitted the improviser in his choice of areas.[29]

Western visual artists were accustomed to place their compositions in an architectural environment, either real or simulated. Some man-made structure is generally included in the picture itself, which usually has a clear definition of locality; seldom is the setting purely natural or landscaped. This omnipresence of architectural forms, as in Roman and Hellenic theaters, suggests a traditional concept of scene in medieval art, and may have adumbrated the playwright's idea of appropriate staging for his scenes. For movement and area he must have been influenced chiefly by past and present ritual in his own church, but for the visual definition of those staging areas he may have been motivated by an architectural concept similar to that of the visual artists.

This sense of the architectural for staging meant negatively that the playwright would never bring in trees and bushes to define a stage area. We have already seen that outdoor travel episodes are almost never major ones, and that the locale of major scenes was usually an interior, a *locus,* a *domus,* or a *sedes* (terms used interchangeably in stage directions for a confined location). Positively, then, the settings of most of the plays were to be created from architectural members. Much was already available in the architecture of the church: doors and doorways, arches and archways, pillars, bays and transepts, chapels and altars, a short but wide flight of steps from the crossing to the choir, the curved back wall of the sanctuary with access to the ambulatory behind it. For a time, while the plays were still playlets and the dramatic impulse generated by the ritual was only partially fulfilled, the existing architectural surroundings were adequate. Subsequently, they were not outgrown, but merely supplemented by theatrical structures to give increased definition and hence greater veri-

---

[29] Young, II, 509–10.

similitude to the major scenes of the longer plays. As with the early use of ecclesiastical vestments as costumes and of ceremonial objects as theatrical properties, the playwright initially did very well with what was at hand.

To judge from stage direction requirements for the most sophisticated plays, there came a time when the ready-made settings were insufficient to match the extent of theatrical realism and symbolism available in the other aspects of production, a time when "in similitudinem" demanded more scenic definition. This point of development did not happen simultaneously all over Europe and surely varied from church to church and from decade to decade. Moreover, it was determined by other factors as well, some of which should be mentioned.

In ritualistic activity there may often have been little audience. Even in a sizable monastic community most members were probably participants rather than spectators; one could hardly have distinguished between them. Whenever this distinction did exist, the spectators would have followed the procession of celebrants wherever in the abbey the ritual was held, and would have stood during its brief enactments. As these communities grew larger, and as they and the cathedral schools drew more patronage from the princely courts, two conditions became unsatisfactory. Unless the action was in a raised sanctuary, neither the onlookers nor the actors were more than slightly elevated, and the number of onlookers who could see what was going on was extremely restricted: three rows deep was probably the limit. Furthermore, when courtly patrons and their retinues began to be drawn to the special occasions for which a play had been prepared, they were certain to have been treated with special consideration, which meant not only that they should see what the actors were doing and singing (lip reading is half of verbal comprehension) but also that they should be seated on faldstools or raised benches for the performance. (There were no pews in the medieval church; the first were probably a Reformation derivative of the raised benches brought in to accommodate a courtly medieval audience.) Once these conditions appeared, the church theater was confronted with some drastic changes. No longer could a small audience follow the play around the church, stopping for a brief scene here, another there. The staging area would have to be restricted to what the seated, immobilized courtiers could see and hear from left to right.

Meanwhile something had to be done to bring the other members of the new audience into good vertical view of the play. An audience that in a typical Romanesque church might have numbered over a thousand would of course grow restless, inattentive, and even noisy, if many of them could see nothing but the tops of the actors' heads.[30] The classic theatrical solutions have always been either to raise the audience, as in the Greek amphitheater, or to raise the actors, as in the Elizabethan public theater, the ideal solution being to raise both—as to some extent the Greeks and the Elizabethans did. The medieval solution, perhaps as early as the end of the eleventh century, seems to have been mainly to elevate the actors on *sedes,* which term was then extended to include a platform as the floor of the interior location. At the same time the benches may have been slightly elevated on other platforms.[31] The combination of a seated audience with a standing crowd was what in all likelihood brought about the use of the platforms, which robbed the medieval theater of some of its fluidity and scope, but compensated with greater scenic definition.

One of Chambers's main points, in explaining "the transfer of the plays from the interior of the church to its precincts" is that "the growing length of the plays, the increased elaboration of their setting, made it cumbrous and difficult to accommodate them within the walls." He cites the "complicated requirements of, say, the Fleury group . . . the half-dozen *loca, domus,* or *sedes* demanded by the *Suscitatio Lazari* or the *Conversio Pauli. . . .* It is in the twelfth century that the plays first seek ampler room outside the church." [32] This reiterated generalization, emphasizing the lack of space for the *sedes,* has been picked up and echoed even by such responsible later historians as George Freedley. But the development of the *sedes,* in response to a growing demand for more similitude, actually concentrated the staging area and required less of the total church space, not more. Whatever the reasons for the religious theater's departure from the church, lack of space was surely not one of them.

In developing platforms as an accommodation to the audience, the playwrights must have also had some contact with the ancient Roman comedy, at least enough to recognize that if they set up two platforms the open space between them became an outdoor space in the manner of the Roman stage-street between two houses, a *platea.* The medieval playwrights' use of the same theatrical term is in itself evidence of their acquaintance with Roman practice.

[30] See Kenneth J. Conant, *Carolingian and Romanesque Architecture 800–1200* (Baltimore, 1959), p. 306 (hereafter referred to as Conant).

[31] *Pew* is related to Latin *podium* and French *puy,* both of which denote an elevation, a rise.

[32] Chambers, II, 79. His evidence for the "half-dozen *loca, domus,* or *sedes* demanded by the *Suscitatio Lazari* or the Conversio St. Paul," is considerably overplayed. Three *sedes* take care of the Fleury *Lazarus* (see below, pp. 167–69), and the *Conversion of St. Paul* is extraordinary for its inept use of every element of theater, including the *sedes.*

The number of plays of the repertory that use the word *sedes* in the stage directions is an indication of how widespread the use of platforms was. They are: the *Lazarus, The Image of St. Nicholas, The Son of Getron, The Play of Daniel, The Annunciation,* and *The Purification.* Internal evidence implies *sedes* in *The Play of Herod, The Visit to the Sepulcher, The Procession of the Prophets, The Conversion of St. Paul, The Wise and Foolish Maidens, The Three Daughters,* and *The Three Clerks.* Only two plays, both in fourteenth-century versions, for diverse reasons do not imply a platform set: *The Shepherds* and *The Lament of Mary. The Pilgrim* may or may not have required a *sedes* for the inn at Emmaus.[33]

No permanent location for the platforms was then likely, since the platform requirements for the plays of the repertory vary (from none to three), and the erection of the platforms was necessarily temporary and occasional. In Chaucer's late-fourteenth-century *Miller's Tale* they are called "scaffolds," a term which further suggests that they were temporary structures. Because they had no fixed and traditional location, the platforms could be placed wherever they would be most effective in relation to the proportions of the existing architecture and to the space requirements of the audience. If the latter were the chief consideration, the platforms would probably have been stationed just inside the entrance to the choir, so that the audience could occupy the large space in the crossing and in the nave. In plays which apparently used the high altar—*The Visit to the Sepulcher* and *The Pilgrim,* for example—the platforms, if they were used at all, would have been set up in the back of the choir area or in the front of the sanctuary, the altar being farther back and higher, and the audience standing somewhere in the choir area.[34]

Once established, the platforms could not have remained bare and unmasked at the rear, front, or even sides. The parapet screens which often sectioned the nave would have been a fairly practical means of masking, as would the drapery curtains which apparently were traditional as a backing or a divider for a special ceremony.[35] Curtains of this size are to my knowledge mentioned only once, in the fourteenth-century Rouen stage

[33] See below, pp. 113–14.

[34] E. Martin Browne has effectively staged medieval plays in such arrangements of audience and actors, notably at the National Cathedral in Washington in 1968.

[35] Conant, p. 22, has a description of parapet screens. For a modern illustration of curtaining in the Sistine Chapel, see *L'Italia,* No. 238 (April 1968), p. 38. See also a miniature in the famous *Traite sur l'Oraison dominical,* reproduced by A. Laborde, *Les miracles de Nostre Dame, compilé par Jehan Miélot* (Paris, 1929). The curtains are stretched between the capitals of Romanesque pillars, and hang in pleats at the sides of the altar. No platform is involved in this fifteenth-century curtaining. See also Young, II, 510.

direction for the Midwives to reveal the Madonna and Child, "cortinam aperientes" (opening the curtain), in *The Shepherds.* This reference is of course not to back or side curtains but to a front draw curtain. Unfortunately for us, the playwrights did not in any of the plays need to specify curtains for the platforms, the term *sedes* being capable of comprehending a stage set, its accompanying platform, and necessary curtaining. The same Latin word may, I suspect, have colored the etymology of the modern English "set" in its theatrical use.

The medieval artist does not offer much help in visualizing the curtained platform. An eleventh-century *Lectionary* from Reichenau, illustrating the resurrection of Lazarus (plate 40), shows the characters of the story (or play) on a level above that of the spectators, with a drapery valance over the front edge of the floor of the supposed platform. The *Peterborough Psalter,* from the middle of the thirteenth century, has several illustrations that could be taken for platform settings, with fleur-de-lis curtains draped from center top to the front corners, and some kind of back curtain within (plate 25).[36] A similar hint of a back curtain is illustrated in the *Pseudo-Bonaventura Meditations* of the thirteenth century (plate 23). The best evidence for the back curtains is the practical need that the platforms, which are often specified in the stage directions, have curtains to mask off the sides, back, and underpinnings. We know that *sedes* were used in most of the plays, and we may reasonably posit from circumstantial evidence the existence and necessity of curtains to complete them.

The existence of a front draw curtain on the *sedes* is, however, rather unlikely.[37] No matter how thin the curtain material was, when it was drawn to the sides it would have made a gathering of at least a foot in width at each end, which would have had to be subtracted from the width of the visible playing area, and which would have been a formidable obstacle for spectators at forty-five degrees to the front of the platform. From medieval art works one gathers that slim, ornamented posts (as in plate 25), would usually have been all that framed the front opening.

Inside that opening, and at its ends, may have been a sort of double door, a stylized set-piece which dated from the era of the classical Greek

[36] A more realistic drawing of this type of curtain is in Pierpont Morgan Library MS 724, English (twelfth century). Reproduced by Arthur Watson, *The Early Iconography of the Tree of Jesse* (London, 1934), plate XXVIII.

[37] Young, II, 404, regrets that in *The Conversion of St. Paul,* "The personages of the play, including Ananias lying on his bed, take their positions in full view of the spectators at the outset, and thus preclude the possibility of pleasurable surprise at appropriate moments in the subsequent action."

theater, and which may be traced in art illustrations throughout the Middle Ages. Although it is not mentioned in the stage directions of any of the plays, the illustrations attest its presence on the *sedes*. Unless one dismisses the whole piece as a painter's fetish that somehow lasted fifteen hundred years, there is something both provocative and illuminating in juxtaposing illustrations of the Greek stage from *phlyakes* vases of the fourth century, B.C. with certain works of twelfth-century artists (plate 1

1 *Phlyakes* Doors, shown at left as depicted on a southern Italian vase, fourth century B.C. From Margarete Bieber, *The History of the Greek and Roman Theater*, 2d ed. (Princeton: Princeton University Press, 1961), fig. 509, p. 139.

with plates 21, 22, 27, 32, 34, 35, 48, and 66). The subjects are entirely different, legendary Greek as against medieval biblical, yet the swinging double door remains amazingly constant, sometimes stage right, sometimes stage left, sometimes centered. This double door—reminiscent of the french doors of the Ibsen-Shaw era but not, like them, centered for the entrance of the star—swings *in* as a proper stage door should. It is a symbol for an entrance door, differentiating on-stage from off-stage, interior from exterior. The Roman theater had the convention of houses left and right of the central *platea;* possibly the Romans, influenced by Greek theatrical customs as always, used the same door, redoubled, to represent their stage "houses." Twelfth-century producers, somehow aware of Roman but certainly not of classical Greek theatrical practice (except through the Byzantine), may have maintained the convention, perhaps also influenced by the graphic artists' illustrations around them in abbey and cathedral. This scenic adjunct of production cannot be precisely defined, but neither can it be denied. The playwright, unfortunately for us, would not have needed to explain such an obvious matter on expensive parchment.

The high altar is a critical item of theatrical furnishing in *The Visit to the Sepulcher, The Pilgrim,* and *The Shepherds.* In the latter two plays there is a sustained dramatic action visible behind the altar, which the modern mind imagines as backed by a reredos (retable), a screen so closely attached to the altar table that no action would be possible behind it. Actually, however, in the production of some of the music-dramas, the altar usually was not encumbered with such a screen but was free-standing, and the priest himself officiated behind the altar. As Hans Weigert observed,

Except for a small Crucifix, chalice, and missal, the mensa remained empty, so that the priest who at first celebrated the Mass from behind the altar, facing the congregation, could be seen. In the twelfth century, for some reason unknown to us, perhaps because of a change in the teaching of Transubstantiation, the priest moved to the front of the altar, and instead of administering the Sacrament on behalf of Our Lord, he became the representative of the congregation. The altar could now be enriched with a reliquary, a free-standing figure of a saint or the Virgin, and a retable.[38]

In the Beauvais version of *The Pilgrim,* the scene of the supper at Emmaus, if not performed on a *sedes* as it may have been in some later twelfth- and early thirteenth-century versions, took place at the altar before it was backed by a reredos and encumbered with a reliquary casket and a saintly statue. Similarly, the Nativity scene in *The Shepherds* must have been originally designed to be enacted in the manner of the visual portrayals: the image of the cradled Christchild above on the altar, with Mary below on a pallet (plate 31).[39] The addition of the draw curtain and revelation of the two characters together, in Renaissance style, could only have been necessary or effective after the installation of the screen and the altar ornaments. The Salzburg *Lectionary* illustration of the Nativity (plate 29), though dated "middle twelfth century," reflects the priest's change of position. When an Angel appears "retro altare," as in some versions of *The Visit to the Sepulcher,* his point of entrance is

[38] In Harald Busch and Bernd Lohse, eds., *Romanesque Sculpture,* trans. Peter Gorge (London, 1962), pp. xviii–xix.
[39] This enamel plaque is variously assigned to the eleventh and twelfth centuries. See Thomas P. F. Hoving's note to plate 25 of *A Medieval Treasury,* ed. James J. Rorimer (New York, 1965). In view of Weigert's distinction, the earlier date is better.

an indication that he is in a play that was organized after the reredos and the statuary had been put up, sometime in the twelfth century. The reredos was, then, a rather new piece of scenery, a theatrical backdrop, and together with the other additions to the altar, it revolutionized the staging of scenes at the high altar in the same way that the changes in the audience affected the fluid concept of staging and brought in the *sedes*.

It should also be remarked again that for twelfth-century playwrights these revolutions, destructive as they always are, made possible more intensification of their scenes and a greater degree of the verisimilitude for which they were apparently reaching.

Young's summary of the findings of Brooks and others in respect to the structures erected in churches for use as Easter sepulchers includes a masterly condensation of information about actual full-size buildings, from the original Anastasis at Jerusalem to its pseudoforms in supposedly eleventh-century Aquileia and in postmedieval Europe.[40] In relation to the production of twelfth- and thirteenth-century music-dramas on the theme of the resurrection, particularly *The Visit to the Sepulcher* and the *Lazarus,* what we need to know, if it can be ascertained at this late date, is the kinds of structures that might reasonably have been used for the staging of these plays. For this purpose, visual representations of the Sepulcher, and my hypothesis about the *sedes* as a theatrical structure, may be combined with what the Fleury and St. Quentin playwrights of *The Visit to the Sepulcher* may have used as images of the anastasis and the sarcophagus. In this instance, the use of anachronism as verisimilitude is not, and was not for those playwrights, a valid approach to the staging of their works. The Crusades had brought back firsthand accounts of the actual Anastasis, and had thereby shaken the confidence of playwright and audience in setting up a frankly anachronistic, Romanesque theatrical structure as a satisfactory sepulcher. The artists betray the same uneasiness, and either invent their own versions, based on hearsay from crusaders and pilgrims and on the drawings of earlier artists, or avoid the problem by showing only a sarcophagus, instead of struggling to relate it to the apparently engrossing structure of the Anastasis. As I have explained in more detail in the chapter on *The Visit to the Sepulcher,* the playwrights were unable to avoid an anastasis because the sarcophagus would have been too slight, stark, and inadequate, even ridiculously like a

---

[40] Young, II, 507–13. I consider the permanent structure at Aquileia either a sport or misdated. The other permanent structures did not appear until "the close of the Middle Ages, and thereafter" (Young, II, 511).

horse trough, if it were the only furnishing for the scene. The *sedes* was, furthermore, a common stage structure, and could have had an anastasis, tomb, or monument satisfactorily built upon the raised platform. A domed canopy over the *sedes,* not unlike that of the tenth-century Hartker illustration,[41] with foreshortened Romanesque arches and a sarcophagus at the level of the platform, would have satisfied nearly everyone, including the stunned Soldiers profiled against the front skirt of the platform. The location of the platform and its anastasis was no doubt influenced by architectural conditions; it did not have to encompass the altar or even be close to it. Chambers gives evidence that its usual position was on the north side of the choir.[42] Young's only example of the sepulcher's being placed "apart from the main altar," is from sixteenth-century Bamberg.[43] But the Fleury and St. Quentin playwrights, to judge from their scripts, could not possibly have produced their plays at the altar, and must have been compelled to use more sophisticated production techniques.

For only three plays of the repertory do we have today the architectural surroundings in anything like their condition at the time of performance. Fire and dissolution have destroyed three churches in which five plays of the repertory were originally staged. The Romanesque church of St. Martial at Limoges, the site of *The Wise and Foolish Maidens* and *The Procession of Prophets,* was dedicated at the right moment to have presented the plays, but the church fell to ruins and was demolished in the eighteenth century. The Carolingian choir of the Beauvais cathedral, the original stage for *The Play of Daniel* and *The Pilgrim,* was destroyed by fire in 1225, long after the plays had been performed there, and the present choir was not finished until 1272. The Romanesque cathedral at Rouen for which *The Shepherds* was probably composed was almost entirely destroyed by the great fire of 1200. Because the present cathedral was then rebuilt from west to east, its new chancel was not completed in time to accommodate this play, even supposing that it was not composed until the latter part of the thirteenth century. Nothing today remains of the abbey at Origny-Sainte-Benoite, the home of a superior version of *The Visit to the Sepulcher;* it was repeatedly put to the torch until its complete destruction in 1761.

The most vexing problem in relating the plays to their original surroundings is that of establishing a twelfth-century connection between the "Fleury Playbook," in which nine of the practical repertory are contained, and the Abbey St. Benoit de Fleury at St. Benoit-sur-Loire. Un-

---

[41] See p. 20n.   [42] Chambers, II, 22, note 6; and II, 83.
[43] Young, II, 510; and I, 323.

fortunately there is no reference to Fleury in the nine plays, as there is to Beauvais in the *Daniel,* and as there are to the Paduan cathedral and baptistry in the stage directions of *The Annunciation* and *The Purification.*

The ascription of the Playbook to this abbey rests on evidence which definitely connects the manuscript with the abbey only as far back as 1552.[44] One therefore cannot at this time proceed to study in detail the production of the nine plays in the still extant Romanesque abbey, on the assumption of a twelfth-century connection. Presumably these plays were performed in a monastic church, to judge from stage-direction references to the "fratres" and the "monasterium," and one may, as a profitable exercise, visualize them as being played in the commodious choir and elevated sanctuary of Fleury rather than at another abbey.[45]

For architectural authenticity, we are thus limited to *The Annunciation* and *The Purification* in the Duomo at Padua and *The Lament of Mary* in the Cividale Cathedral. Both of these cathedrals "suffered" (as the art historians say) drastic remodeling and restoration, but fortunately the three plays can be shown to have been performed in specific transept areas whose dimensions have remained unchanged. (These demonstrations are presented in discussion of the staging of each play.)

MAKEUP: BEARDS AND HAIRSTYLES

Whether or not beards were in fashion during the period of the plays is an oversimplified question. If the premise is that the visual arts of the pe-

[44] Solange Corbin in "Le Manuscrit 201 d'Orléans: Drames Liturgiques Dit de Fleury," *Romania* LXXIV (1953), 1–43, wishes to remove Fleury from consideration as the locale of the Fleury plays, and to substitute St. Lomer de Blois as the twelfth-century source. Her hypothesis does not work any better than the assumption she disturbs, that the play had some twelfth-century relationship to the Abbaye St. Benoit de Fleury. Père Lin Donnat of the Fleury abbey is preparing an article in which he will describe in full detail the composite nature of Orléans MS 201, as revealed by his direct examination, and will establish the positive rapport of three other bonafide Fleury manuscripts (Orléans MSS 73, 126, and 216) with that portion of MS 201 which contains the plays. The Fleury Playbook may thus be definitely connected with Fleury as far back as 1552 when the bonafide manuscripts were catalogued (Bibliothèque Nationale, MS latin, nouvelles acquisitions 137). Grace Frank, *Medieval French Drama* (Oxford, 1954), p. 44, note 1, has similar objections to Corbin's argument. On the other hand, C. W. Jones, *The Saint Nicholas Liturgy* (Berkeley and Los Angeles, 1963), p. 91, believes that "it is, in fact, not even certain that the Fleury play book was copied at Fleury, let alone that the plays were composed there . . . some wandering scholar collected an anthology of favorite pieces where he could find them."

[45] The contents of the Playbook were first published in 1860 by Edmond de Coussemaker, *Drames liturgiques du Moyen Age* (facsimile edition: New York, 1964); hereafter referred to as Coussemaker.

riod reflect contemporary custom in beards as well as in clothes, and that for biblical or legendary characters in the plays the anachronism of fashion was often modified by the traditional attributes of those characters, one may still discriminate among characters, and attempt to discover which sorts of men in those times and plays often wore a certain style of beard, which sorts wore other styles, and which were clean shaven. Yet even these generalizations would hide as much as they would reveal. In our own times, in a span of only sixty years, we have seen beards first the rightful property only of old men and now the nearly exclusive possession of youth. How would one characterize the beard-wearer of the period 1910–1970?

Within the comparable period 1100–1300, when fashion changed so much more slowly, we may at least sample the art works and establish probabilities. The lack of absolute consistency may reflect changes of fashion within the period, though none can be detected with certainty because of the underlay of tradition in respect to the characters of the plays. A survey of several hundred pictures and sculptures of men of the period yields the following sartorial guidelines:

Herod always wore a beard. I find no illustrations of a clean-shaven Herod. Apparently this does not mean that beards were a symbol of villainy, like the black mustachios of the villains of melodrama, for the Christus wears much the same kind of beard in three-quarters of the pictures surveyed. St. Paul is invariably bearded, and so is St. Peter. Does this mean that only men having authority let their whiskers grow, as a badge of office? Apparently not, for while other kings, like the First Magus of the *Herod* and Marmorinus of *The Son of Getron* are always bearded, Darius and Belshazzar of the *Daniel* are clean-shaven. Authority cannot have been the index, for the old Silenus figure in *The Shepherds* gets part of his comic effect from his receding forehead and bushy beard. The foreigner is sometimes distinguished by his beard. The Jew in *The Image of St. Nicholas,* who in Hilarius's unproduceable version is called Barbarus, is always represented in art with a heavy black beard, because he is a pagan, a barbarian, and therefore assumed to be bearded.

In groups of three men in the same walk of life the visual artists usually beard only one, often the leader. Thus the first of the three Magi, one of the three Shepherds, one of the three robbers in *The Image of St. Nicholas,* and one of the three courtiers in the *Herod.* Possibly this arrangement was merely for the sake of variety; if so, the play-producers could have been acting upon the same aesthetic principle.

There appears to have been at least one invariable rule: Never beard a

35

very young man, no doubt because it will blunt his youthfulness. For this reason John, Daniel, the Soldiers in the *Herod* and elsewhere, the young Clerks in *The Three Clerks,* the Archangel, and the younger Shepherds were never bearded by the artists. The only apparent exception to this rule is a sole surviving portrait of the Suitor of *The Three Daughters.* His beard may, however, suggest that he is not a handsome young man but an older fellow, interested more in the dowry than in romance.

A second principle seems to have operated. Beards either dignified or degraded the wearers; if there was risk entailed in which effect beards would produce, they were avoided. A third principle has to do with the cut of the beard: a light, well-trimmed chin beard was stylish and dignified, while a heavy, bushy, unkempt one was either villainous or comic. One notes that the Christus' beard was usually rather short and well trimmed, as were those of his disciples, of kings, and of St. Nicholas. The beards of the Jew, of the First Robber, of the Old Shepherd, and of the Spice Merchant in the St. Quentin version of *The Visit to the Sepulcher* were, on the other hand, longer, bushier, and untrimmed.

Men's haircuts were considerably longer than has been the modern custom, but considerably less than shoulder length. Wigs are not obviously needed for any character in the plays except John in *The Lament of Mary,* and neither in that play nor in any of the versions of *The Visit to the Sepulcher* in which John appears is a wig specified for him in the stage directions, although its propriety may be inferred from most illustrations of the postcrucifixion scene (e.g., plate 16). Although wigs may occasionally have been required to conceal the tonsured or bald head of a monastic actor, the playwright would hardly have immortalized the individual actor's problem in the permanent form of the playscript.

Women's hairstyles are consistently long, well down their backs. In the extreme, Mary Magdalene's hair hangs down to her knees, so that she may dry the Lord's feet with it. For the medieval boy actor of the role, this would have entailed the addition of at least a hairpiece. Sometimes women's hair was parted in the middle, as in some illustrations of the Wise and Foolish Maidens. Often one cannot tell from the pictures because the head is veiled, there having been an ancient and stringent prohibition against women's heads being uncovered either in public or in church. Sometimes, as with the Midwives of *The Shepherds,* the hair is netted in a snood, though this seems to have been appropriate only for the lower class. Fillets helped to dignify persons of either sex, to bind the front hair of the Marys or of the Christus "in His glory."

We may presume that the medieval producers took as much pains with the tonsorial aspect of their productions as they did with costumes. Otherwise, a tonsured monastic countertenor, dressed as Mary Magdalene, would have looked absurd. Similarly, a clean-shaven actor, serious or comic, would have been furnished with a beard if his role traditionally called for it or would be enhanced by it. Shakespeare's parody, in which Bottom ponders what color beard he should wear for the Pyramus role, suggests that four hundred years later even the rankest of amateurs expected to be bearded for a play, and may reflect medieval practice. Beards are, like costumes, attractive for the dramatically inclined of any age or culture, and are easier to contrive than scenic effects.

Medieval use of facial makeup for the stage, through charcoal lining and pigments, seems unlikely, though the Elizabethans used these techniques, and probably did not invent them. Unless the makeup at the close range of the medieval audience was more subtly naturalistic than the brushwork of the twelfth- and thirteenth-century frescoes and miniatures, one doubts that makeup would have been used, especially at the risk of being unintentionally fantastic.

The use of masks seems to have been restricted in the church music-dramas to Devil roles, represented in the repertory by the "Daemones" of *The Wise and Foolish Maidens.* The disrepute into which secular "maskings and disguisings" had brought the mask, as reflected in Innocent III's mention of *monstra larvarum* in his ruling,[46] eliminated it from theatrical use in the church, except for the diabolical roles. A twelfth-century devil, sculptured on a capital at the Abbey St. Benoit de Fleury, appears to be masked as he tempts St. Benedict with a whore. This illustration, and one from Vézélay (plate 50), are more typical of the period than the abundant and monstrous pictures of devils produced in the fourteenth and fifteenth centuries.[47]

LIGHTING

The use of artificial light in a medieval church combined the functional and the dramatic. Processions, which were routine for the beginning or ending of a liturgical office, were accompanied by bearers of tapers. They were essential for lighting the way of a procession at Matins, and at other monastic Hours after sundown and before dawn, as well for the

[46] Quoted by Young, II, 416. See also above, p. 6.
[47] As reproduced by Nicoll, pp. 190–93.

Easter vigil Mass. They also provided an element of the ceremonial, the symbolic, the mystic; by the early Middle Ages they had become so much a part of liturgical observances that they were—and still are today—routinely used even in the daytime. We may therefore assume that both tapers and thicker, shorter candles were the basic lighting for church music dramas.

In a Romanesque abbey or early Gothic cathedral, such illumination was hardly adequate, even for medieval eyes, accustomed to lower levels of light than ours. To judge from illustrations, the intensity had to be increased by means of candelabra, on pedestals or on the altar, and by a quantity of torches and lamps fueled by oil or spirits. The lamps had several advantages: they could be suspended on adjustable chains from a pillar bracket or a high arch, and would in that overhead position be out of the way of ceremonial and dramatic movement, while attracting moths and mosquitoes to a higher level. Also, they burned much longer and more steadily than wax candles and thin tapers. These suspended lamps were of two types, both widely used if we may accept the pictorial evidence of the times. One was a vase or amphora-shaped lamp of glass within a gilded metal frame; the glass bowl was filled with fuel in which floated a wick (plate 29). The other type of suspended lamp is of particular interest to this study because it was used in at least two plays as a medieval analogue of the modern spotlight. Known as the *corona* or *corona lampadarum,* the crown light could be set ablaze more quickly than a bank of candles or a vase lamp, and was much more powerful. The rim of the lamp was in the shape of a crown, with openwork in the rim, and crosses or other appropriate ornaments mounted on the top edge. Centered in this metal structure was a large glass bowl, with a cluster of smaller bowls around it, in line with the openwork. Each bowl was filled with fuel and contained a floating cotton wick.[48]

Two medieval illustrations are of direct relevance to the drama. They show a crown light hanging over a scene from *The Visit to the Sepulcher* (plate 10) and over a *Herod* court scene (plate 32).[49] Corroborating the theatrical use of this light in *The Visit to the Sepulcher* is a stage direction from the thirteenth-century Monza version of the play:

[48] F. N. Arnoldi, "Liturgical and Ritual Objects," in *Encyclopedia of World Art* (New York, 1964), IX, 305. Hereafter referred to as Arnoldi.

[49] Other period illustrations of the crown light in use are in P. Metz, ed., *Das Goldene Evangelienbuch von Echternach* (Munich, 1956), plate 31; George Swarzenski, *Die Salzburger Malerei* (Leipzig, 1908), plate II; and Jean Porcher, *L'Enluminure française* (Paris, 1959), p. 16, fig. 14. See also W. H. Forsyth, *Metropolitan Museum of Art Bulletin,* n.s., III (1945), 165.

Et cum sumus in ecclesia, stamus et dicitur antiphona: *Et valde mane una sabbatorum veniunt ad monumentum, orto iam sole. Alleluia,* archipresbitero sedente super foldestorio. Et hoc dicitur ter, et chorus semper similiter respondet. Et cum intramus chorum, custos, levata cruce aurea cum candelis accensis desuper, ponit ignem in corona lampadarum circumdata et tota cooptera bombice, quod dicitur farum.[50]

(And when we are inside the church, we stop and let be sung the antiphon, *And very early in the morning, the first day of the week, they came unto the sepulcher at the rising of the sun, Alleluia!* [51] the high priest sitting on a faldstool. And this [the antiphon] is to be sung three times, and the choir always sings the same responsory. And when we enter the choir, the bearer of the gilded cross, with lighted candles at its top, raises it aloft and ignites the crown light which has been fueled and wicked all the way around, like a chandelier.) [52]

The scribe appears to make the point that this is not an ordinary chandelier, a bank of candles, but is a crown light, fueled and wicked so that the blazing candles on top of the gilded staff-cross can quickly ignite all the wicks, unlike the slow candle-lighting process. At the same time the effect is—"quod dicitur"—like that of a lighted chandelier.

The *Et valde mane* antiphon includes Mark's phrase "orto iam sole" (the sun now rising) and this phrase is immediately imitated by the speedy illumination of the prepared crown light. In many versions of *The Visit to the Sepulcher* the procession of the Marys to the sepulcher is preceded by the singing of the antiphon, and by the Angel's striking down the Soldiers with lightning and sitting on the sarcophagus. The Monza version is ingenious in suggesting a further preliminary action, that the Angel light the crown light as a symbol of the rising of the sun, and as a focal point of destination for the Marys' movement.[53] So used, the crown light may fairly be claimed as the first special or spotlight or area light in the history of the Western theater.

Another theatrical use of the crown light is documented by art illustrations and by a stage direction from a fourteenth-century Magi playlet from Rouen, and while this is a late manuscript, the dates of the illustrations (plates 10 and 32) attest that the use of the crown light was not a post-Romanesque development. The stage direction reads:

[50] Young, I, 228.

[51] Mark 16:2. The antiphon adds only the customary *Alleluia.*

[52] Ronald E. Latham, *Revised Medieval Latin Word-List* (Oxford, 1965) cites such uses of *pharum* in the eighth and ninth centuries.

[53] See below, pp. 291–92, for a detailed discussion of the use of the crown light in the *Visit to the Sepulcher.* Young, apparently unaware of the nature and theatrical function of the crown light, describes the action in the Monza version thus: "a crown of lights, of candles and cotton, is set ablaze over a gilded cross" (I, 229).

Dum autem processio navem ecclesiae intrare ceperit, corona ante crucem pendens in modum Stellae accendatur, et Magi, Stellam ostendentes, ad Yma-ginem Sanctae Mariae super Altare Crucis prius positam cantantes pergant: *Ecce Stella in oriente. . . ."* [54]

(But when the procession is ready to enter the church, let the crown light be lit, hanging in front of the cross as if it were the Star. And let the Magi, point-ing out the Star, move to the Image of Saint Mary, placed earlier over the altar of the Holy Cross, singing *Behold a star in the east. . . ."* [55]

The most spectacular lighting effect, unique to the Magi plays, is the special "stella" which is specified in the stage directions of the Limoges and Rouen versions as being suspended, and which "appears"—we are not told how—in the Fleury, the *Carmina Burana,* and the Montpellier versions, where it may also have been suspended. [56] The Limoges version refers to the star's being hung on a rope ("pendentem in filo") which may have been joined to the three chains of the crown light, and which could have been controlled by pulleys. In any event, there can be no doubt that the "corona" of the Rouen Magi play is the "corona lampa-darum" of the Monza stage direction for the Sepulcher playlet. The Rouen version locates its manger scene, with figures of the Virgin and Child, at the altar of the Holy Cross, so that the crown light star very properly hangs over the manger. In addition to the similar altar locations of both plays and their common use of the "Quem quaeritis" formula, the crown light is a hitherto unrecognized way in which the Nativity and Sepul-cher themes were joined. Since the crown light was used in the Sepulcher set, there was every reason to use it over the Manger set. We may therefore infer that the apparitions of the star, a feature of four other versions of the Magi-Herod play, were in actuality the long ignored crown light. [57]

Although the abundant illustrations of the crown light in the period of the plays give a fair idea of dimensions and construction, they do not show the precise design of the interior fuel bowls. Because the crown light was so common in medieval churches, one would expect to find at least a few survivors today, although a cursory investigation in French and Italian churches of the period and in several museums has failed to

[54] Young, II, 44.

[55] Young, II, 45, as in I, 229 cited above, mistakenly translates "corona" as "a star-shaped cluster of lights."

[56] For the Limoges version see Young, II, 34–35; for the Montpellier, II, 68–72.

[57] Smoldon, in Noah Greenberg and W. L. Smoldon, eds., *The Play of Herod, A Twelfth-Century Musical Drama* (New York, 1965), p. 77, reflects the current impres-sion of the "stella" in describing it as "apparently a candelabrum."

locate a single specimen. Access to the genuine object, rather than merely to illustrations, would allow us to blueprint its construction for accurate reproduction in modern productions. Either this style of lamp went out of fashion or it was too easy a mark for marauders and sackers, its gilded bronze being a ready source of war materials. Two larger cousins of the crown light give us some idea of its construction. According to F. N. Arnoldi, "the unique pieces in the Cathedral of Aachen and in the Church of St. Maurice, Coburg, were inspired by the imaginary architecture of the Heavenly Jerusalem, and depict a wall with gates and towers; they may date from the twelfth century." [58] The wall of Jerusalem on these lamps corresponds to the rim of the more modest crown light, the towers to the earlier crosses. From the base of the monstrous Aachen model, one gathers that there was a large central bowl, and around it a series of smaller fuel cups, and that each container had its own wick of wadded cotton, the "bombice" of the Monza crown light. At the other end of the crown light's history is a prototype of its shape in the Cairo Museum. Dated fifth to seventh century, it has a solid rim, around the top of which are mounted ten candlesticks in the shape of dolphins. Three chains, as usual in illustrations of the suspension of the crown light, hold it level.

Other types of fuel-burning lamps were the portable amphora and the torch. Both are treated below in discussion of *The Wise and Foolish Maidens.*

SOUND EFFECTS

St. Paul's rather slighting reference to what St. Jerome later translated as "aes sonans aut cymbalum tinniens," and Tindale as "sounding brass or a tinkling cymbal," is ironically the prototype for the sound effects of a medieval church play.[59] The early Christian church took over much of the ritual of the synagogue of St. Paul's day, and continued the singing of psalms (the prototype of the medieval antiphon), the sounding of brass bells and the tinkling of finger cymbals. The generally celebrative sound of such bells was thus a traditional element of dramatic ceremonies at Easter, Christmas, and other feast days of the medieval church.

The extremes of size, pitch, and timbre of these traditional bells are implied in St. Paul's phrase. The powerfully resonant tower bells, the *campanae,* of the abbey or cathedral, customarily alerted the entire re-

[58] Arnoldi, p. 305.   [59] 1 Corinthians 13:1.

ligious community to the fact that a service was about to begin or conclude. The standard verb in the many stage directions for their use in the plays is "pulsare," which suggests their pulsing, throbbing quality.[60] At the other extreme were the high-pitched little finger cymbals, the timbre of which is brighter than the modern English "tinkling" denotes; the medieval *tinniens* is onomatopoeically more accurate, the sound resembling a bell more than a cymbal.

Between these extremes were the hand bells and chime bells. The latter were usually hung in a rack, tuned in the range of about an octave, and in this arrangement were more stationary than portable. The chime bells were struck with a leather-covered wooden mallet, while the hand bells, held one in each hand, had clappers. Their use is illustrated in a detail from a Mosan reliquary of the early thirteenth century,[61] and they are referred to by the sixteenth century antipapist, Barnaby Googe, in *The Popish Kingdom* (1570): "The boyes before with clappers go, and filthie noyses make." [62] Googe's unsympathetic description of bells in a procession is countered by a parallel twelfth-century stage direction: "Pueri primum ferentes tintinabula" ("the leading choirboys carrying hand bells").[63] There were in fact many liturgical moments, in and out of the plays, when the chime bells, the hand bells, and the finger cymbals were used to underline a dramatic moment.[64]

We cannot always be sure which type of bell is required by the rubrics of dramatic ceremonies and by the stage directions of the plays, but we do know that liturgical bell ringing was intensified during the period of the plays. As an example of this increase, solely in relation to the ceremony of the Elevation, Young quotes a historian of the liturgy: "We do not realize at once how much of novel and imposing ceremonial is involved in the addition, in the twelfth and thirteenth centuries, of the single act of the elevation of the Host and Chalice, with its accompanying lights and torches, censing, bell-ringings, and genuflections." [65]

Finger cymbals are technically classified as percussion instruments, though their tone is more bell-like, as I have remarked. Unlike the chime

---

[60] See, for example, Young, I, 141, 559, 620, 621; II, 248, 253.

[61] James J. Rorimer, *The Cloisters,* 3d ed. (New York, 1963), p. 140, fig. 68. See also a twelfth-century illustration in *Grove's Dictionary of Music and Musicians,* 5th ed. (London, 1954), VI, plate 48 (facing p. 536).

[62] Reproduced in Young, II, 532–37.

[63] From a primitive version of the *Visitatio* from Soissons (Young, I, 304).

[64] See, for instance, Hardison, p. 213.

[65] Edmund Bishop, *Liturgica Historica* (Oxford, 1918), p. 9, as quoted by Young, I, 42–3.

bells, the little cymbals were not arranged in a scale of pitches, and hence their use was percussive. In the plays, to judge from modern revivals, the finger cymbal added a touch of strangeness and beauty. Larger cymbals, not more than eight inches in diameter and with the more characteristic timbre of modern cymbals, were also used in this period. They had sufficient volume to be rousing and shocking, particularly when clashed in the very "live" acoustics of medieval stone or brick churches. Drums of several sizes were apparently also available for percussive use in the plays, and whether or not these instruments were used in the original productions, their dramatic effectiveness has been proven by the New York Pro Musica's revivals of the *Daniel* and the *Herod.*

The playwrights, probably considering the drums and larger cymbals a sound effect (what they termed a "noise"), never scored these or any other accompanying instrument in their scripts. Occasionally, as in the Beauvais version of *The Pilgrim,* a stage direction suggests that a chime bell is sounded at least once, but this is in imitation of an action in the Consecration division of the Mass.

As with the costuming and props in these plays, which are so bound up with traditional liturgical practices, the fact that other, nonpercussive instruments are not mentioned in stage directions does not preclude their use, particularly on the kind of special occasion for which many of the plays were composed. On the other hand, the liturgy of the medieval church is so fully melodic, monophonic, and vocal that the plays must also have been primarily so intended. Dr. Smoldon, in a laudable effort to forestall modern excesses, states flatly that "the evidence for the use of instruments of any sort during performances of these dramas within the church is very slight indeed." [66] The only exceptions to this generally proper conclusion are the courtly plays: the *Herod,* the *Daniel,* and *The Son of Getron,* in which the influence of the courtly audience may well have encouraged a certain amount of secularization and musical pomp. In the *Daniel,* for example, there is a stage direction for harpists to lead the procession of the pagan Darius. The closer a play of the repertory is

---

[66] Smoldon, *Visitatio,* p. iv. and W. L. Smoldon, "Medieval Church Drama and the Use of Musical Instruments," *The Muscial Times* (London), Dec. 1962, No. 1438. In opposition to this point of view, see a series of three articles by E. A. Bowles in *The Galpin Society Journal,* X (1957), XI (1958), and XII (1959). The experience of the present writer is that instrumental bridges between items of a medieval music drama are rarely needed. A production of the *Lazarus* in Washington in 1971 (see below, p. 157) demonstrated that for at least that play no instrumentation was needed or even desirable.

to the tone and quality of its liturgical antecedents, the less likely it is that instruments other than the portative organ and the bells discussed above would have been considered necessary or appropriate as accompaniments to the sung dialogue. In the more detailed discussion of possible sound effects for each of the plays of the repertory, I have therefore been conservative in my suggestions of "noise" of any kind.

The Plays of the Repertory

1. The Visit to the Sepulcher

2 Postcrucifixion and Spice Merchants. Lintel, right portal, west façade, St. Gilles Church, twelfth century. Courtesy of the Fogg Art Museum, Harvard University.

3 Spice Merchants (detail of plate 2).

4 Spice Merchants. Capital, Museo Civico, Modena, ca. 1175. From Francovich, *Benedetto Antelami,* plate 54. Courtesy of Görlich Editore.

5 The Marys Approaching the Sepulcher (below left), the central Mary grinding spices. Relief, St. Pieterskerk, Utrecht, ca. 1160. Courtesy of Mrs. A. C. F. Vorstius Kruijff.

6 The Three Approaching the Sepulcher (below right). Capital from the sanctuary, Abbaye Saint Benoit de Fleury, Saint-Benoit-sur-Loire, end of eleventh century. Courtesy of the photographic service of the Abbey.

7   The Malmesbury Pyx (or Ciborium). 1160–75. The Pierpont Morgan Library.

8 Four Pyxes. Thirteenth century. Courtesy of Victoria and Albert Museum, Crown copyright.

9 The Marys and the Angel at the Sepulcher, with soldiers below. "Brandenburger Evangelistar," fol. 56ᵛ, early thirteenth century. Brandenburg (Havel), Library of the Cathedral of Peter and Paul. From *Brandenburger Evangelistar*, facsimile edition (Leipzig, St. Benno-Verlag, 1961). Courtesy of St. Benno-Verlag and Domstift Brandenburg.

10   The Marys and the Angel at the Sepulcher, crownlight above, soldiers below. Ivory
plaque from Cologne, second half of twelfth century. Courtesy of the Metropolitan
Museum of Art, gift of George Blumenthal, 1941.

11 The Marys and the Angel at the Sepulcher, with soldiers below. Book of Hours, ca. 1250. Brussels, Bibliothèque Royale, MS 2935, fol. 8ʳ. Courtesy of Bibliothèque Royale Albert Iᵉʳ.

12 Mary Magdalene Recognizes the Christus. "Miniatures," French, second half of twelfth century. New York, The Pierpont Morgan Library, MS 44, fol. 12ʳ.

13 Mary Magdalene Recognizes the Christus. English Psalter,
early thirteenth century. London, British Museum, MS
Arundel 157, fol. 11ᵛ. Courtesy of the Trustees of the
British Museum.

14 Mary Magdalene Recognizes the Christus. English Gospel Book, early twelfth century. Cambridge, Library of Pembroke College, MS 120, fol. 4ᵛ. Courtesy of the Masters and Fellows of Pembroke College, Cambridge.

The Visit to the Sepulcher

Visitatio Sepulchri

TONE AND QUALITY

THE resurrection theme, as everyone knows, is a central concern of all the medieval arts, and was the most fertile ground for dramatization of the liturgy. Of the three plays dealing with resurrection, including the *Lazarus* and *The Pilgrim,* none treats the theme more fully than *The Visit to the Sepulcher.* Its popularity is attested by the vast quantity of extant versions, good and bad, which outnumber those of any other play at least ten to one. The famous *Quem quaeritis* trope was apparently the foundation for a play that was built during a stretch of four centuries and in many places.

In its final condition, this play is a work of consummate art, not through historical accident but because its theme was more intensely vital to actors and audience than that of any other play of the repertory. What this play expresses is no less than a basis of hope for the individual and for the world. The grim fact of death, and the possibility of fearlessly overriding its stark finality for oneself or others, are the deep, ageless, personal concern of every man. In his natural, physical world mankind has always seen in the return of spring a symbol of life succeeding death, of personal renewal, of fertility, and even of immortality. In his social world he has interpreted the earth's renewal as assurance that though the times have seldom been worse, they will not be the last. To Christians, now as then, the events of resurrection are those of Christ's death and burial and his astonishing reappearance to his closest friends.

These specific, dramatic events are set forth in the simple but strong narratives of the New Testament. This narrative material served as the subject matter of pictorial and sculptural art for many more centuries than it did for dramatic art. The explanation for the delay is that the medium of lyric theater was also the medium of the liturgy—song. For a long while the expression in terms of antiphons, psalms, and hymns was sufficiently dramatic to inhibit theatrical expression in the form of music-drama. In fact many versions of *The Visit to the Sepulcher,* even in the great period of dramatic composition, were not much more than a patchwork of antiphons, sung with ritualistic movement and gesture in semi-dramatic style. Thus we find in the visual arts more frequent and more artistic portrayals of the scenes at the sepulcher than we do in the Sepulcher play before the twelfth century. For this reason art representations of the period have a clarity of expression that only the latest and best of the plays are able to match. One can best discover the tone and quality intended in the Fleury and St. Quentin versions of *The Visit to the Sepulcher* by study of the many pictorial representations. These have much in common yet are not stereotypes; each has its own way of expressing the same thing the play expresses. The examples in this study are reproduced in plates 2 through 6 and 9 through 14, all of them created within the twelfth and thirteenth centuries.

MAJOR EPISODES

To judge from corresponding art works, the two major episodes of the narrative dealt with in the Fleury and St. Quentin versions of *The Visit to the Sepulcher* are the Angel's revelation to the three Marys and the meeting between Mary Magdalene and Christ in the disguise of a Gardener. In both of these episodes the visual portrayals choose a moment that is not at the beginning of the episode but at its climax. In each of the four examples (plates 2, 9, 10, 11) the Angel is seated and is pointing into the empty sarcophagus, his words to the Marys almost audible: "Non est hic!" [1] Only plate 8 apparently has other dialogue; it seems to depict a point slightly later in the Angel's speech, when he informs the Marys that Christ is risen, and so points upward. The St. Quentin stage direction echoes this pose in specifying that the angels "demonstrer au doit" (point with their fingers). In all of the examples the Marys are responding by looking with some amazement at the empty sarcophagus and the graveclothes draped over its side, not at the Angel. There are clues here as to how this episode in the Fleury and in the St. Quentin versions of the play was performed.

The meeting between Magdalene and Christ as the Gardener is perhaps the most touching episode of the play, and is uniformly shown in art at the moment when Christ, having revealed his identity to her,

[1] The St. Quentin version has "Non iacet hic" in order to versify the speech of the Angel. See Young, I, 416.

stops her impulsive move to reach out to him by saying "Noli me tangere." In an English Psalter miniature (plate 13) there is even a dialogue strip attached to Christ with those words upon it, not an uncommon device. Others (plates 12 and 14) do not need the words to identify the moment and the speech. The Fleury and St. Quentin versions agree in reproducing this speech, in traditional plainchant style, without effort to versify the verbatim quotation from John 20:17.

The setting for the meeting with Mary Magdalene is unusual in that the pictorial artists—no doubt prompted by Christ's disguise as a gardener—usually fill in their compositions with a flowering shrub. (See plates 12–14). One would expect them to follow the setting of John 20, which assumes the same setting "ad monumentum" as was used in play and picture for the encounter of the Marys with the Angel, and that of Mary Magdalene with the two Angels. But there is no sign of the sarcophagus in any of the hundreds of illustrations of the Magdalene-Christ episode. The play versions, on the other hand, give no indication of a change of place, though this is not conclusive evidence that a garden set-piece was not used for this scene, the stage directions often being reticent about such matters. No other versions of *The Visit to the Sepulcher* mention a shrub or other garden set-piece. I infer that the artists created their own setting, independent of either the play or the Gospel, in order to complete their compositions with a different object from that used in the scene between the Marys and the Angel. Certainly a filler was often needed, with only two figures present in the composition. In the event that the producer of the Fleury or the St. Quentin version felt that he needed to move Mary Magdalene away from the sepulcher, that the scene was becoming static at the sarcophagus, he would have the garden setting of the illustrators as his authority. The pictures may indeed be an indication of a medieval point of view toward the matter of frequent changing of scene in order that the story, or the picture, or the play, might move around. I have remarked above on how accustomed both the producer and the audience were to frequent changes of location.

The episode in which the Marys buy spices with which to embalm the body of the dead Christ appears in the St. Quentin version but not the Fleury. This scene is frequently illustrated in the art of the period. See, for example, plates 2–4, which confirm this as a major episode, even though the leading character of the play, Mary Magdalene, takes no active part in it. In the Saint-Gilles lintel (plate 2) the spice-merchant scene is sculptured immediately to the left of that of the sepulcher. This juxtaposition is again an indication of what were considered major episodes. In the text of the play there intervenes the episode of the Marys' travel to the sepulcher, singing as they go a twelve-line song of lament, and upon arrival at the place the customary *Quis revolvet* antiphon. None of this incidental travel is portrayed in the illustrations and sculptures.

On the other hand, none of the play versions contains an episode of the Marys preparing their spices after they have bought the material. One miniature does show the Marys working with a large mortar and only two pestles (Mary Magdalene having some time ago had her spices prepared, according to the initial stage direction in the St. Quentin version).[2] However, this illustration is late, well beyond the period of the great plays, and so has only slight relevance to the choice of major episodes by a playwright of that period. Furthermore, it introduces the Virgin as a bystander in the scene, a character not one of *The Visit to the Sepulcher* plays ever included in the cast, for the reason that throughout this play Mary Magdalene has the lead, and could not have had it if Mary Major had been there.

More apposite is a recently discovered relief from St. Pieterskerk in Utrecht (plate 5), dated about 1160, showing the three Marys at or in procession to the sepulcher. The central Mary holds a mortar, and is stirring or grinding with a spoon or pestle. The other two Marys hold conventional pyxes. It is conceivable that this action with mortar and pestle could be fitted into the prescribed movement of the Marys over the distance from the Spice Merchants' booth to the "luis du Sepuchre" (the place of the sepulcher), which takes roughly forty-five seconds to cover.

We may conclude that while the visual arts confirm the major emphasis of two scenes in the Fleury version of the play, and three in the St. Quentin, there is a lack of complete correlation between the visual and the dramatic choice of scenes. The climax of the Fleury version in performance (the St. Quentin version breaks off before this point) is obviously reached when Mary Magdalene places the graveclothes on the altar, and the three Marys turn and sing the ecstatic "Resurrexit hodie," followed by the appearance of the glorified Christ, singing *Nolite timere vos,* and the return of the "Resurrexit hodie" theme. None of this magnificent, obviously major episode is shown in any visual art representation known to me, even though the episode has strong pictorial values.

[2] Oxford, Bodleian Library, MS CCC 410, fol. 147 verso (thirteenth century).

CHARACTERIZATION

Attention was called above to the fact that Mary Magdalene's is the leading role in the play, at least in its Fleury version. In the St. Quentin version we may assume her similar leadership at the climax, but her passive role in the spice-merchant scene slightly undercuts her pre-eminent position, and gives one some concern in sorting out the intended character emphases in that version. On the other hand, the first words of the first item of the St. Quentin version are "Maria Magdalene et alia Maria, . . ." which certainly sets her up as the chief Mary in the play. The remarks which follow about Mary Magdalene are nevertheless applicable chiefly to the Fleury version.

The evidence of her leadership is everywhere. In the words of the first stage direction she could hardly be other than "prima earum" (the first of them), and she is the only one of the Marys who is particularized in the headings of any speech. She leaves the other two Marys for a solo at the sepulcher, and rises and runs to call out to Peter and John. After they have left, she alone has the scene with the two hidden angels, and there follows her scene alone with the Christus as Gardener, which concludes with her solo speech to the audience. After the two angels have invited the Marys into the sepulcher structure (the anastasis), all three Marys come out and place the graveclothes on the altar. But it is obviously Mary Magdalene ("Prima") who begins the glorious announcement, "Resurrexit hodie Deus deorum," and sings the beginning of the repeated announcement, "Resurrexit hodie, rex angelorum." In the Smoldon edition of the play, the editor interpolates an item (No. 30) from the *Victimae Paschali* hymn as a solo for Mary Magdalene, before the re-appearance of Christ in his glory and the choral conclusion of the play. In performance, this addition to the play not only provides a quiet moment after the fortissimo choral end of the "Resurrexit hodie" and a transition to the solemn re-entrance of the Christus, but also emphasizes still further the role of Mary Magdalene.

As a quantitative measurement of her predominance, a count of items (one cannot count bars, for some of her items are in free rhythm) reveals that she sings in no less than nineteen of the twenty-nine musical items in the manuscript of the play. Of these nineteen, fifteen are solos. In other words, more than half the total substance of the play is hers.

Mary Magdalene has in this cornucopia of items a greater range of emotional expression than the Virgin Mary has in *The Lament of Mary,* where the role of the Magdalene is appropriately subordinated. She expresses profound grief, excitement, sensuous tenderness, reverence, and ecstatic joy. Apart from the general dominance of the Christus in all of the resurrection plays, including the *Lazarus,* she is indisputably the leading figure in that cycle, for she not only dominates *The Visit to the Sepulcher* but has other large roles in *The Lament of Mary* and in the *Lazarus.* While the Virgin appears in *The Lament of Mary, The Shepherds,* and in the short plays of *The Annunciation* and *The Purification,* her total bulk of lines and bars does not compare with that of Mary Magdalene. She has nine of the twenty-one items in her best play, *The Lament of Mary*—considerably smaller than the proportion of Mary Magdalene's in *The Visit to the Sepulcher.* Moreover, even in *The Lament,* Mary Magdalene sings five items (a fourth of the play) while the Virgin is not even in the cast of *The Visit to the Sepulcher.*

The popularity of Mary Magdalene is greater in the plays than in the visual arts, for the Virgin's annunciation scenes, nativity tableaux and *mandorle,* passion and pieta tableaux, and enthronements as the Queen of Heaven in medieval stone, metal, and paint are innumerable. The reason for the greater attention to Mary Magdalene in the plays seems to rest on her warm humanity. She is an approachable human being, and is accepted as a woman, almost as a lover, in contrast to the necessary restriction of the virgin's roles to those of mother and of friend to the other Marys and to the disciples. Venerableness is not as approachable. The colors of their costumes, prescribed in the plays and in all the arts of the period, emphasize this contrast: the Virgin is in blue, Mary Magdalene in red. Blue is cool, red warm, whatever their shades. Red is the color of blood and of wine; Mary Magdalene is the patron saint of wine growers. Furthermore, her red costume is a reminder of her former occupation, and mankind always feels more kinship with a reformed sinner than with a virgin saint. Christ makes this point repeatedly in such parables as those of the prodigal son and the lost sheep.

The role of Mary Magdalene is, then, full of a dramatic potential that the playwrights were happy to use. To judge from the ardor of her dramatic songs, and from even the most monastic artists' portrayals, the medieval mind accepted Mary Magdalene as a character of appeal, and had no false piety or puritanical reservations about her.

Those of us who live in a culture that does not daily confront us with images of Christ in art have difficulty in accepting or even imagining an actor playing the Christus. Even for medieval actors of the role there must have been some adjustment to make, some sense of unworthiness to represent Christ. But only in recent times has there been a psychological block against showing Christ in a play. The authors of *Family Portrait* (1939) took pains to contrive an account of his life without his once appearing on the Broadway stage. Audiences would have cringed at the idea of a realistic appearance, there being no recent dramatic tradition to authorize it, yet were willing to accept him at Oberammergau or in a revival of an English craft play, where he was not a part of our world and its mirror, the stage. Perhaps this is the clue, that in a play in a church, and the play not modern realism but high music-drama, we can accept and believe his appearance.

The medieval realist also knew that the shock could be too great to bear. This may be the reason why in *The Visit to the Sepulcher* and in *The Pilgrim,* Christ's first appearance is in disguise as a gardener or a pilgrim, ordinary human beings. After these encounters the medieval actor and audience were prepared for the later appearances "in his glory"— which may well reflect the playwrights' sense of what was dramatically feasible for actor and audience.

The visual artists of the period show the Christus in every conceivable moment of his worldly and resurrected life. The ever-present crossed nimbus, the special halo, helped the painters to ennoble their portraits, even though the human likeness of the face is for us sometimes distractingly inadequate. When he is portrayed in his glory, the costume, the nimbus, and often the sheer physical elevation of the portrait, as in a fresco in a vaulted arch or a sculptured figure at the top of a church portal, provide enough distance and otherworldliness to make him more easily accepted. The playwright, however, has to begin with Christ as a man, and build to his glory. The Passion plays of the repertory avoid his appearance on the cross in the flesh, even in *The Lament of Mary,* where he is a central figure but was, I feel sure, to be represented only by an approximately life-size crucifix in stone or wood. His role in the *Lazarus,* discussed in relation to that play, is rather less difficult than in *The Visit to the Sepulcher* or *The Pilgrim,* inasmuch as in the *Lazarus* he is still presented in his human nature.

The characterization of the Angels in *The Visit to the Sepulcher* is not a matter of great difficulty, even though like the Christus they have super-human qualities. In the Fleury version of the play there first appears a single angel, who may be equated with the Archangel in *The Shepherds, The Annunciation,* and *The Wise and Foolish Maidens.* He is followed much later, after the Christ-Magdalene scene, by two angels, whom some scholars identify as guardian angels, paralleling the function of the Midwives in *The Shepherds.* There is no indication in the Fleury script as to whether one of the two angels is the Archangel from the earlier scene, or whether the latter could properly not appear in the company of another angel of lesser rank.

The visual artists are of small help here. Usually the scene represented by them is that of a single angel sitting on the sepulcher and singing "Non est hic!" in the manner described above. Occasionally a scene with two angels is portrayed, but at an entirely different dramatic moment, when the two angels invite the Marys to "Venite et videte" where Christ was but is no longer. Certainly the pictorial artists were aware from the New Testament accounts that this occurred at a later point in the story; they merely chose not to represent one angel or two for an undefined sepulcher scene. In visual representations I find no essential difference in elaboration of costume or spread of wings to suggest that the two later angels are of lesser rank than the earlier single angel. No single artist seems to have illustrated both angelic scenes, and our comparisons must therefore be less direct and conclusive from artist to artist.

The only remaining possibility is that the two angels became un-differentiated from the single angel whenever a shift was made from use of the anastasis type of sepulcher to that of the sarcophagus.[3] If the two angels are located exactly as the single angel was, sitting on the sarcoph-agus, there would remain small reason to differentiate their characters. This is their location in the Osnabruck and Frankfort illustrations of the earlier scene, and in an eleventh-century Byzantine miniature.[4] Modern experience suggests that for practical purposes, at least in the Fleury version (which as we shall show below probably used the anastasis type of sepulcher), there needs to be a strong differentiation between the Archangel and the two later Guardian Angels. In the St. Quentin version, in which the sarcophagus form may have been used,[5] two angels also appear in the earlier scene, and must therefore be the same two. This may have been an attempt on the part of the playwright to simplify the cast, reducing it from a total of three angels to two, but the Fleury dis-tinction is more usual and rather more dramatically effective.

[3] See Young, Appendix A, "The Easter Sepulchre," II, 507–13.

[4] Mount Athos, Greece, Dionysin Monastery Library, MS 587 (740), fol. 172 verso. Reproduced by K. Weitzmann, *Aus den Bibliotheken des Athos* (Hamburg, 1963), plate 15.

[5] The Angels "descouvrir le Sepuche un peu," which could hardly have been managed with the older anastasis type of sepulcher, but may refer to the gates to the Chapel of the Sepulcher.

The circumstances of production at St. Quentin were certainly different from those at Fleury. At St. Quentin—shorthand for a convent near St. Quentin at the Abbey of Origny-Sainte-Benoite—one would assume that some or all of the roles in *The Visit to the Sepulcher* were played by women. The manuscript from which Coussemaker first published the play includes a charming section by one Héloise de Couflans, in which she records that the manuscript "Book of the Treasury" was translated into French by her in 1286, when Isabelle d'Acy was abbess. Some fifteen men are listed by name as canons of the abbey at that time, along with eight prioresses who served with them, and six women clerks (escolières), presumably including Héloise.[6] From this group of men and women the cast must have been chosen, with the men singing only the male roles. The same manuscript also contains a French translation of a more primitive Easter Matins dramatic ritual, containing specific details as to the proper vesting and conduct of the three women who were to play the Marys ("faire les Maries").[7] There can therefore be little doubt that the women of the convent played the Mary roles in the full-scale play.[8] In this semidramatic office there is no scene with Magdalene and the two angels. Instead, the Marys themselves enter the chapel of the sepulcher, close its gates behind them, go to the altar of the chapel, and later emerge with the graveclothes and their announcement to the congregation that "Surrexit Dominus de sepulchro."[9] The angels who confront the Marys before they enter the chapel of the sepulcher are priests ("li prestres doivent dire"). We may therefore deduce that all the angel roles in the St. Quentin *The Visit to the Sepulcher* were played by men, the priests and canons of the abbey.

In this same semidramatic office the first scene or location of the ritual is "devant l'autel de le Magdelainne" (before the altar of the Magdalene), an indication of the popularity of Mary Magdalene at this abbey. A further indication of the extreme importance of the Magdalene role in the St. Quentin version of the play is imbedded in the end of this office,

---

[6] Coussemaker, p. 338.   [7] Coussemaker, p. 340.

[8] Young includes five versions of the *Visitatio* in which women take the roles of the Marys: from Barking, I, 381; Troyes, I, 603; Essen, I, 333; Bresci, I, 221; and Origny-Sainte-Benoite (St. Quentin), I, 685. All of these date from the end of the thirteenth century to the fifteenth. R. Marichal, "Les Drames Liturgiques du 'Livre de la Trésorerie' d'Origny-Sainte-Benoite," *Mélanges d'Histoire du Théâtre du Moyen-Age et de la Renaissance offerts à Gustave Cohen* (Paris, 1950), pp. 37–45, presents some evidence that the staging of the full-scale St. Quentin *Visitatio* is "très imparfaitement adaptée aux coutumes et aux particularités de l'abbaye," as described by Héloise de Couflans. I find her description sufficiently compatible with the play to provide a valid interpretation of the original production.

[9] Coussemaker, p. 341.

when the "tresoriere" (keeper of the treasury) supplements with other relics the graveclothes held by the two Marys. One of these relics from the treasury is "les cheviaus de le Magdelainne" (some of Mary Magdalene's hair); another is similar to a lantern (ensi comme une lanterne"). There will be occasion later in this study to use information derived from the St. Quentin office in considering movement, staging, and costuming for the St. Quentin play.

The spice-merchant scene, omitted in the Fleury play, is not unique to the St. Quentin version. In fact, the considerable number of versions which include this scene, with a variety of emphases on the character of the Spice Merchants, has led scholars a merry chase in their attempt to trace the development of the scene, and to assess the import of the Spice Merchants. Hardison summarizes the situation thus:

> However it originated, the mode of presentation of the spice-merchant scene is up to the dramatist. Latin texts containing the scene show a wide variety of treatments. In some cases the merchant appears but does not speak. In others, he demands exorbitant payment. In still others, he is a pious believer who offers his wares free of charge. He is sometimes alone, but sometimes has competition from another merchant or is rebuked by a shrewish wife. In contrast to these later treatments (thirteenth century), the Ripoll text [twelfth century] is surprisingly down to earth. The merchant praises his wares (there is no suggestion here either of satire or of the medicine man of folk drama whom Stumpfl considers his prototype), and quotes his price. Mary pays without comment and resumes her lament.[10]

In whatever version, the Spice Merchant is clearly an invented, not a traditional character. He does not exist in the Gospels; Mark 16:1 mentions that the Marys bought spices, but does not narrate the action or say from whom they were bought. The Spice Merchant appears to have been introduced into the resurrection story no earlier than the twelfth century. Only the Ripoll version of *The Visit to the Sepulcher,* as Hardison points out, is twelfth-century; others containing a spice-merchant scene are thirteenth and fourteenth. The unique version of *The Wise and Foolish Maidens,* in which two Oil Merchants have an eight-line role, is dated late eleventh or very early twelfth century, and may or may not have given dramatists the idea for the invention of the spice-merchant scene in *The Visit to the Sepulcher.* The evidence from art is similar. There exist only two representations of the Spice Merchants, one from the portal of Saint-Gilles church (plates 2, 3), the other a capital by the great Italian

---

[10] Hardison, p. 246.

architect and sculptor, Benedetto Antelami; both date from the twelfth century (plate 4).[11]

The variety of treatments of the character of the Spice Merchants follows, as Hardison suggests, from the fact that they were invented during the high period of medieval art and drama. The impulse toward character invention was not typical of the best medieval artists when they were dealing, in drama or art, with a traditional subject, and surely no subject is more traditional than that of the visit to the sepulcher. The Spice Merchant anticipates the genre character, as do some of the creations of Chaucer and of fourteenth-century visual artists. His appearance in earlier art and drama is premature—some seeds of decay germinate early.

With this orientation one may look to the text and music of the Spice-Merchant role in the St. Quentin play. I see no real possibility of interpreting the Merchant's words or his style of bargaining as comic, or the playwright's intent as satirical. The bargaining is quite conventional; one still buys merchandise this way from a street merchant in Mediterranean countries. The two Marys' attitude toward him is friendly, and he returns their friendliness by his repeated expressions of sympathy and his wish to go with them to the sepulcher, "Because he has loved us so fully" (Car il nous a mout volentiers ames). If the Merchant were a sharp dealer, it is doubtful that the playwright would have made him young and kind. The Marys address the "jouvenes marchans" as "gentius" (kind), and as "tres bons, vrais, et loiaus" (very good, true, and loyal), and he could hardly fail to live up to that recommendation. Incidentally, the melodic range required of him in the St. Quentin play is the same as that of the Marys, which may indicate that his youthfulness is further expressed by his tenor voice.

The two portraits of the Spice Merchants—there are two in each illustration, although only one Merchant has a singing role in the St. Quentin version—tend to confirm this characterization. In the Saint-Gilles scene (plate 2) both merchants are bearded, perhaps indicating that they are older, but the upper parts of the faces have been so vandalized that their age is impossible to judge. In Antelami's version (plate 4) the leading merchant has a beard, and the other apparently is clean-shaven, suggesting that he may be an apprentice. The leading merchant's face shows a smile and enthusiasm, as if he were speaking of Christ's love. The Marys' faces are grief-stricken, the corners of their mouths drawn far

[11] Antelami's work has been exhaustively researched and interpreted by Geza de Francovich, *Benedetto Antelami: Architetto e scultore, e l'arte del suo tempo* (Milan and Florence, 1952).

down. This visual scene seems to reflect the same mood as that of the dramatic verse.

The possibility of doubling the roles of the later two Angels with those of the Spice Merchants may occur to the student or producer, since there is sufficient time for a change of costume. The melodic range for the two Angels, however, once goes a fourth below what is required for the Merchants.

Another character in the St. Quentin version, not required by the Fleury version, is the Priest who leads the procession and has the opening lines at the beginning of the procession. There is the possibility that this role might be doubled by the Christus, since the Priest has no lines or action after he reaches the chancel. With change of costume he would become Christ as the Gardener, and as the glorified Christ at the end of the play would lead out the company of actors and the choir in the *Te Deum.*[12] Such a double would insure that the processional at the beginning would be led with strength and dignity.

John and Peter are contrasting types. John is young, red-headed, and as we shall see in *The Lament of Mary,* tender, almost effeminate, and intellectual. Peter, on the other hand, takes his character from his name; he is a swarthy, tough, mature man. The visual arts of the period understand this matter, and invariably portray John as young, tender, and red-headed, and Peter as dark, heavy-jawed, and bearded.

To complete our discussion of the characters of *The Visit to the Sepulcher* there remains only consideration of the Soldiers who are sent by Pilate to guard the tomb, and who are struck senseless by their fear of the Archangel on his first appearance. These events are narrated in Matthew 27:62–66, and 28:2–4, and soldiers appear in illustrations of the sepulcher scene from the fourth century on.[13] Following this lead, some of the more advanced versions of the resurrection play, which go further back in the narrative than our two produceable versions, use the soldiers extensively.[14] Only the Coutances version, opening approximately at the same moment as our versions, gives any indication that the soldiers were part of the cast. This version has a preliminary dumb show, in which four clerks, armed and dressed like soldiers, approach the sepulcher, at which point "two angels appear bringing lightning in their hands in the form of two candelabra, each holding ten candles. At the sight

[12] A page is missing from the manuscript at the end of the St. Quentin version; this deficiency can be supplied from the Fleury version or some other.

[13] Lowrie, plate 27b.

[14] For example, the "disordered" Tours and unproduceable *Carmina Burana*-Klosterneuberg versions, reproduced by Young, I, 438, 432, 421.

of these, the soldiers fall down as if dead, and remain in that position until after the *Te Deum* at the end of the play." [15] If this were all the evidence of the presence of the soldiers in our versions, one could well dismiss the idea of using them. The Coutances version, however, is fifteenth-century, and other advanced versions of the resurrection play, while of the right period, are more panoramic and less focussed upon the Marys.

What strongly suggests the use of the soldiers in our versions is the survival of hundreds of visual representations of them as sleeping figures in the scene showing the visit to the sepulcher by the Marys (e.g., plates 2, 9–11). Two of these works are of the twelfth century, the others of the thirteenth. In liturgical art, the tradition of including the soldiers in this scene may be traced as far back as a tenth-century miniature found in Hartker's *Antiphonary.*[16] The soldiers are indeed missing from the sepulcher scene only when the artist, in stone or fresco, could not for dimensional reasons include them. With so strong a tradition operating over eight centuries, the inclusion of the soldiers in any play version seems almost obligatory. That they are not mentioned in any but the Coutances version of *The Visit to the Sepulcher* play is not particularly significant, for we have noted the reticence of the stage directions, and we may suppose that nonsinging, walk-on roles were usually assumed rather than noted in the directions.[17]

The number of soldiers is anyone's choice. In the illustrations here exhibited, the number varies from two to four. The Coutances version specifies four, and two of the advanced versions mentioned above call for five. How they are to be arranged in relation to the sepulcher, without being in the way throughout the play (a matter to be considered in the next section) may affect the choice of number.

MOVEMENT AND GESTURE

In this section are discussed only such matters of movements and gesture as can be considered apart from determination of probable acting areas and furnishings, whether anastasis or sarcophagus. Most of these matters are applicable both to the Fleury and to the St. Quentin version.

Although the stage directions do not mention it, a dumb show at the sepulcher between the Soldiers and the Angels might well have opened

[15] Young's summary of the stage direction, I, 410.   [16] See above, p. 20n.
[17] For references to soldiers in an antiphon used in the popular Vigil Mass and in a preceding Deposition ceremony, see Hardison, pp. 137, 165, 295.

both the Fleury and St. Quentin plays. The *Carmina Burana* version and the fragmentary Tours version suggest the sequence of actions and a pattern of movement for this scene.[18] The Soldiers march in and take their places at or before the sepulcher. Then, according to Tours, "Modo veniat Angelus et iniiciat eis fulgura; Milites cadant in terram velut mortui" (Let the Angel then come and let him brandish his lightning at them; let the Soldiers fall to the ground as if dead). The matter of lighting and properties involved in this stage direction will be discussed later. After striking down the Soldiers, the Angel, in accordance with the Fleury stage directions, would seat himself "foris ad caput sepulchri," in the doorway of the anastasis, either beside the sarcophagus (plate 2) or on it (plates 9–11). He would then be ready for the approach of the Marys. The dumb show with the Soldiers gives him a strongly motivated entrance, and he can plausibly sit as soon as the Soldiers have fallen, long before the Marys reach him and sing the "Sed nequimus hoc patrare" stanza. The description of the Angel's hand props in the Fleury stage directions supports this interpolation: "palmam in sinistra, ramum candelarum plenum tenens in manu dextra" (a palm frond in his left hand, a branched candelabrum full of lighted candles in his right hand). The flaming candelabrum is obviously the thunderbolt brandished (not, of course, thrown) at the Soldiers. The Saint-Gilles lintel (plate 2) shows the candelabrum in the Archangel's right hand after he has seated himself near the head of the sarcophagus, the light shining into the sarcophagus to reveal its emptiness as he sings the line, "Non est hic, sed surrexit," and points upward with his left hand on "surrexit." This same lintel shows two of the paralyzed soldiers at the Archangel's left, the other two soldiers to the left of the sarcophagus.

Where the Soldiers fall and remain is of course a matter of some importance. In the Saint-Gilles lintel they are subordinated only by being seated in tangled, slumped pairs (very comfortable positions for actors to hold for the remainder of the performance). The play requires that they be farther from the anastasis than the Saint-Gilles lintel indicates. Often in visual representations the fallen soldiers are placed below the level of the Marys, Archangel, and sepulcher, as in plates 9–11. This suggests an arrangement of the Soldiers on the steps to the choir, either centered below the anastasis, which is of course at one side of the choir, or to far stage right, beyond the plane of the anastasis. For composition they are better centered below, but for freeing the very active area around the

[18] Young, I, 435, 439.

sarcophagus for the movements of the Marys and of John and Peter, the position at extreme stage right would be more practical.

The interpolation of this dumb show into the two versions of *The Visit to the Sepulcher* under consideration is, I believe, justified by the standard inclusion of the fallen soldiers in the art of the period, and by the stage directions for their fall in other versions of the play. The Soldiers' presence in the Fleury and St. Quentin versions adds another symbol of the triumph of Christ not only over death but also over the military authority which had tortured and crucified him. Since the soldiers usually carry lances in the visual representations of this scene, and should in the play, the audience might feel that these Soldiers' lances, or others like them, had been used shortly before to pierce Christ's side, or that these may be the soldiers who cast lots for his garments. As the play goes on, moreover, there is a continuous contrast between the deathlike stillness of the fallen soldiers and the lively movements of the resurrected Christ and his friends and disciples. Finally there is the appearance of Christ in his glory, with a lancelike cross in his right hand ("crucem cum labaro in dextra"), as the Fleury stage direction specifies. He gives the promise of everlasting life; the Soldiers, of old mortality.

From whatever point the three Marys begin their procession to the sepulcher, and whether their journey is interrupted by a stopover at the Merchant's booth (St. Quentin) or is continuous (Fleury), the space to be covered from the opening of the play to the arrival at the sepulcher can effectively be large, probably as far as from the narthex to the choir.[19] During this movement the Marys (Fleury) sing nine stanzas of a conversation in the form of a lament and a plan of action, each singer performing three stanzas, at the conclusion of which the Fleury stage direction reads, "Cum autem venerint in chorum" (Let them by this time have arrived at the choir).

How this long journey was to be performed, with the women singing and carrying their pyxes and thuribles, is specified in a preliminary Fleury stage direction. Let the Marys, it says, "procedant . . . pedetemtim et quasi tristes" (proceed slowly, feeling their way with their feet, and as if grieving). At least three other versions of the *Visitatio* use the dramatically vivid word "pedetemtim" to describe the movement of the Marys; one of these versions is from the tenth-century Winchester *Regularis Concordia,* one from an unidentified thirteenth-century German monastery, and one from fifteenth-century Sainte-Chapelle. A fourth

[19] Throughout this study the word *choir* is used both to define an area of the chancel and to name the singing chorus that gave its name to the area.

dramatic use is in the Fleury *Pilgrim.*[20] The international currency of the word—in three countries over a span of six hundred years—seems to have been exclusively as a theatrical term; the most recent edition of the *Revised Medieval Latin Word-List* has no nondramatic entries for its medieval use in England.[21] Livy, a millenium earlier, worked it into his hexameter "Quaerentis pedetemtim vadis in terram evasere," from which one or another of the monastic playwrights may have pre-empted it for theatrical purposes. There may be nothing more than coincidence in the fact that "quaerentis" also appears in Livy's line, and that two of the five uses of this word are in two Fleury plays and a third in the *Regularis Concordia,* which professed its indebtedness to earlier Fleury customs.

No doubt this very precise direction was written into the script because the play can so easily begin awkwardly if the Marys either stroll or stride briskly up the nave in the dark. The remainder of this preliminary direction, "alternantes hos versus cantantes" (singing the following stanzas in alternation, i.e., as marked in the script for the Prima, Secunda, and Tercia Mariae) is a key to the formal movement pattern, the procession. After the Soldiers' dumb show, the first Mary, certainly Magdalene, will lead the other two Marys during the singing of her first stanza, having moved from the preliminary grouping at the foot of the nave only after the startling wail "Heu!" which begins the stanza. When the second Mary (Jacobi) begins her stanza with the same "Heu!" Mary Magdalene pauses, and Mary Jacobi moves up to take the lead for her stanza. Similarly, the third Mary's (Salome) "Heu!" stops Mary Jacobi, and Mary Salome moves into the lead for her stanza.[22] The next three stanzas are a series of questions, to be asked of each other either in the same alternating movement or with the group stationary. The seventh stanza, Magdalene's again, proposes decisive action: "Eamus ergo propere" (let us therefore go quickly). Here the "pedetemtim" movement, performed by each of the Marys in turn as pathfinder in the dark, quickens.

Still in the dark, the Marys increase the tempo of the procession, and of their singing, which shifts from a duple to a faster triple rhythm. During the last three stanzas they approach the crossing and eventually mount the steps into the choir. The Marys being in fuller view of the audience by the time they reach the crossing, their repeated references to the pyxes they carry is a basis for inferring appropriate individual gestures. Visual

[20] For all four uses, see Young, I, 249, 287, 313, 473.

[21] Ed. Latham, s.v. *pedetemptim.*

[22] The names "Jacobi" (i.e., the mother of James) and "Salome" do not occur in the stage directions; I give them these designations, following the Gospel narrative, for the sake of clarity. Cf. Smoldon, *Visitatio,* p. viii.

representations of this scene usually show the Marys carrying the pyxes in their left hands, and this would almost be a physical necessity, because at least one of them customarily carries a thurible, which must be manipulated by the right hand. In order to be able to gesture effectively with the pyxes as they approached the sepulcher, the Marys would presumably have to move in an arc from the center of the crossing to stage left and hold there during the Soldiers' dumb show. Then they would move toward stage right in single file, gesturing with their pyxes as they mounted the steps to the choir and approached the sepulcher.

This movement, sparked by the Marys' references to the pyxes, may indicate that the anastasis type of sepulcher was not centered in the choir at Fleury but was considerably to stage right. We shall notice, in the consideration of that structure below, that at Fleury it must have been placed at one side of the choir space in order to clear the sight lines for the climactic scene at the high altar. In this connection, an ivory plaque from Cologne (plate 10) shows the Marys in profile arriving at the sepulcher, although, atypically, Magdalene has only a thurible, and the other Marys carry their pyxes in their right hands, which would reverse the side of the choir in which the sepulcher was placed and the side from which the Marys approached it. The effect, however, is the same, and at the very least suggests that the Cologne artist and the Fleury playwright thought an approach in profile, single file, would be a good composition (or blocking) for this scene.

The St. Quentin version, largely because it introduces the spice-merchant episode as the first scene after the procession, seems to call for rather different organization of the movement of the Marys from starting point to sepulcher. The opening stage direction describes a ceremonial, candlelight procession of the Marys and a priest.

Chascune des Maries doit avoir en se main un cierge alumeit, et Marie Magdelainne doit avoir unne boiste en se main, et les autres deus nient, dusques adont quellez aient acate au Marchant. Et li prestres doit aler devant iceles, et doit avoir en se main un encensier atout lencens. Et li cuers ensiut iceles, et chascune diceles a I cierge en se main alume.[23] (Each of the Marys must have in her hand a lighted candle, and Mary Magdalene must have a pyx in her hand and the other two none, which pyxes they will have to buy from the Merchant. And the priest must go before them and must have in his hand a lighted thurible to spread the incense around. And the choir follows them, and each of them in the choir has one lighted candle in hand.)

[23] Young, I, 413.

If the semidramatic office from St. Quentin may be trusted to speak with some relevance about staging conditions for the St. Quentin play version—their dates cannot be much out of line and they are in the same manuscript—we find that the Marys pick up (among other articles) a thurible at the altar of the Magdalene and proceed to the choir and straight to the sepulcher, where they stop because the door to the sepulcher is closed, and sing "Quis revolvet." The altar of the Magdalene, presumably to stage right of the Chancel, would seem to have been intended as the imagined location of the Spice Merchant's booth.

The fact that the choir follows the Marys suggests that in the St. Quentin play the three stanzas by the Marys and the choir's refrain after each stanza take place between the starting point of the procession (at the back of the nave) and the Marys' sidetrack to the chapel of the Magdalene. The three-stanza form of the dialogue, specified only as for "les trois Maries," may well have been handled individually by the Marys as in the Fleury version described above. At this point I surmise that the priest with his thurible, followed by the choir, leads the procession into the chancel, the Marys meanwhile encountering the Spice Merchant. The effect of the choir's passing the Marys while it sings the choral refrain "Dominum quaerentis in monumento" for the third time, is that of leading the way for the Marys as soon as they have bought their ointments. This passing movement also provides a cover for the entrance and seating of the Spice Merchant before that scene is revealed ("apparrillies"). Altogether, the amount of singing in procession, counting the dialogue between the priest and choir as well as the Marys' three stanzas and the choir's responses to them, is roughly three-fourths of that involved in the Fleury processional, and the movement could have been similarly patterned up to the point of the Marys dropping out at the Magdalene chapel for the merchant scene.[24]

The two illustrations of the merchant scene (plates 2–4) show a simple counter beside which the merchants sit, and to which the Marys approach from stage left. The counter is not large, and one does not expect much movement from the Marys once they have come to its left side. But they sing two stanzas of the "Peres trestous puissans" dialogue, followed by another stanza by Mary Jacobi and Mary Salome, before they take their last steps to the counter. Mary Magdalene, the stage direction says, remains behind, having bought her spices some time before. One

[24] There is also a suggestion in the semidramatic office from St. Quentin that the Priest is, or could be, the Archangel, inasmuch as other priests, already in the chancel, are to sing the "Quem quaeritis" line. See Coussemaker, p. 341.

gathers from the Merchant's first line to the two Marys ("Ca aproiches vous") that it cues their movement toward him.

At the conclusion of this scene the two Marys, pyxes in hand, rejoin Mary Magdalene, who is appropriately stage left in the chapel (and to stage right of the chancel) and they continue directly on their way to the sepulcher, singing together as they go the two stanzas of the "Ille quippe." At the end of this item, they have, according to the stage direction, arrived at the door of the sepulcher, by perhaps the same maneuver as was suggested for the Fleury entrance to the choir. The Marys' lack of thuribles, however, would make it possible to compose the scene in the manner of the Cologne plaque (plate 10), allowing the Marys to gesture with the pyxes in their right hands.

In the Fleury version the Archangel's colloquy with the Marys ends with his "Resurgere cum gloria." His gesture (and that of the two Angels in the St. Quentin version) is aptly illustrated by the gesture of annunciation in plate 68. Although there is no stage direction to remove the Archangel, this is certainly the moment for his exit,[25] for the Marys then are directed to turn toward the audience ("conversae ad populum") and sing to it, which they would not do if the Archangel were still "on stage." In the St. Quentin version the two Angels do not leave after their similar line "et in die tercia resurgere." Instead the two Marys are directed to leave, and Mary Magdalene then has a long duet with the Angels.

In the Fleury version the two Marys leave only after they sing to the people of their experience with the Archangel. The stage direction does not call for them to leave; it merely says, "Post haec Maria Magdalene, relictis duabus aliis, accedat ad Sepulchrum" (After this item has been sung, let Mary Magdalene, leaving the other two, go to the sepulcher.) What happens thereafter to the other two Marys is not easy to discover. In neither version is there a further reference to them until after Mary Magdalene's "Noli me tangere" scene with the Christus. At that point in the Fleury text the two Archangels appear in the doorway of the anastasis ("exeant ad hostium Sepulchri, ita ut appareant foris"), and apparently invite only Mary Magdalene, who has been singing to the audience, to "Venite et videte locum . . ." (come and see the place . . .). But in reply the Women ("Mulieres," presumably the other two Marys), leaving the sepulcher ("discedentes a sepulchro"), announce to the people "Surrexit Dominus de sepulchro" (The Lord has risen from the sepulcher). The inference is that the two Marys had earlier retired around the side of

[25] Smoldon so indicates the Archangel's exit, *Visitatio*, p. 11.

the anastasis structure when Mary Magdalene left them to go to the exposed front of the anastasis, where the sarcophagus was on view, and that they went in at the rear of the anastasis and now come out the front. They were inside during the Archangels' "Venite" item, and they now come forward and exhibit the graveclothes to the audience in their next song, "Cernite, vos socii." Mary Magdalene joins them, and the Archangels retire again inside the anastasis. The two Marys could not have entered the anastasis at the front because Mary Magdalene went directly there when she left them. The two Marys must, however, re-enter from the front because that is where they must pick up the graveclothes draped over the side of the sarcophagus.

The only alternative to this pattern of movement at Fleury is for the Marys to re-enter from around the side of the anastasis—they must have been out of sight during the "Noli me tangere" scene—and to reappear upon the Archangels' invitation to come inside. This solution seems to me not only more awkward but also less faithful to the intention of the Fleury stage directions. The key to the solution is the proper translation of "discedentes a Sepulchro." Although Smoldon translates it as "retiring from the sepulcher," "re-entering from" makes more theatrical sense and indicates their whereabouts during their long stay "offstage." [26]

The St. Quentin version is of no help here. It gets the two Marys "offstage" at the proper time, but does not say how or where. At the end of the "Noli me tangere" scene Christ suddenly goes to the two Marys, who prostrate themselves before him. He sings to them, and then, according to the stage direction, "parts from Mary Magdalene, goes to the two Marys, and sings with them the 'Eya, nobis internas.' " Christ must disappear at this moment, following which the *three* Marys sing at the sepulcher. How the two Marys got back on stage one cannot tell, but since they are not required to re-enter through the anastasis with the graveclothes, as they are in the Fleury version, they may well have come around the side of the St. Quentin anastasis. The remainder of this version, like the Fleury, proceeds smoothly enough with considerable possibilities for movement and gesture.

Before leaving this subject, I should add that in the "Noli me tangere" scene the kneeling or prostrating of Mary Magdalene in the Fleury version, and of all three Marys in the St. Quentin, was a gesture requiring some decision. It is variously illustrated in plates 12 through 14. Only in the

---

[26] The Smoldon edition of the Fleury *Visitatio* does not cope with the whole problem, but has two Marys reappear, then has them "retiring from the Sepulcher" with no indication as to how they got in it or how they later pick up the graveclothes.

miniature from the Arundel *Psalter* (plate 13) does Mary Magdalene actually touch her knees to the floor. Full prostration, with kissing of Christ's feet, is illustrated in the movements of the *Lazarus* (plates 40, 41). The four illustrations of the "Noli me tangere" scene, from the hundreds in the file of the Index of Christian Art, also suggest four appropriate gestures for the Christus on his line, "Noli me tangere," there being apparently no traditional gesture involved here.

In tracing the blocking of the many characters in this play one is impressed by the dramatic quality of their entrances, which can almost be described as rhythmical, and certainly keep the play alive with action. Mary Magdalene, who has only one entrance, remains "onstage" as the protagonist throughout the play. In the arrangement of entrances I believe there is evidence of the playwright's art. One may prefer the more classic pattern created by the Fleury version to that of the later St. Quentin, but both are impressive. Some of this pattern is of course inherited from other versions known to these playwrights, but some of it is unique to each. There is an odd coincidence in the fact that both playwrights have trouble with entrances only once, and that at the same moment, with the whereabouts of the two Marys. Of course, the trouble may be our own, not theirs.

In the Fleury version, the episode of the race between Peter and John requires some consideration. There is no race in the St. Quentin version. The Fleury stage direction to begin that scene reads: "Deinde pergat velociter ad illos qui in similitudinem Petri et Johannis praestare debent erecti, stansque ante eos quasi tristis dicat. . . ." (Then she [Magdalene] rushes toward those actors who in the likeness of Peter and John must be standing and ready, and, in front of them, she sadly sings. . .).[27] The difficulty is that if she has to run very far she will be too winded to sing well. If on the other hand they are only a short distance away, their race to the sepulcher is going to be ridiculously attenuated. Modern experience in production has shown that the race down the nave is a very effective piece of dramatic movement. Formally, it parodies the earlier, slow procession of the three Marys. The only solution is to have Mary Magdalene rush only a few feet, to the steps at the crossing, and project her "Tulerunt Dominum meum" from there down the nave. This is somewhat at odds with the Fleury direction, and the only excuse for suggesting it is that if the Fleury version was performed in the twelfth century abbey, only the first four bays of the nave had been completed by 1184, the last three not

[27] I follow Young's restoration of this stage direction and the next (I, 394), adding only a final *m* to his "similitudine."

until 1218. This would still require a run of about a hundred feet from the chancel to the provisional side door on the north. The distance from the chancel to the end of the north or south transept, completed in 1108, is only about sixty feet, and this may have been the staging area for this scene.[28]

One may also note that while some other versions have the race of Peter and John, none requires Mary Magdalene to race first, and that in the St. Quentin version, from a nunnery in which Mary Magdalene was undoubtedly played by a nun, the race is omitted entirely. Smoldon's interpolation of the *Currebant duo simul* for the choir during the race of Peter and John is a good accompaniment to the race and protects the moment of the apostles' arrival at the sepulcher and their pantomimic action inside the anastasis, before they come out and sing to Mary Magdalene of the wonders they have discovered inside. Without this choral addition there is a stretch of silence rather too prolonged in so musical a play as this. For the meeting and gesticulating between the two apostles and Mary Magdalene, the Salerno altar frontal provides some clues for gestures.[29]

COSTUMES

A costume survey of the ten music-dramas from the "Fleury Playbook," all of which are produceable versions (some uniquely so), reveals that with one exception (*The Conversion of St. Paul*) the stage directions of the two Easter plays—*The Visit to the Sepulcher* and *The Pilgrim*—are the only ones that explicitly require actors to be realistically costumed, to be "in similitudinem" of the characters they play. In most of the other Fleury plays there are some stage directions, often quite detailed and specific, but none concerns the costumes of the actors. I have used the Fleury repertory for this survey not only because it includes the finest version of *The Visit to the Sepulcher,* but also because it is by far the largest extant repertory that seems to be from a single source. Not that much importance

---

[28] For the chronology and dimensions of the Fleury abbey, see Dom A. Hardy, *Saint-Benoit-sur-Loire et Germigny-des-Prés* (Paris, 1959), p. 18; Conant, p. 155; and G. Chenesseau, *L'Abbaye de Fleury à Saint-Benoit-sur-Loire* (Paris, 1931). A ground plan of the abbey and recent photographs of the chancel, with the postmedieval steps to the sanctuary removed, are in Dom J.-M. Berland, *Saint-Benoit-sur-Loire* (Paris, 1960).

[29] Lowrie, plate 117c.

is to be given to the fact that those plays were collected in a single twelfth-century manuscript that may have been associated with Fleury.[30] The importance of the results of this survey lies in their being derived from a representative source of data about a group of twelfth-century dramas that have proven eminently playable. Having eliminated the amateurish plays, the closet dramas, and the random specimens, we are in position to interpret the results of a survey of plays that were in all probability actually produced.

It is surprising to find that only the scripts of the Easter play are much concerned with costuming. Does this mean that only plays on this greatest of feast days in the Christian year were thought worthy of realistic costuming, the others (except *The Conversion of St. Paul*) being costumed in improvised ecclesiastical vestments, as all plays had been in the tenth and eleventh centuries? Or, conversely, does it mean that after the many generations in which the play had been acted in adaptations of ecclesiastical dress, it became necessary to specify in the twelfth-century script that these newer, professionally composed versions were to be performed in the realistic, not the old liturgical style? For plays with a shorter history, like the Fleury St. Nicholas plays, there would have been no need to specify realistic costumes. Although *The Pilgrim* has no such ancient tradition behind it, the earliest version dating only from the twelfth century, the fact that it is an Easter play, and therefore subject to mishandling by contamination with the old style of producing the adjacent *Visit to the Sepulcher,* is perhaps enough to account for its explicitness concerning costumes.

In any event, the costumes of *The Visit to the Sepulcher* were certainly intended to be contemporary, and twelfth-century illustrations of them are plentiful. Detailed description of the costumes of the Marys is found in the section below, "Notes on Production." The costumes for the Christus, both as gardener and "in his glory," are adaptations of ecclesiastical vestments, as the stage directions of several play versions and the many artistic renderings of the "Noli me tangere" scene and the Ascension clearly indicate. These roles, like those of Angels and Archangels, are supernatural and their actors would therefore be properly costumed as ecclesiastics, particularly since the early playlets had improvised their costumes from the sacristy wardrobe. Fleury's directions are for Christ in his glory to be dressed in a white dalmatic (dalmaticatus candida dalmatica"). He had a long tunic under it, according to the Fleury stage

---

[30] See the discussion of this matter above, pp. 33–34.

directions and the illustrations of the Doubting Thomas scene in *The Pilgrim,* where the Christus again appears "in his glory" (plate 21).[31]

These directions are only for the basic costume, yet even so are rather more specific than those of other versions of *The Visit to the Sepulcher* or *The Pilgrim.*[32] The Fleury playwright continues with a unique stage direction as to the ornamentation of the basic, readily available vestments. On the Christus' head is a white fillet or band, ornamented with amulets ("candida infula infulatus, filacteria preciosa, in capite"). While the Rouen *Pilgrim* version adds the standard amice vestment, there is no indication of its ornateness.[33] Superb ornamentation was obviously essential to represent the glorified Christ and to place his costume beyond competition from that of the Angels, who had been displayed earlier in the play in lavish costumes. The artists knew this necessity, and no doubt the scribe of the Fleury playscript knew it too but had only to mention the white dalmatic and the unique headdress to remind himself of the production requirements. The artists had to spell it out visually, however, and in so doing have shown us what the full extent of the playwright-producer's intent was. The Christus in this costume enters at the moment when the crest of the play's wave has broken. He has now to deliver a final coup de grace as he sings the prophetic and comforting "Nolite timere vos," is confirmed by the stirring choral response, "Leo fortis, Christus, filius Dei," and then leads the company of actors out of the chancel and down the nave in the traditional and ineffable *Te Deum laudamus.* A costume nonpareil must surely accompany this genuinely glorious finish to the play.[34]

Worn earlier in the play as a humble yet still ecclesiastical disguise, the Christus' costume as the Gardener is by contrast much less elaborate. One is at first surprised to find that it is not, as we today might suppose, a medieval gardener's costume. A stage direction of only one version gives any hint as to the nature of this costume. The Nuremberg version specifies a long tunic with a short cloak over the shoulder, a crown, and bare

[31] The tunic worn by the actor of the Christus in these versions of *The Pilgrim* must have an open seam on the right side.

[32] This fact is not noted by Young or other commentators. No other versions of *The Visitatio* mention the "glory" costume, while the Fleury version of *The Pilgrim* has another specific description of this costume.

[33] Young, I, 462.

[34] Smoldon, *Visitatio,* p. 25, quotes the Fleury stage direction for the costume, and comments: "It may be that a modern producer will choose to modify the details of the costume described above." Young in his appreciation of the play makes no mention of the importance of the costume to the catastrophe.

feet.[35] These are not, of course, the practical working clothes of a gardener. The costume consistently represented in the visual arts (plates 12–14, for example) is composed of the same long tunic he will wear later in the Fleury version under the white dalmatic, along with a knee-length cloak. His head and feet are bare. As will be explained below, he has in hand a plain cross, which is both a gardening implement and the instrument with which in some versions of the play he proceeds, without time for costume change, to harrow Hell (see plate 12, which is typical of many). Perhaps this circumstance explains the absence of costume directions in all but one version of this scene. Also involved was the theological point that the Christus was the supreme ecclesiastical figure, the head of the Church, and could not be represented as a mere peasant, even in disguise.

As for the Angels' costumes, the stage directions of several versions, with help from visual representations of the period, suggest what the medieval practice was. The Fleury stage direction describes the Archangel of the first scene at the sepulcher as "vestitus alba deaurata, mitra tectus caput etsi deinfulatus" (vested in a gilded alb, a tight coif around his head but without a fillet over the coif). The St. Quentin direction is merely that the two Angels are "vestus de blans aournemens" (vested in white with ornaments). Other versions of the play, if they mention the Angel costume at all, direct: "alba stola indutus" (clothed in a white stole), "vestitus alba dalmatica" (vested in a white dalmatic), and "unus . . . vestem rubeam, alter vero vestem albam" (one vested in red, the other vested in white).[36] The dalmatic is the standard vestment; it should be white unless there are two angels, in which case one dalmatic may be red. Fleury calls for an "alba deaurata," which I am inclined to think is really describing a white alb with gilt trim, not a white alb with gold threads worked into it. By "aournemens" St. Quentin may also suggest the trimming of the white vestment.

Fleury is, once again, more specific about other details of the Archangel's costume, in requiring a plain headdress, without the fillet reserved and later specified for the Christus. One may interpret this distinction in the Fleury stage directions as an indication that the playwright was, as I suggested above, aware of the danger of comparison between Angel's dress and Christus' dress. The Fleury coif seems to be well illustrated on the angel of the Cologne plaque of *The Visit to the Sepulcher* (plate 10).

[35] Young, I, 399.   [36] Young, I, 382, 385, 435.

Other illustrations of angels in the sepulcher scene—angels elsewhere as in *The Annunciation* and *The Shepherds* are in another category because they are not subject to comparison with the Christus—show very much the same tight coif, so closely wrapped about the angel's head that one cannot always be sure that he is wearing more than his own coiffure (plates 2, 9–11). In none of these typical illustrations is there any indication of the fillet that Fleury warns against.

Angel wings were, I think, desirable, and were usually designed to be no larger than those in the Tuscan relief of the Annunciation (plate 68). They are occasionally specified in versions of *The Visit to the Sepulcher,* as in the Besançon playscript printed by Young, I, 290: "super humeros alas habentes." The word "super" here means "over," not "on," and suggests the upright position of the wings in most illustrations. "Super" also suggests the position of the wing harness, which must have been worn over the shoulders.

The costume of the Soldiers is another of the special and contemporary outfits. The Roman Soldiers are dressed in the chain mail of twelfth- and thirteenth-century soldiers. Frequent illustrations in the art of the period (e.g. plates 2, 9–11, 32, 36, 43) give details of this uniform, and include a reminder that the chain-mail tunic had to be long enough so that in a sitting position the knees were covered to avoid a comic tableau. The same uniform is of course used for soldiers in *Herod* and *The Conversion of St. Paul.*

Costumes for John and Peter are not described in Fleury stage directions, but from those of the related Dublin version we may legitimately borrow suggestions. They are to be clad "albis sine paruris cum tunicis, quarum Iohannes amictus tunica alba, palmam in manu gestans, Petrus vero rubea tunica indutus, claves in manu ferens" (in albs, untrimmed, and tunics, of which John is clothed in white with an amice and carries a palm, and Peter in fact is clothed in a red tunic, and carries keys in hand). The red of Peter's tunic was presumably darker than that of Mary Magdalene, and the material much coarser than that of her silk. The portrait of Peter in the *Lazarus* scene shows him carrying one large key (plate 40) as a costume accessory, though other illustrations and their source in Matthew 16:19 call for several keys.

The costumes of the Spice Merchants are self-explanatory in plates 3 and 4. The Saintes-Gilles portrayal shows the Merchant on the left with what appears to be an ankle bracelet on his right leg. What they and their colleagues in the Antelami portraits have on their heads is not clear, but may well be fillets to bind their hair.

STAGING AND THE DEFINITION OF
ACTING AREAS

When the Fleury stage directions refer to "Monumentum" and "Sepul-chrum," they are naming two distinct structures, both of them placed in the choir of the abbey, the "Sepulchrum" inside the "Monumentum." The St. Quentin directions mention only the "Sepuchre" but seem to intend the two structures. The "Sepulchrum" was a sarcophagus with a lid, and this smaller furnishing was placed a few feet inside the front archway of the "Monumentum." The monument, a tomb, was a "circular or polygonal structure of varying dimensions. . . . In their cone-shaped roofs . . . they copied, more or less suggestively, the original in Jerusalem." [37]

In the period of the great plays, Crusaders and pilgrims must have greatly heightened Western interest in the Anastasis at Jerusalem, a rotunda-shaped monument built over the original sepulcher in the time of Constantine.[38] The edifice had been reconstructed by Greek architects in the eleventh century, and somewhat modified by the Crusaders in the twelfth. Twelfth-century illustrations often provide a sketch of what the Anastasis at Jerusalem looked like. Typical are the two round domes and their Corinthian-capitaled columns that frame the top and sides of the Cologne plaque of the sepulcher scene (plate 10). It is noteworthy that the idea of the Anastasis in the tenth century, as conveyed by the Hartker illustration aforementioned, is not very different from that of the later Cologne artist, though the Anastasis had been reconstructed in the intervening two centuries. Nor are these images greatly different from those of much earlier artists, whose illustrations of Christ's and Lazarus's tombs go back respectively to the fourth and sixth centuries.

The importance of these similarities is that they confirm the traditional architecture of the "monument" as it must have been envisioned and built for the mature Fleury or St. Quentin play. While Young is loathe to distinguish between the permanent anastasis, of which there are many surviving specimens in Western Europe and England, and the temporary scenic structures built especially for the Easter plays during their hey-day,[39] there can be little doubt that the stage directions of the Fleury

---

[37] Young, II, 508, summarizing Neil C. Brooks, *The Sepulchre of Christ in Art and Liturgy* (Urbana, 1921).

[38] See Lowrie, plates 8c and 78d.

[39] Young, II, 508–13.

and St. Quentin plays call for the temporary structure. Such scenic structures are common in the larger productions of the period.[40] The Fleury direction even tells us where to place it: in the choir. If my reconstruction of the movement for the approach of the Fleury Marys to the monument is plausible, this structure must have been placed in the choir at stage right. Some further corroboration of this position is to be found in Young's statement that "in England . . . the *sepulchrum* is virtually always in the choir, or chancel, on the north side." [41]

[40] This is Young's conclusion, II, 400.   [41] Young, II, 510.

2. The Lament of Mary

15 The Virgin at the Postcrucifixion. Wooden statue, Italian, thirteenth century. Courtesy of the Metropolitan Museum of Art, the Cloisters Collection, gift of John D. Rockefeller, Jr.

16 St. John at the Postcrucifixion. Wooden statue, Italian, thirteenth century, companion piece to statue in plate 15. Courtesy of the Metropolitan Museum of Art, the Cloisters Collection, gift of John D. Rockefeller, Jr.

17 Postcrucifixion Scene, with Mary and John. Byzantine ivory plaque, eleventh (?) century. Courtesy of the Metropolitan Museum of Art, gift of J. Pierpont Morgan, 1917.

18   Crucifix and North Transept, the Duomo at Cividale (Basilica di Santa Maria Assunta): the focal point of *The Lament of Mary*. Thirteenth century. Photo Bront.

The Lament of Mary

Planctus Mariae

TONE AND QUALITY

THE tone and quality of *The Lament of Mary* are strongly individual, and not altogether typical of the high medieval period; in fact the tone is Gothic rather than Romanesque, florid and psychological.

The action of the play is simple; there is no chorus, and the cast of characters is small. Their expression, on the other hand, is apparently more lyric than dramatic. There is considerable evidence that the Passion play, of which the Cividale is the only surviving produceable version in the form of music-drama, had an immediate ancestor in a lyric dialogue known as the *planctus*.[1] The relationship with that lyric form is similar to that of classical Greek drama to the dithyramb, and of other medieval church plays to the liturgical lyric. In some instances the lyric in dialogue form led directly to high drama; in others, as in *The Song of Songs,* the earlier lyric has maintained its dominance, and the dramatic version has been recognized as derivative and inferior. *The Lament of Mary* seems clearly a development into drama from the lyric *planctus,* even though one may entertain the notion that the Cividale playscript could be adequately presented in concert, without acting the roles.

The play miraculously manages to transmute its essential lyric materials and to offer genuine drama to its audience. How this is contrived will be suggested in later sections on the production of the play. Here we need only remark that the action of the play is not as introspective as it seems. The disposition of its four actors into very emotional relationships to each other, and most importantly to the large crucifix, is dynamic, not static. There is more here than a conventional tableau of the Crucifixion, although this was a favorite subject for the medieval artist.[2]

---

[1] Young summarizes the scholarship on this matter, I, 538.

[2] At Cividale, for example, there have survived from the period of the play ten illustrations of the postcrucifixion scene. These are reproduced by Antonino Santangelo, *Catalogo delle Cose d'Arte e di Antichità d'Italia—Cividale* (Rome, 1936), pp. 136–42, 155, and 158. All are in the National Archeological Museum in Cividale del Friuli, and are of local origin.

The only external event in the story has happened only a few minutes before the play begins. The officials, executioners, and soldiers have left, but the crowd lingers. The mother and closest friends of the dead man, who still hangs limp above them on the cross, remain to take their farewell of him, and to try to understand what has happened.

The role of the crowd is thrust upon the play's audience. The Virgin's first speech is to us in the crowd: "O fratres et sorores." This seems so conscious a construction on the playwright's part that one suspects he knew what it would take to make a play out of a lyric song, and acted at once to establish his medium as theater. In other plays of the repertory the audience is addressed from time to time by the actors, as in *The Visit to the Sepulcher* and *The Annunciation,* but never in the first lines, as if the audience is also to act in the play.

The actors then begin to ask the inevitable and not immediately answerable questions about death: where, why, who? "Cur," (why) is used six times in the course of the play. "Why was he who was without sin crucified?" is the agonized question, asked from various angles by the Virgin, Mary the mother of James, Mary Magdalene, and John, of each other and of the crucified. There are no glib answers among the four, and the figure on the cross does not answer. But out of their efforts to comfort each other with affection, not arguments, the play moves along, and moves the audience.

Lest the audience think itself no longer in the cast after the fourth item, Mary Jacobi asks in Item 16, "Who is there here who would not weep to see the mother of Christ in such sorrow?" The Virgin, aware that the question was addressed to the audience, herself turns to them with the magnificent "O vos omnes," and they can hardly fail to sympathize with her as they are asked to. But absolution is not so easy. In the last item of the play, the Virgin speaks bitterly to the crowd: "O mentes perfidas, et linguas duplices" (O perfidious minds, and lying tongues).

THE DETERMINATION OF MAJOR EPISODES

Unlike any other play of the repertory except the very brief *Purification,* this one has only a single, sustained episode. The dead Christ, the four friends, and the crowd are all there at opening; no one leaves the stage, and no additional character appears. This is easily the longest single episode in the repertory.

Excellent as is the artistry of the visual representations of this scene, a static, posed quality is difficult to avoid. Only intensity of feeling for the event and for the persons represented redeems these portrayals from wooden lifelessness (see plates 2, 15–17), and this quality may all too easily be transferred to the actors of the play. Between the static and the bathetic is a fine line, to which medieval artists hewed. Each artist's problem was magnified by the patent fact that every artist before him had tried his skills on this scene. The playwright faced a different problem, there having been no significant output of mature plays on this subject. His was the necessity of sustaining, intensifying, developing. In this effort one cannot underestimate the value to the play of its hauntingly beautiful melodies. Their subtly varied repetitions and relationships are evidence of a skillful composer at work.

CHARACTERIZATION

The Virgin Mary has the title role, and is clearly the protagonist; her name in the playscript is "Maria Maior." When the other Marys and John are not addressing the dead Christ, they usually speak to her. She sings nine of the twenty-one items, all of them solos. Mary Magdalene, the lead of *The Visit to the Sepulcher,* sings only five, the other seven being divided between Mary Jacobi and John.

I remarked above that the Virgin is harder to approach as a theatrical human being than is Mary Magdalene, because the Virgin, as the mother of Christ, has always been the most venerated of women. In order to act her role, or understand her character in the play, one must make the kind of effort to accept her that I have suggested above for the Christus. Except for her relationship to him, she would be just another courageous woman, of whom much was asked and little given during her life, up to and including the time of the play.

During the play she expresses her loss as almost entirely personal. While she has the respect and sympathy of the other characters, she is not venerated by them, nor does the playwright require this of us.[3] As a woman she is individual and feminine throughout the play. It is not she but the other Marys who accept Christ's death as necessity, as prophesied. She feels only the deep personal loss; she is by turns anguished, pitiful, and indignant, incensed at the injustice as any normal woman would be. She never says with a resigned smile, "The Lord's will be done." By the end

[3] An apparent exception is the "Cur merore deficis" (Smoldon's Item 8), where the other Marys curtsey to her; but this is a gesture only of respect.

of the play there is still no sign of resignation in her, though she has gone through torrents of passion, and is physically exhausted. In the violence of her emotions she frequently embraces the other Marys and John, talks to her dead son, even more frequently beats her breast. The sense that she is a woman possessed runs through the play. There is also a sense that she knew it would come to this, as pictorial representations of the Nativity suggest (plates 28, 29). She cannot accept this rounded necessity now, try as she does in the "Triste spectaculum" item. In fervent words to John she recognizes that:

> Tempus est lamenti.
> Immolemus, intimas,
> Lacrimarum victimas
> Christo morienti.
> (Now is the time to lament.
> Let us, his intimates, offer ourselves
> As sacrifices of grief
> To the dying Christ.)

John sings the "O Maria," they look at her dead son, and she acknowledges his tender offer to take care of her. At this point the emotion is intolerable and can lead nowhere, as the playwright knows. Mary Magdalene, always instinctively knowing what to do, now rushes in to throw herself towards the crucifix and to sing the "O Pater benigne."

Neatly balanced characterization of the other Marys and John will not do here. All of their characters are being tested and moulded in their agonizing dialogue. What can be said? The important fact is that all of them, even Mary Jacobi, have roles to play, necessities to meet, in their attempts to hold themselves together. They do not resort to trite rationalizations. To comprehend the roles one must recognize that these characters are caught in a tragic situation, and are trying to do what they can: honestly, heartily, wretchedly.

MOVEMENT AND GESTURE

Literary and musicological students of this play have remarked enthusiastically upon the unusual quantity of its stage directions. From a dramatic point of view these must be scrutinized rather more critically before they can be accepted as cause for rejoicing. What style of acting do they represent? Are they a genuine reflection of actual performance?

Do the movements and gestures help to pattern the play? Are they fully integrated with the words and melodic phrases, as their arrangement in the manuscript seems to claim, or are they haphazard, or merely literary? All of these questions have to do with the artistic merit of the total play, and the stage directions are no more exempt from such consideration than the verses or the melodies.

Again, as Coussemaker long ago suggested, these stage directions are "un monument unique dont vient s'enrichir l'histoire de l'art dramatique."[4] I trust that the following detailed analysis and critical interpretation of them, in relation to production and to their occasional counterparts in the visual arts of the period, will help to define their actual importance to the history of the theater.

The psychological and therefore representational elements in *The Lament* are more suggestive of the fourteenth century—the date of the manuscript of the play and of its verbal and musical paleography—than they are of the more austere, contained style of the twelfth and thirteenth centuries. The kind of internal life the playwright finds possible to bring out in *The Lament of Mary* is more akin to the psychological introspection of Chaucer in *Troilus and Creseyde* than it is to the spirit of the Cologne or Saint-Gilles sculptures of the Crucifixion.

The seventy-nine stage directions are another symptom of the rather baroque style of the play. None of the twelfth-century plays of the repertory is so avid about gesture as to specify seventeen breast-beatings as well as the hand to be used. More characteristic is the kind of direction given in the Fleury *Visit to the Sepulcher* at a similar moment of anguish, with more than ordinary attention to movement: "pedetemtim et quasi tristes" (feeling their way with their feet and as if grieving). The key to the difference is the "quasi" (as if), which leaves the actor room for interpretation, like a tempo indication in a musical score. No other play-script of the repertory placed the stage directions over and under the music notation, as a running account of what the actor must do. The usual practice was to place the stage direction before the speech, the way the rubrics of the service books had always done it. In fact, most scholars prefer to call the stage directions rubrics, as I suppose the playwright himself did. One would have trouble, however, calling the directions of this Cividale play rubrics.

In addition to the directions for breast-beating, to be considered later,

---

[4] Coussemaker, p. 346. Young made no effort to assess their value. W. L. Smoldon, *Planctus Mariae: A Fourteenth-Century Passiontide Musical Drama* (London, 1965), prints them in translation, but without critical appraisal or interpretation.

some of the instructions ask for a style of acting that can only be called forced. The best example is the direction which accompanies Mary Jacobi's "Quis est hic qui non fleret" (Who is here who would not weep). The direction is "Hic ostendendo circumcircha et, cum manibus ad oculos suos, postea dicat" (Here, gesturing to those around her, and then with her hands to her eyes, she says). In the very next item the Virgin is directed to do the same thing. On the line "Simul mecum flete" (Weep together with me) the direction is "Hic ad oculos suos ponat manus" (Here she puts her hands to her eyes). This kind of gesture is pseudo-dramatic, like the forced efforts of beginning actors. One readily admits that a wide variety of acting styles is effective for different plays, and one is aware that music drama requires more stylization than modern realism. One recognizes also a modern prejudice for naturalistic, by which is meant psychological, acting: to act as if one were not acting. Yet one cannot imagine that playwright-directors of this repertory of highly sensitive and sophisticated dramas would have encouraged such a crude style of acting them as is occasionally demanded in the stage directions of *The Lament of Mary*.

One way to account for this ineptitude is to assume that some of the audience at Cividale knew no Latin, and that the clergy in charge wished the actors to "sign" with their hands, so that the laity would understand that "flete" was *piange* in the vernacular. But there is another possibility. While the majority of the stage directions are eminently practical, as I shall shortly demonstrate, one may speculate that not all the directions were written for the actors but that the offending ones were written later in order to satisfy some untheatrical personage who presided over the writing of the manuscript, perhaps even the scribe himself. This hypothesis would explain the unusual quantity and specificity of the directions, and even the unusual editorial device of including them between the musical staff-lines. It was remarked in the introduction that a paucity of stage directions usually means that the manuscript of the play, as we have it, is closer to the playwright and to his initial production of the play than is a manuscript that is more abundantly descriptive of movement and setting. We have no information about how much control the medieval playwright had over his score after the initial performance and during the time the play was being recorded for inclusion in the ecclesiastical library or for transfer to another institution, but it is unlikely that he had much control or even cared any more about this medieval equivalent of publication than Shakespeare did about the editing and printing of his quartos.

In further support of this hypothesis, that the editor of the Cividale *Planctus Mariae* was someone removed from the playwright and his play, one may adduce the two crashing blunders of the editor in the fundamental matter of assigning speeches to the wrong actor. This happens twice, once in assigning to John Item 6, "Fleant materna viscera," which is clearly not a speech for a man, and again in the middle of Mary Major's Item 9, "Triste spectaculum," when in the midst of a sentence John is specified as singing "Profunde me vulnerat." These are not the errors a playwright or any one close to a production of a play could conceivably make. They are much more like the few incredible stage directions for bad acting, in that no one involved with the acting of the play was likely to have written them.

PROPERTIES AND FURNISHINGS

The only furnishing required for *The Lament of Mary* is a large crucifix. The one almost certainly used in the original production is still hanging on the end wall of the north transept of the Cividale church (plate 18). In view of this extraordinary circumstance, a detailed description of the effigy may be of value in visualizing the original production of the play. The upright of the wooden cross is about ten feet in length, and the Christus upon it is seven feet tall. The feet of the figure in its present and presumably original location, are six feet above the transept floor, and are happily not supported by one of the little platforms often found expedient by medieval sculptors. The effigy is attached to the cross by bars in the usual fashion, and the cross itself is flush with the end wall of the transept, and laterally centered on it. In the description of Antonino Santangelo:

The Christus hangs on the cross with his head drooped upon his right shoulder, and his knees angled to the right of the observer. The gilded loincloth hangs in undulating folds to the knee. . . . The modeling of the body, in flat relief and much simplified . . . has archaic qualities that make one think of the art of the end of the 13th century. . . . In wood, intaglioed and tinted. . . . It has suffered an ancient restoration.[5]

The importance of these facts to our visualization of the original production of the play is evident. The entire Christus is above the heads of

[5] Santangelo, *Cividale,* p. 18 (my translation). The attribution to the thirteenth century is shared by another Italian art historian, P. Toesca, *Storia dell' Arte Italiana* (Torino, 1925), p. 788.

the actors, as the stage directions dictate. It is larger than the actors, and contributes greatly to the play's effectiveness. The crucifix is centered in the stage area, and permits balanced tableaux and movements.

Most medieval illustrations, like those in plates 2 and 17, place the crucifix only a little higher than the level of the characters, an arrangement necessary for a compact graphic composition but totally ineffective for a dramatic production.

The only hand property for the play was optional. Some illustrations of the Passion show John holding a gold Gospel in his left hand, the right being reserved for gesturing. Inasmuch as John is less involved with movement and dialogue than the Marys, the actor of the role may have been glad to have something in hand for his long periods of attentive inaction.

STAGING AND THE DEFINITION OF ACTING AREAS

Even without knowing the actual location of the Cividale crucifix, one would still expect the play to have been set in a smaller space than in the large choir of the cathedral. The audience is taken into the play at several points, most efficiently if the actors and audience are in close relationship to each other and to the crucifix. These conditions are admirably fulfilled in Cividale's shallow north transept, with its lateral dimension of thirty-six feet, and a depth of only twenty-four feet from the north wall of the choir (plate 18). The audience, a collegiate group, must therefore have been small, with hardly more than three rows of spectators in good vertical sight lines. The needs of the stagers for space could not have been great. The cast is small and its blocking intensive rather than extensive; its depth movements are slight. These requirements are reflected in the small dimensions of movement in the stage directions, and the large quantity of gestures. In fact, the extraordinary number of directions for gesture may well be explained by the necessity of acting in a small area —a probably unused maximum of thirty-six feet in width and perhaps twelve feet in depth—in order to keep the focus on the crucifix.[6] The

---

[6] The sense that a small area was appropriate for such a play is found in the description of a semidramatic *planctus* ceremony at Toulouse in the thirteenth century. Santangelo, *Cividale,* repeatedly refers to the Cividale cathedral as a collegiate church.

characters are throughout almost literally "at the foot of the cross," as a modern playwright would describe the setting.

Since the Cividale church has been considerably remodeled since the period of the play, one may gain further insight into the style of its staging from the west facade of the church at Gemona, only a few miles from Cividale, in the same Friuli district. The upper level of the facade has a relief of the Passion scene with the crucifix, the Virgin, and John. It was done by local sculptors about 1290.[7]

MAKEUP: BEARDS AND HAIRSTYLES

As with the Marys in *The Visit to the Sepulcher,* the women of *The Lament* should have their heads so fully covered that the style of their hair is not significant. John is almost always clean-shaven, as in *The Visit to the Sepulcher,* and is invariably represented as having red hair. The style of his hair in the visual representations of *The Lament* is always curled and short, as for example in plates 16–17, and looks like a rather thick wig. I do not know the reason for this convention in the visual arts of the period. It was of great age, to judge from an apparently similar hairstyle for John on the fifth-century door panel of Saint Sabina's church in Rome.[8]

LIGHTING

A Toulouse service book of the thirteenth century describes but does not quote a *planctus* dialogue, sung on Good Friday, "presumably," Young writes, "as part of the ceremony of *Tenebrae.* The two singers stood on a platform surrounded by curtains, and in the course of their performance all the lights were extinguished except one, in token of the fact that, of all Christ's followers, only the Virgin Mary was steadfast in her devotion." [9] While a modern performance would hardly be visible in the light of one candle, and the Toulouse ceremony was probably not a drama, a key to the light plot for the Cividale play is given in the description of the snuffing of the lights until there was only a single beam.

[7] Giuseppe Marchetti, *Mostra di Crocifissi e di Pietà Medievale del Friuli* (Venezia Giulia and Friuli, 1958), p. 18, fig. 13.

[8] Lowrie, plate 93b.

[9] Young, I, 503. There was at Cividale, of course, no platform, in order that the crucifix be as high as possible above the actors.

3. The Pilgrim

19 The Christus and The Disciples on the Road to Emmaus. Ivory dip-
tych, Spanish, twelfth century. Courtesy of the Metropolitan Museum
of Art, gift of J. Pierpont Morgan, 1917.

20 The Disappearance of the Christus from the Emmaus Inn.
English Psalter, early thirteenth century. London, British
Museum, MS Arundel 157, fol. 11ᵛ. Courtesy of the
Trustees of the British Museum.

21 Scenes from *The Pilgrim*. English Gospel Book, early twelfth century. Cambridge, Library of Pembroke College, MS 120, fol. 4ᵛ. Courtesy of the Masters and Fellows of Pembroke College, Cambridge.

22 The Christus and the Disciples on the Road to Emmaus. Byzantine Gospel Book, as copied in the twelfth century. Paris, Bibliothèque Nationale, MS grèque 74, fol. 162ᵛ. Photo courtesy of Bibliothèque Nationale.

23 The Christus and the Disciples on the Road to Emmaus. Pseudo-Bonaventura, *Meditations,* thirteenth century. Oxford, Bodleian Library, MS C.C.C. 410, fol. 159ʳ. Reproduced with the permission of the President and Fellows of Corpus Christi College, Oxford.

24   The Supper at Emmaus. Gold enamel panel, plaque no. 6, ca. 1160. Hildesheim
Cathedral Treasury.

25   The Supper at Emmaus (right) and Doubting Thomas (left). "Peterborough
Psalter," middle thirteenth century. Brussels, Bibliothèque Royale, MS 9961–2,
fol. 92ʳ. Courtesy of Bibliothèque Royale Albert Iᵉʳ.

The Pilgrim

(*Peregrinus*)

TONE AND QUALITY

IN MARKED contrast to *The Visit to the Sepulcher* and *The Lament of Mary,* in which the women's roles predominate and there is no scene or dialogue without them, *The Pilgrim* [1] has no women in the cast. Four men only, and a choir. A man's play, and a manly one, its quality is more direct and muscular and less intensely lyric, as if the playwright had begun with characters in a story rather than with a passionately lyric theme.

The play from Beauvais opens, like the other versions,[2] with a familiar liturgical hymn, four stanzas of *Jesu, nostra redemptio,* sung by two disciples as they sadly walk the road to Emmaus. We are out of doors again, as in all of *The Lament of Mary* and most of *The Visit to the Sepulcher.* The hymn is in effect interrupted by the appearance of a pilgrim, Cleopas, behind the disciples. In a liturgical antiphon setting of the dialogue from Luke, the pilgrim asks them what their trouble is, that they walk and talk so sadly. They reply in a continuation of the same antiphon. Having stated his theme in traditional words and music, the playwright-composer is now free to vary and expand that theme. The next seven items of dialogue are his versifications of Luke, together with his own musical fantasy on the plainchant theme. Now Cleopas breaks back into another liturgical plainchant, the *Mane nobiscum,* and

---

[1] W. L. Smoldon, in his edition of the play, *Peregrinus: A Twelfth-Century Easter Musical Drama* (London, 1965), prefers *The Stranger* as the English title. Medieval Latin *peregrinus* also denoted *pilgrim;* moreover, in the age of vast pilgrimages all pilgrims were strangers but not all strangers were pilgrims. The force of the title is much stronger if it evokes not only the Gospel journey to Emmaus but also the popular pilgrimages to Compostela, Rome, and Jerusalem during the period in which the play was composed. I also note that art works of the period generally portray Christ on the road to Emmaus in the dress of a medieval pilgrim. Another consideration is the force of Cleopas's line, "Tu solus peregrinus es in Jerusalem? . . ." (Are you the only pilgrim in Jerusalem? . . .) A visitor to Jerusalem in the twelfth century was certain to be a pilgrim.

[2] The Fleury, Rouen, Saintes, *Carmina Burana,* and Sicily versions, in Young, I, 471, 461, 453, 463, 476.

immediately thereafter the playwright again expands a traditional antiphon in versification and musical fantasy.[3]

For the supper scene, the disappearance of the revealed Christus, the disciples' search for him, and the choir's comment, the playwright was obliged to use liturgical antiphons and a liturgical *communio,* inasmuch as the central action in that scene is a typological parallel of the last supper and of the Mass. As soon as this scene is completed and the inn setting abandoned, the Beauvais playwright returns to variations on a liturgical theme. This time he gives the musical variation first, in the opening measure of the *Pax vobis! Ego sum!* for Christ's reappearance, and while using some verbal material from liturgical antiphons, expands the preceding original musical variation in much the same fashion as he had the earlier antiphon themes.[4] Even the choir's free-rhythm item after these expansions, in a familiar liturgical text, begins with an expansion of the first measure of the *Pax vobis.* After two original and unrelated items, in which Thomas is introduced, the playwright proceeds to state musically the liturgical theme that had been back of these variations and expansions of it, another *Pax vobis! Ego sum!* The melody of this item is to be found in the modern Antiphonary of the Roman Church, and is presumably the ancient Hartker antiphon melody, unrhythmed but note for note identical with the Beauvais item.[5] The playwright has reserved it for the third and final reappearance of Christ during the play, and the majestic simplicity of the melody appears to emerge from the dramatic complexities of its variations. Followed by the simple melody, it is the musical counterpart of what is happening in this story of reappearances, of resurrections.

I have described these musico-dramatic constructions less as a discovery than as an indication of the playwright's formal intent. How masterfully this intent has been fleshed out, dramatically as well as musically, should become apparent in following sections of this study.

DETERMINATION OF MAJOR EPISODES

The three major episodes of the play are easily identified, and two of them are confirmed as episodes developed in the twelfth century (not

---

[3] Smoldon, *Peregrinus,* does not mention these musical expansions, though he does remark a similar kind of fantasy in his *Visitatio,* p. 10.

[4] The *Pax vobis! Ego sum!* appears also in the *Carmina Burana* version, but without readable notation; it is repeated later in that version, and in the Fleury version. Meyer identified sources in Hartker's *Liber responsalis* (see Young, I, 466, note 3, and 689.)

[5] *Antiphonale Sacrosanctae Romanae Ecclesiae Pro Diurnis Horis* (Paris, 1949), pp. 464–65, 481.

just episodes taken directly from Luke 24 and John 20, or indirectly through liturgical antiphons) by the copious illustration of the scenes. So close are some visual portrayals to the play's version of the story that several scholars have convinced themselves that the illustrations are indebted to the Fleury and Rouen versions of the play.[6] While this is not the place to consider the merits of such claims, a quotation from Otto Pächt illuminates the relation of the third episode to the arts of the period:

Before the twelfth century the story of Emmaus is a comparatively rare subject of artistic representation, and the few pictorial cycles which contain it invariably confine themselves to two episodes: The Road to Emmaus and The Supper at Emmaus. The St. Albans Psalter miniatures are the earliest examples known to Western European art of a sequence of Emmaus scenes with three episodes, that of Christ disappearing from sight being a newcomer to the cycle. . . . Everything points to the fact that the pictorial treatment of the moment of Christ's disappearance at Emmaus was an original contribution of the Twelfth Century. . . . In one way or another it is the impersonation of the Peregrinus of the mystery plays (that is, the Latin dramas of the Church) and not the Jesus of the Gospel text which is reflected in all these twelfth-century representations.[7]

For immediate reference these pictorial moments may be related to the play as follows:

Episode	Smoldon item no.	Moment	Plate no.
A	2–5	Christ as pilgrim meets the disciples.	22, 23
	9	Christ chides the disciples.	22
	14	The disciples invite Christ to the inn.	21
B	16c	Christ gives the disciples bread at table.	24, 25
	16c	Christ disappears.	20
C	23c	Thomas feels Christ's side.	21, 25

The six moments actually amount to only three episodes, dramatically considered, since the supper scene is concluded with Christ's disappear-

[6] Emile Mâle, the noted art historian whose works are too numerous to cite here, first proposed this relationship of the visual arts to the drama of the period. In the course of the present study it will become apparent that such a relationship can hardly be generalized, inasmuch as illustrations of the subjects of the plays in almost every instance antedate the plays, often by centuries. There is, however, no reason why an occasional illustration cannot have been influenced by the artist's having seen the play in question. Even in such instances, however, the extent of his indebtedness is difficult to determine because traditional concepts of scene and story were shared by artists and playwrights.

[7] Otto Pächt, C. R. Dodwell, and Francis Wormald, *The St. Albans Psalter,* Studies of the Warburg Institute, XXV (London, 1960), pp. 73–74. The Psalter is dated 1120–1130, and is from Hildesheim. Pächt's plates 122–24 contain twelve portrayals of Peregrinus episodes. See also his *The Rise of Pictorial Narrative in Twelfth-Century England* (Oxford, 1962).

ance. The three incidents on the road take up nearly two-thirds of the play. This statistic compares closely with the quantitative emphasis of the visual artists represented here. One gathers from this comparison something of what the medieval artist, whether involved with drama or with visual art, saw as the proportions of the story. The Biblical narratives of Luke and John reverse these proportions, and devote nearly twice as many verses to the post-Emmaus story as to the earlier episodes. To judge from these discrepancies and from the sudden increase of dramatic and pictorial representations of this narrative in the twelfth century, that period had its own concept of the major episodes of this story, and of their proportions.

One needs of course to balance this estimate of proportion and emphasis with the Beauvais master's structure. He used the twelfth-century proportions of the episodes but opposed them musically, with emphasis on Christ's three reappearances (*Pax vobis! Ego sum!*) during the play. This counterthrust is as subtly artistic as his variations and expansions are. Together they weave a marvelous pattern for his drama.

CHARACTERIZATION

The Christus, as we remarked above, takes the active lead in this play, and sings nearly half its items. In spite of his disguise as a pilgrim and his sudden disappearances and reappearances, his character throughout the play is remarkably consistent, and remarkably human. While he tests the disciples' faith and understanding in the first scene and Thomas's in the last, and does not spare any of them the embarrassment of their mistakes, he is never enraged or nettled by them. Essentially, he is always the good teacher, working to help people understand themselves, even if it is painful to them. In Luke's account he calls the disciples "stulti" (stupid), and "tardi corde ad credendum" (slow to have heart to believe), which are the words of a teacher exasperated by the weaknesses of his best students. The Beauvais master adds something to this outburst by prefacing the "stulti" and "tardi" with a sarcastic "O cum sitis eius discipuli" (What studious disciples of his you are!), and by rearranging Luke to follow the appellations of "stupid" and "slow" immediately with the more drastic "increduli" (unbelieving). This last touch is an inspiration, for it links the two disciples with the incredulous Thomas of the later scene, and sets up more clearly the point of Christ's final line, "Beati qui non viderunt et crediderunt!" (Blessed are they that have not seen, yet have believed!) Other versions of this play merely quote Luke (or the antiphon) verbatim: "O stulti, et tardi corde ad credendum. . . ." There is a note of agile playfulness in the disguise and in the disappearances, and the touch of sarcasm in "O cum sitis" increases the sense that Christ is chiding the disciples as he had on such occasions as Peter's loss of nerve in walking on the water ("O ye of little faith"). This attitude is, one feels, not severe and vengeful, but seasoned with a kind of dry wit that is sarcasm at its best. This aspect of the character is not recognizable in the portrayals of Christ in other plays of the repertory.

All other characters in *The Pilgrim* are disciples. Cleopas is not one of the most prominent disciples, and there is no reason to individualize either him or the other disciple, who is so vaguely identified in the Gospel story, and hence in the play, that we could call him either Luke or Peter. Luke is customarily preferred, but the custom may be three hundred years younger than the play, there being in the dramatic tradition only fifteenth-century vernacular plays to date it.[8] The only general evidence is the assumption that since Luke wrote the Emmaus story he must have been there. The antiphon *Surrexit Dominus et apparuit Petro* (The Lord is risen and has appeared to Peter), which is sung by the choir after Christ's first disappearance from the two disciples, would suggest that the other disciple should be called Peter, since in many instances the antiphons were the ancient carriers of such traditions. The Beauvais master remained as vague as others about this matter. Although the Fleury version of *The Pilgrim* also uses this antiphon, it names neither of the two disciples. No character in any of the versions ever calls them by name, nor have I found verbal identifications of these disciples in the visual portrayals from any period.[9]

I do not mean to suggest that the two disciples are colorless characters in the play. Their attitude is always straightforward, honest, and friendly. They are not suspicious of the strange pilgrim who stops them on the road, and they are interested in what he has to say, even after he calls them stupid and slow. They let him sit down and teach them about the prophets, and are most hospitable in asking him to be their guest at the Emmaus inn.

Thomas is more an individual because he is less straightforward. He is

[8] See Young, I, 688.

[9] If a modern producer performs this play with *The Lament of Mary* and *The Visit to the Sepulcher,* there is an advantage in calling the nameless disciple Peter, in order to double the actor from the Peter role in *The Visit to the Sepulcher.*

an intellectual skeptic who has to have hard evidence to believe what he has been told. Because of our own skepticism, we are probably more drawn to him than a medieval audience, with their sublime faith, would have been. Only Christ's charity and mercy save Thomas from an ignominy only slightly less than that of Judas. Thomas's contrast with the other two disciples is assisted by Smoldon's having changed the *tessitura* of his voice to that of a baritone or tenor, the other disciples apparently being basses.

The Fleury version introduces the non-speaking role of a person at the inn who "offers bowl and napkin for a ceremonious washing of hands, pours wine, and retires." [10] I can see no dramatic gain in holding up the action of the play for this business. The effect is of a long pantomime which is not compatible with the otherwise continuous action of the play, and which occurs at the opening of a new scene, when the momentum has subsided and needs to be built, not retarded. Dramatically, this is the opposite of the pregnant pause. One's first thought is perhaps that the Servant or Innkeeper provides a means of getting the table set with food and drink, and as such is a valuable interscenic person. But he cannot logically set the table; it must be already set at the beginning of the play, as we shall see later in considering the staging areas. If the ceremonial washing of hands is cut—it takes time and risks unintentional comedy— there is nothing left for the Servant or Innkeeper to do. Finally, the Fleury stage direction, which gave Gustave Cohen an idea which he passed on to Young and Smoldon, does not name this person as a member of the cast.[11] The Fleury stage direction reads, "afferatur eis aqua ad lavandum manus suas, deinde mensa bene parata, super quam sit positus panis inscissus, et tres nebulae, et calix cum vino" (Let there be brought to them water to wash their hands, and then a table well prepared, on which let there be placed the cut loaf, and three wafers, and a chalice of wine). The movement meanwhile is rather crudely planned. During the choir's long *Mane nobiscum* and *Alleluia,* the three men go (quickly, of necessity) to a *sedes,* where all that the stage direction requires, which is quite a tedious lot, is brought to them. The setting of the table would have had to be accomplished during the *Mane nobiscum,* which because of its subject matter would have been a distraction.

Altogether, I cannot see the dramatic point of interpolating a clumsy bit of business from another, inferior version. The reason, I suspect, was

[10] This is Smoldon's adaptation of the Fleury stage direction, (Smoldon, *Peregrinus,* p. 12) which in the original makes no identification of the server.
[11] See Young, I, 476 and note.

Darwinian; Young gives it away: "The person who performs this service is, no doubt, the forerunner of the comic innkeeper of the later plays in the vernacular." [12] Hardin Craig supplies the corrective: "Medieval religious drama existed for its own self . . . and not as an early stage of secular drama." [13]

MOVEMENT AND GESTURE

It would be premature to discuss movement and gesture for this play without settling the location of the three acting areas that are required for the Beauvais version. The stage directions of this and the other versions, however, do not define movement in relation to acting area, and we may as well see what movements and gestures are appropriate in each of the three areas, from the evidence of stage directions and illustrations in the art of the period.

At the opening of the play the two disciples enter at a west door (Rouen version) or walk down the nave or from a transept toward the choir, and slowly approach the front of the nave.[14] In any event, they walk toward the Emmaus inn but must be stopped by the disguised Christus before they are close to it. The first part of the conversation between Christ and the disciples is standing; the Rouen version directs that Christ "stet inter illos" (stand between them). Certainly there is room for shifts in the blocking as the conversation continues. Plates 19, 21, 22, and 23 show a variety of positions for this scene. A remarkable element in all of these illustrations is the animated gestures of the three actors during the conversation. Three versions of the play, but not the Beauvais, quote or paraphrase Luke's description of Christ pretending to go his way ("se finxit longius ire"). One twelfth-century drawing (plate 21) shows the Other Disciple pointing to the inn or the sun during his *Iam sol vergens,* and another shows him using his pilgrim's staff as a pointer.[15] The large, palms-out gestures of two of the figures in plate 19 are no doubt too extreme for modern acting, but are suggestive of the extent to which

[12] Young, I, 476.

[13] Hardin Craig, *English Religious Drama of the Middle Ages* (London, 1960), p. 7. See also Hardison, pp. 18–25, for a discussion of the limitations of the evolutionary concept as applied to medieval drama.

[14] The Fleury version uses the adverb "pedetemtim" to describe the Disciples' later searching for the Christus after his disappearance. The word would have been apt here. See above, pp. 71–72.

[15] Pächt et al., *The St. Albans Psalter,* p. 43.

medieval actors talked with their hands. Here the two disciples appear to be greeting the Pilgrim. That these are traditional gestures may be surmised from the quite similar poses in a sixth-century Ravenna mosaic of the same scene.[16]

Movement and gesture in the inn scene, at the table, are very much the same in visual portrayals of the moment at which Christ gives the bread to the two disciples. Always the Christus is seated back of the middle of the table, the two disciples flanking him but also back of the table, not at its ends (plates 21, 24, 25). The only variation of the simultaneous giving of the bread is the cross-armed gesture (plate 25), which emphasizes the ceremonial nature of the act. For this purpose it would have been done slowly and firmly with no sense of the bread being thrust at the disciples.

The many illustrations of Thomas feeling the wound show a variety of positions for his hand. In the *Peterborough Psalter* (plate 25) Thomas kneels and raises his right arm to touch the wound. With his right hand Christ holds him by the wrist and brings Thomas's hand to the wound. As in all illustrations from this period, Christ bares his right side; Thomas does not fumble inside Christ's mantle. In the St. Albans illustration, the kneeling Thomas touches the wound with his right index finger (plate 21),[17] but in others he inserts all the fingers of his right hand into the wound, and his thumb sticks straight up. In some of the illustrations Christ's gestures reveal the stigmata on one or both palms.

Thomas's gesture of refusal to believe ("nunquam credidero") is reminiscent of that of Cain in the Salerno altar frontal as he asks, "Am I my brother's keeper?" The gesture of the two disciples when they realize that Christ has vanished from the table is illustrated in plate 20 rather more dramatically than in the Fleury stage direction, "aspicientes ad invicem" (staring at each other).

One almost expects some extreme proponent of Mâle's well-known theory—that many works of visual art are records of play performances, particularly of *The Pilgrim*—to suggest that the staging of Christ's disappearance from the table included the use of a pulley hoist (see plate 20).[18] The timing and lighting of Christ's two disappearances did involve a Houdini-like agility on the part of the actor. A momentary distraction would have helped, but could hardly have been enough to have

[16] See Lowrie, plate 78e.
[17] See also *Treasures from the Pierpont Morgan Library: Exhibition Catalogue* (New York, 1957), plate 15.
[18] See also Lowrie, plate 106d.

gotten Christ out of sight unless the table were placed off-center. Since the table cloth in all illustrations is draped in folds over the front of the table (e.g., plates 20, 21, 24, 25), the Christus could have hidden behind the table. The problem then would have been to stage his reappearance with majestic dignity! The simplest solution may have been for the Christus to give the bread to the disciples, who bend over to eat it from their palms (in a customary Communion manner); while they are so preoccupied, the Christus quickly rises from the table and stalks out. When they raise their heads from eating, he is gone. While the medieval predilection for gadgets was strong, and there are records of small Ascension images being pulled up to the roof of the church,[19] one can readily imagine the havoc that would be wrought upon the play were a live actor to be so handled.

Still another possibility for the disappearance from the inn is suggested in an illustration from the *Peterborough Psalter*. The portrayal on the left in plate 25 has the three characters seated in a recessed booth, rather more crowded than would be necessary in staging. If the back wall of the booth were a slit drapery curtain, as it appears to be, the Christus would have an easy and fast means of exit, and would be concealed for his next entrance around the side of the booth. Note that plates 21 and 24 also frame the table scene in arches which suggest a similarly recessed and curtained booth.

STAGING AND THE DEFINITION OF ACTING AREAS

There is one well-defined acting area in this play, a room at the inn at Emmaus. The other scenes require no specific location or setting, and were probably thought of as *plateae,* left and right. Attention must therefore be placed on the nature of this interior set and its means for contriving the instant disappearance of the Christus and his later appearance. Because the Beauvais version is not specific about the location of this set, we must learn the possibilities from other versions.

The Saintes and Sicilian versions merely locate the inn scene at the altar (ad altare), which one would infer was the simplest way of staging the scene, and a very good one. The supper at Emmaus is in one sense

---

[19] The ceremony is recorded in Young, I, 485–89.

an intentional parody of the Mass, and the altar is the Lord's table wherever he may be, even resurrected and at Emmaus. A free-standing altar, or one that could be curtained and platformed at the sides in order practically to represent the scene—as in some instances the sepulcher set in *The Visit to the Sepulcher* was arranged—made a good basis for staging.

Other versions suggest another location, or *sedes,* for this interior scene, and the artists of the period prefer such a set (plates 20, 21, 24, 25). The Fleury version speaks of the Christus and the disciples "sessum in sedibus ad hoc preparatis" (seated in places prepared for this purpose), which suggests a *sedes,* or platform set. Young speculates that "Presumably the *locus competens* representing the road to Emmaus is in the western part of the building, and the table for the supper, in the center of the nave. Jerusalem, where Christ appears to the ten disciples . . . is in the choir." [20]

The Rouen staging is even more specific. The Easter Monday processional to and from the font stops on the way back "in medio navis ecclesiae" (in the middle of the nave of the cathedral) and sings the psalm *In exitu.* Near the end of the psalm, those who are playing the disciples enter the cathedral by the right portal of the western facade, and slowly join the procession in the middle of the nave as the psalm is finished. (The monastics understood dramatic timing). The disciples begin as usual with the hymn, *Jesu, nostra redemptio,* and the procession presumably sings it through the fourth stanza. At this point the priest who is playing the Christus enters from the left portal, catches up to the disciples, pushes the procession aside, comes between the disciples, and sings to them the "Qui sunt hii sermones" which is also used in the Beauvais version. The procession becomes the audience and the choir. The conversation on the road to Emmaus (in the middle of the nave) ends with the invitation to the inn, and the disciples point to it with their staves ("trahentes baculum ostendentes castellum"). They then lead the Christus up the nave to a set ("tabernaculum") prepared in the likeness of the Chateau of Emmaus. When they have climbed onto this set ("ascenderint"),[21] they sit at the prepared table. The audience has presumably followed them and closed in around the front and sides of the platform.

After the disappearance of the Christus at the end of this scene, the disciples sing an *Alleluia* and the *Nonne cor nostrum* to the processional

---

[20] Young, I, 475.

[21] In translation I have changed the mood and tense of the verb from the "let them climb" to "when they have climbed."

audience, and repeat the *Alleluia.* (There is no mention of the *Surrexit Dominus de Sepulchro* antiphon.) The focus now shifts to the pulpit, where Mary Magdalene is asked by the disciples on behalf of the processional audience "Dic nobis, Maria, quid vidisti in via?" (Tell us, Mary, what you have seen on the way.) Her answer, "Angelicos testes" and "Surrexit Christus spes nostra," (Angels testifying that Christ, our hope, is risen), during which she displays the *sindone* (graveclothes), is completed by the processional audience.[22] When the disciples and Mary Magdalene have gotten out of the way ("recedant"), the audience returns to the choir where Easter Monday vespers are finished. We should recall that Beauvais in this period was fond of processions, and included at least eight of them in *The Play of Daniel.* Wherever the audience was at Beauvais (the stage directions are noncommittal about this) the two disciples come along and sing verses of the hymn, *Jesu, nostra redemptio,* and then the Pilgrim approaches them and sings *Qui sunt hii sermones,* and the play is on. Young infers that "the performance occurred in the choir, before the procession to the font." His inference is based, he writes, "upon the form of Vespers found at Soissons."[23] Why not simply base the inference on the more theatrical Rouen processional? Fleury, usually more explicit about production matters, is in this case no more demanding than the Beauvais script about the circumstances of performance. The two disciples "procedant duo a competenti loco" (The two proceed from a satisfactory location). The audience then, processors and all, would have been in the nave, behind and to the sides of the protagonists, during the conversation on the road.

At this juncture the Beauvais stage directions begin to be specific. After Cleopas' *Mane nobiscum,* the Disciples walk along, leading the Pilgrim and urging him toward the inn ("Tunc ambo eum ducant . . . quasi cogentes eum ad hospitium"). During the *Iam sol vergens,* the three men walk to the inn, and the next stage direction, "Et ducant eum ad mensam" (and they lead him to the table), indicates that they have arrived. This location is obviously down the nave, even at the crossing, for we find that after the scene at the inn and the disciples' search throughout the church for the vanished Christ, the choir is already in place when the disciples come back to it. "Tunc convertant se ad chorum, et chorus cantet: *Surrexit* . . ." (Then the disciples come around to the

---

[22] With "Credendum est . . ." and "Scimus Christus." The other two following lines ("alios duos versus sequentes") are mentioned but not specified by the Rouen scribe, although they are common in versions of the *Visitatio.* See, for example, the Cividale version, Young, I, 380.

[23] Young, I, 470 and note.

choir, and the choir sings *Surrexit . . .*). In other words, while the disciples searched for the vanished Christ, the choir made its way up to the chancel, beyond the crossing where the inn scene had been played. The remainder of the procession (the audience) moved beyond the inn set at the crossing, and was ready for Christ's reappearance, the coming of Thomas, and the final scene with him.

If we may assume a peripatetic audience—and Beauvais would hardly object—the central scene at the inn is to be set up in the nave, probably off center of the crossing where there is space for audience and platform. The three actors climb up onto it. Beauvais merely says that the disciples lead him to it ("ducant eum ad mensam"), but Rouen describes the movement as "ascenderint" (climb up on).

This platform set, the kind of typical *sedes* so often mentioned in the more mature plays of the repertory, is visualized by the painters of the period as a large booth, a sumptuous private dining room (plates 20, 21, and 24, 25). Its furnishings are elegant, for this is no little roadside inn; this is the Chateau ("castellum") of Emmaus. As with many of the pictures of the Sepulcher scene, visual illustrations narrow the focus to show only the interior; the exterior of the chateau has already been exhibited in paintings of the scene on the road.

The platform stage is a curtained dining booth, deep enough for a narrow table and a bench or stools behind it. There are probably curtains at the sides, and a split curtain at the back, not only as a background for the scene but also as an exit and masking for the Christus' sudden disappearance and later reappearance around the side of the platform. The top front of the set is a single or triple Romanesque arch, and the side frames suggest the chateau architecture (plate 25). The platform stage is no bigger than necessary to accommodate the three actors, their bench or stools, and the table.

4. The Shepherds

26 The Annunciation to the Shepherds. Miniature, made in diocese of Constance, 1200–32. Brno, Archiv Městský. Reproduced from H. Swarzenski, *The Berthold Missal,* fig. 94.

27   The Annunciation to the Shepherds (top) and the Purification (bottom). "Gmunden Gospel Book of Henry the Lion," fol. 111ʳ, ca. 1175. Courtesy of The Warburg Institute, University of London.

28 The Annunication to the Shepherds (top) and the Nativity, with Mary, Joseph, and the Child (bottom). Enamel plaques, attributed to Wibert of Aix-la-Chapelle, ca. 1170. Courtesy of the Metropolitan Museum of Art, gift of J. Pierpont Morgan, 1917.

29 The Nativity, with Mary and the Midwives. Miniature, Salzburg region, middle twelfth century. Cambridge, The Fitzwilliam Museum, MS McClean 22, fol. 68ᵛ. Reproduced by courtesy of the Syndics of The Fitzwilliam Museum, Cambridge.

30 The Annunciation to the Shepherds. "Miniatures," second half of twelfth century. New York, The Pierpont Morgan Library, MS M44, fol. 2ᵛ.

31 The Nativity (left) and the Annunciation to the Shepherds (right). "Echternach Gospel Book," 962–1056. Nuremberg, Germanisches Nationalmuseum, MS 156142, fol. 18ᵛ. Courtesy of Germanisches Nationalmuseum.

The Shepherds

(*Officium Pastorum*)

TONE AND QUALITY

I HAVE remarked before the ability of the medieval mind to integrate the most earthly with the most holy, and have suggested that the tradition of the Christmas shepherds has broad comic implications. In the Rouen version of *The Shepherds,* the only well-developed version that is independent of the *Herod* play, there seems no reason not to see in them and the play that mixture of religious elation and homespun horseplay that is elsewhere characteristic of medieval celebrations of Christmas. Even the mighty Herod, in the sequel to *The Shepherds,* becomes in some thirteenth-century versions mock-heroic. In the version produced at Padua, Herod and his attendant on their first entrance throw their wooden spears at the choir; Herod reads the ninth lesson with great fury ("cum tanto furore"); and his ministers, armed with inflated bladders, run around the chancel beating the bishop, the canons, and the choir, and even go out and clobber the men and women of the congregation (in imitation of the slaughter of the innocents?). A moment later Herod, all smiles, carries the Gospel Book to the bishop and canons to be kissed, while his rascally attendant censes them. The choir is then censed also.[1]

Something of this tonal blend is implicit in *The Shepherds* play from Rouen, even though the horseplay is not spelled out in the stage directions as it is in the Paduan play. The Archangel's annunciation to the Shepherds at the beginning of the play is a kind of parody of the annunciation to the Virgin. The later scene at the manger, as scholars long ago pointed out, is a parody of *The Visit to the Sepulcher* in words and melodies, the two midwives being homespun equivalents of the two Angels, and the *praesepe* itself an imitation of the sepulcher.[2] The annunciation parallel has not been so often observed, with the *Nolite timere*

[1] The text is printed in Young, II, 99.   [2] Young, II, 8.

by the Archangel (Gabriel, one supposes, on both occasions), paralleled by Gabriel's *Ne timeas, Maria* in the original annunciation. All of these parodies are intentional; they could not be accidental. They are informed with the best sense of parody, which is testing and interpretation through comedy, but in medieval hands, without irreverence.

If a modern production of *The Shepherds* neglects this parodic quality, the music may be rendered beautifully and the staging like a Christmas pageant with sheets for angels and the shepherds cowering in pitiful fear, but our sober inability to see the reverent joke would surprise the medieval playwright. The germ of the joke may go back to Jerome's translation. He describes the shepherds' reaction to the archangel as "timuerunt timore magno" (they were afraid with great fear), the alliterations of *t, m,* and *r* suggesting the farcical. The dance of the shepherds as they sing the rollicking melody of *Pax in terris nunciatur* must have been as lively a peasant dance as anything Brueghel or Dürer later came up with in their portrayals of folk celebrations. Artists of the twelfth and thirteenth centuries likewise exploit the comic reaction of the shepherds to the archangel, as plates 26 and 27 show.

What is genuinely surprising is the transformation of the Shepherds' bucolicisms into an exaltation by the end of this short play. To go from the bumpkin antics of scene one to the beatific serenity of the end of scene two is something every playwright would like to know how to do. Shakespeare tried it with Bottom, but had to come out with asses' ears, while the medieval playwright quietly succeeded in exalting the humble by having them magnify the Lord.

DETERMINATION OF MAJOR EPISODES

There are two episodes in the play. As in *The Pilgrim* the first is an outdoor scene, the second an interior. Illustrations of the two scenes are copious, and there is no problem of emphasis. What these pictures do not cover is the transitional scene in which the Shepherds, during their singing of the *Transeamus usque Bethlehem,* move from the first major scene in the fields to the second at the manger. One artist shows them simultaneously with the archangel and within a sheep's length of the manger scene (plate 29), but this is to be understood as a frequently employed, medieval artistic license.

CHARACTERIZATION

In nearly all the visual portrayals of the Christmas shepherds, and in all other versions of the play, there are only two or three shepherds, not five as the Rouen stage direction uniquely specifies. When an artist depicts only two, one is an old, bandy-legged Silenus type of stock comic character, the other young and a little foolish (plate 26).[3] When three shepherds are shown in the illustrations, the third is young and carries a wind instrument usually of the shalm or bagpipe family (plate 27), but sometimes a simple recorder, shepherd's pipe, or horn. The instrument is usually drawn as a playable instrument, not just an ornamental property. The Coventry craft cycle, two centuries later, includes a song "As I Outrode This Enderes Night," in which the narrator describes the Shepherds' annunciation scene, and comments, "These joli shepherds theyr pipes can blow." Shepherds did not become philosophical and arcadian until the literary Renaissance of the late sixteenth century forced them into that pastoral pose.[4] In the twelfth and thirteenth centuries they are jolly, their fright is clownish, and one of them can lace out a good instrumental double for the song and dance of *Pax in terris.* The comic shepherd's scene in the fifteenth-century *Second Shepherds Play* of the Wakefield cycle, universally praised for its strongly comic parody of the Nativity, did not alter these medieval characterizations. The Wakefield Master merely echoed them, and we have been so ignorant as to think he invented their comic aspect along with the parody of the plot.

The Archangel has been characterized before, in discussion of *The Visit to the Sepulcher.* His is a straight role, not a comic one. The Multitude of the Heavenly Host numbers seven in this Rouen version, but could be larger; they are merely the best singers in the choir, however many that may be. At Rouen the seven were removed from the choir, which may account for the smallness of their group, in order to sing the *Gloria in excelsis* from a high place ("in alto loco"). Fewer at that distance would hardly be a multitude.

Mary in this play is either a statue or is as motionless as one (plates

[3] Emile Mâle, *L'art réligieux du xii⁰ siècle en France,* 2d ed., (Paris, 1924), pp. 116–17, observes the number and ages of the shepherds as traditional, but misses the comic intent.

[4] See Rensselaer W. Lee, "Erminia in Minneapolis," *Studies in Criticism and Aesthetics, 1660–1800,* ed. H. P. Anderson and J. S. Shea (Minneapolis, 1967), pp. 36–39.

28–29). Mâle, reporting the pictorial tradition, describes her as looking "intently before her at some invisible object." [5]

MOVEMENT AND GESTURE

Plates 26 through 28 were chosen principally to illustrate some of the possibilities of comic movement and gesture in the acting of this play.[6] In plate 26 the older shepherd clutches his hat as the angelic breeze sweeps over him, and the younger fellow is caught going two directions at once, a suggestion for a delightful comic turn at the sound of the Archangel's voice, or perhaps better at the sound of introductory bells or horns. Both poses would probably be held throughout the Archangel's *Nolite timere* and the Multitude of the Heavenly Host's *Gloria in excelsis,* to be relaxed for the Shepherds' dance to *Pax in terris.* Their song and dance is clearly in two sections, the first composed of the beginning and last stanzas. The melody of the middle section, from "Mediator, homo" through "Quod annuntiatum est," is a fifth higher in range. The Shepherds therefore parcelled out these sections among themselves, probably combining for the *Eya*s.

Movement from the scene of the annunciation does not begin until the next item, when action is decided upon in the *Transeamus usque Bethlehem.* This is a relatively short piece, sung while walking (not dancing) toward the curtained manger, with its two guardian Midwives standing outside the curtain on the right and left. They inquire of the approaching Shepherds "Quem quaeritis?" The Shepherds, nothing daunted this time because the Midwives are of their class and kind, reply staunchly. The Midwives then draw aside the curtain and reveal the tableau of Mary and the Child (plates 28, 31). By this period (late thirteenth century) the Child is in her arms, not upstage and above her as in earlier times.[7] Mary is, I think one would conclude with Mâle from the art of the pe-

---

[5] Emile Mâle, *The Gothic Image,* trans. Dora Nussey (New York, 1958), p. 185.

[6] For others with comic intent, see Hanns Swarzenski, *The Berthold Missal: The Pierpont Morgan Library MS 710, and the Scriptorum of Weingarten Abbey* (New York, 1943), p. 46, fig. 62; p. 46, fig. 64; and plate V. See also Porcher, *L'Enluminure française,* p. 163, color plate 42; Lowrie, plate 113a; Départment de Manuscrits, Bibliothèque Nationale, *Evangiles avec peintures Byzantines du XIe siècle* (Paris, 1908), II, plate 97; Busch and Lohse, *Romanesque Sculpture,* plate 218; and Erwin Panofsky, *Renaissance and Renascences in Western Art* (Copenhagen, 1960), II, fig. 127.

[7] See above, pp. 31–32, for the distinction between the earlier setting with unencumbered altar and the later arrangements after introduction of the reredos, reliquary, and statuary.

riod, unaware of the curtains having been pulled, and makes no visible response to the adoration of the Shepherds. In later vernacular versions the Shepherds present the Child with gifts of a ball or a bob of cherries, while Mary holds him on her knee as she does in the Latin plays only for the Magi (e.g., plate 34). The contrast of the tableaux of the shepherds with that of the Magi is worth preserving, for it permits the Shepherds to answer the Midwives' question directly and familiarly, to listen to their joint *Ecce virgo,* and to sing with them the *Alleluia,* before silently kneeling to the utterly still Virgin and Child, and then to rise and sing (as sweetly as the Paduan actor of Herod carried the Gospel Book to the bishop) the lovely prayer, *Salve virgo singularis.* They kneel again after this song, and then rise and turn to the choir or the audience for their joyous double *Alleluia,* in the mood of the earlier *Eyas.*

By this time the clowning is over. The Shepherds have been so exalted by their experience that they can sing their *Iam vere scimus Christum,* a form of the *Victimae paschali* verse that Mary Magdalene sings at the climax of some versions of *The Visit to the Sepulcher.* These humble bumpkins have come a long way in a short while. There are also directions that after the play the Shepherds help to conduct the Mass; they rule the choir ("regant chorum"), read the epistle and the lesson, and are generally elevated to positions of dignity among the officiating clergy.

The running time of the play itself is only ten minutes, but in performance its compressed dramatic substance gives it the dimensions of a much longer play.

5. The Play of Herod

32 Herod and His Court. "Echternach Gospel Book," 962–1056. Nuremberg, Germanisches Nationalmuseum, MS 156142, fol. 18ᵛ. Courtesy of Germanisches Nationalmuseum.

33 Herod. Miniature, Italian or Eastern French, thirteenth century. Cambridge, The Fitzwilliam Museum, MS McClean 31, fol. 206ᵣ. Reproduced by permission of the Syndics of the Fitzwilliam Museum, Cambridge.

34 The Magi at the Nativity (top) and the Magi Leaving Herod's Court (bottom). "Echternach Gospel Book," 962–1056. Nuremberg, Germanisches Nationalmuseum, MS 156142, fol. 19ʳ. Courtesy of Germanisches Nationalmuseum.

35 Herod Ordering the Slaughter of the Innocents (left), and the Slaughter (right). "Echternach Gospel Book," 962–1056. Nuremberg, Germanisches Nationalmuseum, MS 156142 fol. 19ᵛ. Courtesy of Germanisches Nationalmuseum.

36 Herod Ordering the Slaughter of the Innocents (top), and the Slaughter (bottom).
Psalter, second half of twelfth century. Berlin, Staatliche Museen Preussischer Kulturbesitz, Kupferstichkabinett, MS 78 A 6, fol. 8ʳ.

The Play of Herod *with*
The Slaughter of the Innocents

Ordo ad Representandum Herodem with *Ad Interfectionem Puerorum*

TONE AND QUALITY

REMARKS on *The Play of Herod* and *The Slaughter of the Innocents* must be prefaced by attention to the modern production by The New York Pro Musica at The Cloisters in 1963 and elsewhere since then, and to the subsequent acting edition of this work by Noah Greenberg and W. L. Smoldon. This thorough edition, with transcriptions and "Historical Notes" by Smoldon and an introduction by Greenberg, makes superfluous a full treatment of the play in the present study. Greenberg himself is disarmingly modest in writing, "There is, of course, no *one* way to present such a work as *Herod.* The New York Pro Musica Cloisters performance should not be thought of as a definitive presentation, but rather as one possible approach."

Certainly his production is special, and can hardly be considered as representative of medieval performance of the play. It is special, however, in so many beautiful and inimitable ways that it will undoubtedly stand for some years as the modern image of the play, in the same manner that occasionally an actor or producer makes a play so much his own that others in his generation will not place their versions in competition with it. The *Herod* is indeed in danger of being less widely produced than it should be in our time because of the extraordinary resources Greenberg was able to bring to his production. Ironically some of these resources—the magnificent medieval band of the Pro Musica and the lavish costuming of Rouben Ter-Arutunian—are very much in the spirit of the play, yet far beyond what medieval productions could command. The intention of the present study of the play is therefore only to encourage its further consideration and understanding, and to discover more fully the medieval idea of the play, in order to make possible its evaluation as a work of art, both as the Pro Musica performs it and as the twelfth-century playwright composed and directed it.

The Play of Herod and *The Play of Daniel,* which the Pro Musica produced five years earlier but also kept in repertory, are plays of courtly pomp and splendor. There is a colorful elegance about them that seems to anticipate the Renaissance and places them in a different orbit from the Easter plays discussed above. The secular, political figures of Herod, Belshazzar, and Darius were no doubt modeled on certain medieval potentates nearly to the extent of Shakespeare's kings and nobles. As Shakespeare had Holinshed's *Chronicles,* so the Fleury and Beauvais playwrights had their Bibles, and neither limited their materials to these source books in respect or disrespect to these tyrannical characters. Herod the King became, as the archvillains of plays so often do, one of the most popular characters in the medieval repertory of plays, and his fame was not diminished when the Magi play later left the church and its sung Latin, for the town and its ranting, spoken vernacular.

Greenberg, not willing to put forth the *Herod* as just another *Daniel,* emphasized the differences between the two plays, and considered the *Herod* as "a series of highly contrasting scenes, each developing its own mood—the gentle naiveté of the exchanges between the Midwives and Shepherds; the joyousness of the Three Kings; the dark character of the Herod court; the simple happiness of the adoration of the Magi." [1] Yet there can be no doubt that the play is Herod's. All of the events of the play, as the several advanced medieval versions of it show, are organized as much around the machinations of Herod as they are around the birth of the Christ Child. In fact the source of dramatic development in the play is, inevitably, more the threat of Herod than the promise of the Christ Child, and the only direction the play can go is farther into Herod's malevolent actions, even unto the massacre of the children. The Magi are more ceremonial figures than live kings; one cannot have three kingly protagonists developed from completely common motivation. The three Shepherds are, as we saw them in *The Shepherds* play, more strongly individualized, which is a symptom of the oblationary character of the Magi. The only significant counter to this central drive of the play, apart from the immemorial beauty of the Nativity in its fragile humility, is the lyric role of Rachel, coming in after the massacre to neutralize its gall with her soaring lament.

[1] Greenberg and Smoldon, *Herod,* p. vii.

One has the feeling too, that the Fleury playwright, in resuscitating the slaughtered children, dumb-showing the death of Herod, and bringing back the Holy Family for Joseph's "Gaude" to the Virgin, none of which events are in any other version of the play, tried desperately to get the Magi play back to rights after Herod ran off with it. The intention of the playwright was good, but the damage had already been done and could not be undone so quickly, in a single item, merely with a dumb show of Herod's death, a magical resurrection of the children (like that of the Three Clerks), and an Archangelic assurance to Joseph that the Holy Family could go home again. If we believe the last, nasty words of Herod's son, to be performed in a manner most disrespectful to Christ ("despective loquens ad Christo"), we wonder how the Archangel can be so sure.

There is no hard evidence that the Fleury playwright of the *Ad Representandum Herodem* and the *Ad Interfectionem Puerorum* intended the two plays to be presented together, and some of the difficulties described above may even be created by playing the sequel with the original, as with those who join Parts One and Two of *Henry the Fourth.* As a matter of fact, there is some difficulty in reconciling the dramaturgy of the Fleury Magi play with that of the Innocents. The construction of the Magi play, no more or less influenced by other versions than is *The Innocents,* is so much superior to the latter that one doubts that the same playwright even composed the two, let alone intended them to be played together. The frantic effort to patch things up after the massacre and the lament is not very successful. It involved the playwright not only in too much late exposition via dumb show, report, and fiat, but also in a double break in time and in space: Herod is dead and Archelaus is now king, and Joseph and Mary are in Egypt. The information that Egypt is the last scene of the play is not even given in pantomime or dialogue, only in stage direction, though the opening scene makes clear that the Holy Family was to go to Egypt. The Fleury playwright(s) of *The Visit to the Sepulcher* and of the *Ad Representandum Herodem* would not descend to that kind of botched ending, nor did the authors of other versions of the Innocents play, either as an *Ordo Stellae* or an *Ordo Rachelis.* They knew that after the lament of Rachel they could do nothing more than offer the traditional consolation of immortality and stop. One might almost prefer to see the Fleury play of the Innocents, when not played with the Fleury Magi, concluded with the children's ascent to heaven singing the traditional antiphon, *O Christe, quantum patri,* even though this ending would omit the effective "Joseph, Joseph, Joseph!" of the Archangel.

CHARACTERIZATION

It has already been suggested in one place and another in this study that the leading character of Herod is bold, virile, kingly, competent. His rage is understandable only as *hubris*. He has been so successful in the world of power politics that he cannot face an adverse prophecy. His own court, his military officers, and even his own son have surrounded him with a sense of infallibility. Once it is cracked by a prophecy that someone greater than he has been born, he loses control and begins to fall apart.

Curiously, the medieval illustrations of Herod do not generally show his breakdown. Instead they show him as the successful tyrant, either in regal pose for his portrait (as in plate 33), or holding court before the Magi (plate 32), or still very much under control, ordering the massacre (plates 35, 36). In view of the fame of his rages for several centuries during and after the Middle Ages, including Shakespeare's "It out-Herods Herod," one should expect the illustrators to enjoy portraying his more violent acts, such as throwing down the Book of the Prophets.

Long before the twelfth century, the Magi had been everywhere identified as kings, and some individualization of the three was common.

In windows, bas-reliefs, and manuscripts the first king invariably appears as an old man, the second as a middle-aged man, and the third as a young and beardless man. . . . 'The first of the Magi,' says the pseudo Bede, 'was Melchior, an old man with long white hair and a long beard. . . . The second named Caspar, young and beardless, with a ruddy countenance. . . . The third named Balthazzar, with dark skin ('fuscus') and a full beard. . . .'[2]

To refer, as Greenberg does, to the gentle naiveté of the Midwives and Shepherds is I believe to underestimate their charm. When the Shepherds' annunciation and adoration scenes are prologue to the Magi play, as they are in the Fleury version and some others, these scenes and their characters are somewhat subordinated. Their song and dance, *Pax in terris,* is omitted, and they are hurried along to the Manger. When they later encounter the Magi—an addition to the play, whether original with the Fleury playwright or not—they have time only to sing two conventional antiphons and leave, before the Magi launch into the glorious

---

[2] Mâle, *The Gothic Image,* pp. 213–14. Mâle also notes that only after the period of the music-dramas does the third king have "the appearance of a negro" (p. 215).

Quem non praevalent. The Rouen version of *The Shepherds,* as we have seen, mostly balances the comic and transmuted Shepherds, and even permits them to talk familiarly with the Midwives, as well as to "rule" the choir. True, the Fleury version does give the Shepherds their moment by having them turn to the audience in the "Venite, venite, venite," and invite everyone to "Come, let us adore him." If this business was handled as I think the Fleury stage direction intended, the *venite*s were sung, one by each shepherd as a kind of curtain bow, to the audience. "Populum circumstantem" is to be interpreted "the audience standing around," for we have already remarked that in the medieval church the audience did not sit in pews, but literally stood around the acting area. The phrase "tribus vicinis" appears to mean "to the nearest people in the audience," and directs each Shepherd to sing his individual "Venite" to those up close, not to the equivalent of the nonexistent back row.[3] The effect of these invitations by the traditionally comic Shepherds would have been humorously appealing.

In the larger setting of the *Herod,* and with another bland and not very characteristic scene, the Shepherds have more difficulty. It is no longer their play, and they tend to get a little out of focus. Without trying it, one cannot be sure it would work, but there is a good chance that if their "gentle" were taken out of Greenberg's "gentle naiveté," and they were given back their comic bumpkin roles in the annunciation scene, they might start off more firmly and make a stronger appeal to our interest. In the Pro Musica production they got lost in the shuffle, and all the cards came up Kings. Or was it Ter-Arutunian's enveloping costumes that they got lost in?

The character of Archelaus needs attention. In order to assure us that he is too weak and silly ever to be as destructive as his father, he should in my opinion be played as a foppish young man, badly spoiled, and badly trained in the kingly arts, an ancestor of Shaw's Dauphin Charley. His urging of Herod to act "Contra illum regulum" (against this little king, this new-born babe) is so effeminant, and is followed so precipitantly by his fear, that it should convey amusement and comfort to the audience rather than a second threat to the rest of the world.[4]

---

[3] Young, II, 85, reads the manuscript as "vicibus"; Smoldon in Greenberg and Smoldon, *Herod,* p. 83, reads "vicinis." The latter is better in the theatrical context.

[4] In this connection, in the dialogue song beginning "Salve, pater inclite," which has four stanzas, the first and last are obviously and entirely Archelaus's, the two middle stanzas entirely Herod's.

MOVEMENT AND GESTURE

The amount and extent of movement in the medieval production of the *Herod* must have been large. On the road at one time or another are the Magi (twice), the Shepherds, and the Armiger. The Fleury stage directions refer to several sections of the church in order to orient these journeys. There is therefore some difficulty in a modern production that does not have space within sight lines to allow the Shepherds to sing the *Transeamus usque Bethlehem* as they travel, or the Magi to follow the engineered star and to sing the long *Quem praevalent.* These travelling scenes are like those of *The Pilgrim, The Visit to the Sepulcher,* and *The Shepherds,* and were built by the playwrights for the broad and open spaces of an unfurnished cathedral or large abbey. Something of the physical pattern of their plays would have been denied if acting areas, and consequently the movements of the actors, had been restricted to the crossing and the chancel.

The cast of the Magi play is unusually large. The solution for the medieval playwright, having invented or more often having been given such a cast, was a series of *sedes* and *plateae,* at which the major scenes were played and along which the travelling groups moved.

Many of the medieval illustrations of these major scenes are close-ups, which ignore movement, and concentrate on gesture. There are countless illustrations of the gestures between Herod and the Magi, of which plates 32 and 33 may serve as representatives. In these, Herod's right arm is in gesture, not just the hand, though its index finger leads the big muscles of the arm. In plate 32 the Magi also gesture, each Magus having his own individual gesture, variously interpreted by the artists. Herod's sword or scepter occupies his left hand, the symbolism being that in diplomacy one talks with one's right hand and holds the sword or scepter in the left, but when the diplomacy leads to war, as it does in this play, the right hand will grasp the sword and no hand will talk. The Magi, accompanied by pages to carry their gifts to the Christ Child, but often clutching staves (as in plate 32), speak to Herod with right or left hand. Their gestures are likewise diplomatic; these men know how to parley with kings.

The blocking and gestures for the scene between the Scribes and Herod are carefully spelled out in a Fleury stage direction, and the scene is marvelously illustrated in the "Echternach Gospel Book" (plate 32).[5] The stage direction is quoted in full below in connection with the "Book of the Prophets" property (p. 314). As I interpret the stage direction, the Scribes find the prophecy (they may even excitedly *speak* its first words, "Videmus, Domine," to identify their discovery), show the book to Herod, and point out the passage to him. He does not understand a word of it, and gestures to them to read it. Then the Scribes *sing* the "Videmus, Domine."

The same attempt at individualizing the three Magi is observable in illustrations of their presentation to the Christ Child. Luke's narration contributed the symbolic differentiation of their gifts: gold, frankincense, and myrhh, and their postures vary accordingly. The first Magus bows with worldly *savoir-faire* as he presents his gold with "Salve, Rex saeculorum." His posture at this moment, and those of the Magi to follow, are pictured in plate 34. The posture for the second Magus would be more devout, on his "Salve, Deus deorum," which exceeds his predecessor. The third Magus tops both of them, with a gesture nowhere pictured but somehow actable or the Fleury playwright would not have given him the capping line, "Salve, Salus mortuorum!" The resurrection theme again.

Gestures of Shepherds and Angels and Midwives have been discussed in relation to preceding plays. All that remains as germane to the Fleury *Herod-Innocents* play is the movements and gestures of Herod's soldiers before and during the massacre. In the visual arts there is no differentiation between the courtiers and the soldiers who slay the children, no significant difference between the courtiers at stage left of plate 32 and the soldiers of plate 36. The courtier-soldiers seem eager to go to work (plates 35, 36), and happiest when they are at it (plate 36).

STAGING AND THE DEFINITION OF ACTING AREAS

In discussing movement in this play I remarked that the playwrights appear to have expected for it the rather full use of the nave and aisles. The importance of such mobility is suggested by the many travelling scenes, together with the necessity to follow the rigged stars over considerable distances if this gadget were to justify the effort of installing it.

[5] Hand gestures are large in the illustration of this scene on the Salerno altar frontal. See Lowrie, plate 112a.

Only two scenes in the play, the scene at the manger and at Herod's Court, require a location with definite settings, and therefore platforms, curtains, and furnishings. Dramatically, the contrast between these two scenes appears so clearly intended that the positioning of the two platforms may be assumed to have followed this intention. Since there was no necessity for a fixed audience focus, the two platforms could have been set elsewhere than in the chancel, and Fleury definitely wanted the manger "ad ianuas monasterii" (at the door to the monastery). The elaborate scene of Herod's court (as in plate 32) is located by the Fleury script "ad hostium chori" (at the entrance to the choir). Thrones for such great kings as Herod were of some elevation, as witness plates 32, 33, 35, 36, and 67. But it should also be noted that the dais for the Virgin and Child, as in plate 34, is of equal height and elegance. This balance is another feature of the continuing parallel between the two major sets.

The setting for the scene between the sleeping Magi and the warning Angel is somewhat clarified by visual representations, notably plate 34. The Fleury stage direction merely says "Magi incipiant dormire ibi ante Praesepe," (the Magi fall asleep there before the manger), and the Pro Musica production had the Magi curl up on the platform in front of the closed curtains of the Manger set. The Echternach illustration suggests, however, that Magi do not sleep on the floor or on the ground like mere Shepherds, but in neatly covered cots. Presumably these could be quickly pulled out, already made up, by the three accompanying Pages and the two Midwives, from the sacristy or some other concealed point. While the Magi respond to the Angel's warning with "Deo gracias," the Pages and Midwives remove the cots. The Echternach illustration considers the setting an interior, as is evidenced by the set piece at stage right, complete with a "practical" door for the Magi's exit. If this set-piece were incorporated into the over-all design of the manger set, outside the curtain line, as it seems to have been in the manger scene at the top of the same Echternach illustration (plate 34), this addition to the staging would have occasioned no difficulty and would have added to the finish of the production. The "practical" door would probably not be adequate as a way of bringing the cots on and off stage.

Since this study does not preclude the production of the *Innocents* play, either alone or in tandem with the *Herod,* some attention must be given here to the staging of its scenes. The play begins with the direction that the Innocents move in a joyous procession "per ecclesiam" (through the church). The modern Pro Musica production interpreted this phrase as directing "The Innocents to enter the nave and proceed slowly down the center aisle." [6] The next Fleury direction is for the leader of the children, the bearer of the "Lamb," to lead them "huc et illuc" (hither and thither), rather than slowly and straight down the nave. By whatever route in a medieval nave devoid of furniture, the procession of the children while they sing two antiphons, *O quam gloriosum* and *Emitte agnum,* brings them to the front of the nave. They need not arrive at this point until the Joseph-Angel scene (in front of the now open manger set) has been concluded, the Holy Family and the Angel have departed, and the manger curtains have been closed. On their "Agno sacrato," the Innocents move to the crossing and the imminent scene of the massacre. It would be an advantage to have the Holy Family remain in the sight lines when they reach Egypt, rather than disappear left of the choir, as they did in the Pro Musica production, but the logistics of their moving to the left or right transept are complicated. One solution would have been for the Holy Family to go from the manger set down the nave, cross over in the narthex, and return up the opposite side of the nave to take up their tableau in a transept after the Innocents had moved to the crossing. "In any case," as Young concluded, "the space for the performance had to be sufficiently large to provide places for Jerusalem, the manger at Bethlehem, Egypt, and the locality in which the Innocents were slaughtered." [7] These localities were necessary, as was space for the processions of the Shepherds, the Magi, the Armiger, the Innocents, and the Holy Family.

[6] Greenberg and Smoldon, *Herod,* p. 51.   [7] Young, II, 117.

6. The Procession of the Prophets

37 Moses with Horns (right). Psalter, twelfth century. London, British Museum, MS
Lansdowne 383, fol. 15ʳ. Courtesy of the Trustees of the British Museum.

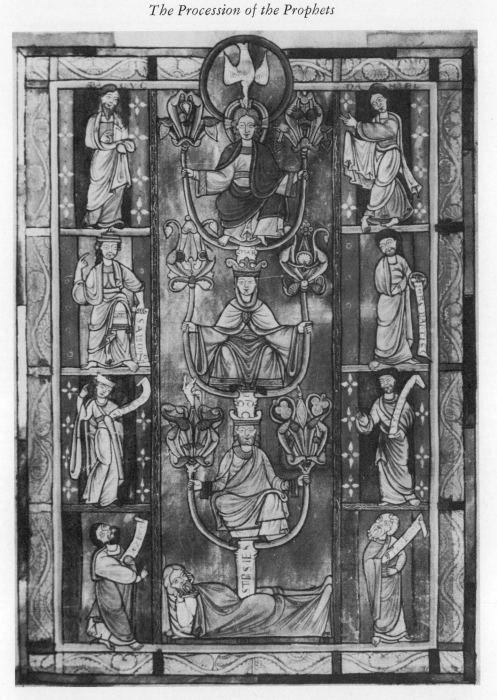

38 Prophets: (left, from top) Habakkuk, Solomon, Sibyl, Ezekiel; (right) Daniel,
John the Baptist, Isaiah, Jeremiah. *De Laudibus,* French, twelfth century. Douai,
Bibliothèque Municipale, MS 340, fol. 11ʳ. Courtesy of Bibliothèque Municipale de
Douai.

The Procession of the Prophets

Ordo Prophetarum

TONE AND QUALITY

EVERYTHING has been done to *The Procession of the Prophets* except to consider it as a play. Young found that it did not fit his definition of a play "because of the absence of rubrics indicating impersonation." [1] Sepet, long before, theorized that the play is a kind of breeding ground for dramas that fly away as soon as the breeding season is over.[2] More recent scholars have continued to be interested in the play, if it is one, as an antecedent of such later works as the vernacular *Mystère d'Adam* of the second half of the twelfth century.[3]

It is obvious that no one wishes to commit himself about the play's intrinsic value. The form of the play is unusual; it is not exactly modern realism, by which the more recent scholars have been conditioned. Nothing happens except the summoning and testimony of thirteen prophets of Christ, with an interlocutor to introduce each.

Yet from the succession of witnesses, all recognizable Old Testament prophets—with the delightful exceptions of Virgil [4] and Sibyl—a dramatic story develops. Recently we have learned to accept this as one way of organizing a play; Brecht did it repeatedly, and so did Peter Weiss in *The Investigation* (1966). Any such play could be questioned on the same grounds of nonconformity to naturalistic standards, and condemned on the grounds of monotonous repetition when of course the whole point *is* the reiteration, the variations on the theme, the procession (in the root sense of a process). If the process is artistic, the play works and the audience is pleased.

Like most of the Latin church plays, this one is impossible to savor without its music, and hardly anyone has known what the melody and

[1] Young, II, 145.

[2] M. Sepet, *Les Prophètes du Christ* (Paris, 1878). For a summary of Sepet's conjectures, see Young, II, 170–71.

[3] Frank, *Medieval French Drama*, p. 74.

[4] Virgil's fourth *Eclogue* was supposedly related to the Isaiah prophecies; hence his medieval status as a prophet.

its subtle counters and variations sound like. Coussemaker defended the play for its music, printed it, and insisted that fellow scholars pay attention to it, but even he did not recognize or ever hear the measured rhythms, he being convinced that it was all free-rhythm plainchant.[5]

With something of the same skill at variations that the Beauvais master shows in *The Pilgrim,* and like him creating the variations out of dramatic necessities, *The Procession of Prophets* takes a melodic theme and gives it subtle twists and turns to match the convolutions of the procession of witnesses.

While the Limoges version, the only one that has decipherable music notation, lacks the stage directions that would help us to visualize the individual prophets, the very similar Laon version is rich with ideas about costume, and what it misses the Rouen version supplies. At the very least, then, the audience can count on strong musical and visual appeal, and, if one can follow it, the skillful Latin verse provides additional pleasure. The dramatic validity of the piece will not be properly estimated until it has been tested in modern performance. Before *The Lament of Mary* was performed, many expressed grave doubt that it was a truly theatrical play, and not merely a monotonous lament. We shall probably discover that *The Procession of Prophets* bears the same relation to *The Shepherds* and *The Herod* as *The Lament of Mary* does to The *Visit to the Sepulcher* and *The Pilgrim.* In this sense, since it was performed during the Christmas season, it serves as an interesting and mood-setting prologue to other plays of that season.

CHARACTERIZATION

When the portraits of the thirteen witnesses are examined, and are compared with the stage directions of the Laon and Rouen versions of the play, characterizations begin to emerge (see plates 37, 38, 62, 63, 65). Relevant passages in the *Old Testament* may also be consulted for their bearing on characterization. It is obvious that the prophet Habakkuk is literally a slapstick character.[6] One imagines that Sibyl's gyrations also inspired laughter. In the Limoges version these two comic characters are well spaced; Habakkuk is sixth, Sibyl thirteenth in order of appearance. The name and character of the interlocutor are discussed in "Notes on Production."

[5] Coussemaker, pp. 314–15.   [6] See below, p. 149.

MOVEMENT AND GESTURE

Performed in the chancel, perhaps with a platform set to which each witness may enter on call from the interlocutor, as in a trial scene, the play's movement is somewhat limited but not static or necessarily monotonous. Entrances would have been made from upstage through the back curtain of the platform, and from left and right, with some element of suspense about the point of entrance as well as the physical appearance of the famous character. A triple-arch frame for the set would have increased the variety of locations for the singers. Each entrance and exit would have been made in character.

Since there is no covering speech for the exit, no great amount of space was needed on the platform. On the other hand, there was no need to go from one item to the next without pause, and in fact there may have been reason to interpolate brief instrumental interludes to space the appearance of each character and to assist his pitch. Key transpositions, effected by these interludes as a further means of variety, were limited, because each episode was begun by the interlocutor's question, and the prophet's answer could not often be delayed for a contemplative modulation. Variety in the color of the male and of the female voices would have helped, as would the punctuation of chime bells suggested in "Notes on Production."

STAGING AND THE DEFINITION OF ACTING AREAS

The *Carmina Burana* version of this play sets it up as a kind of courtroom debate between Augustine's prophets and Archsynagogus's unbelievers. If Augustine is the cantor-summoner, then he is the attorney for the prosecution, his prophets are his witnesses, and the audience is either the jury or witnesses for the defense. In the Limoges version the latter never testify, and the former are ready to render the verdict that Christ is the Son of God when the play is over. How much of medieval courtroom atmosphere was reflected in the platform staging I do not know.

In any event, the entire set would have been centered at the crossing or in the choir. In the interest of increasing the variety of movement (i.e., blocking) as partially suggested above, the platform or acting area might have been divided by three Romanesque arches, somewhat as in plate 24, but with considerably more width for the procession of individual prophets. The three arches would have served as alternating locations for the appearance of the prophets through back or side curtains. If this design were followed, however, the cantor (Augustine) would have had to be elsewhere than in one of the arches.

A simpler solution, which would have provided more contact with the audience, would have been to have the prophets appear, one by one as summoned, from the audience. In this blocking, Habakkuk would have whacked a few "gentes" with his palm branch on his way to the witness stand. Some such action as this seems to have been intended in the comedy-inspiring stage direction of the Rouen version: "Abacus, . . . habens in peram radices, et longas palmas habens unde gentes percuciat, comedens . . ." (Habakkuk, eating radishes from a pouch, and brandishing a long palm stick with which he slaps people [the audience]). This palm frond was the kind used by the Archangel in *The Visit to the Sepulcher.*[7]

[7] See below, p. 288.

7. The Raising of Lazarus

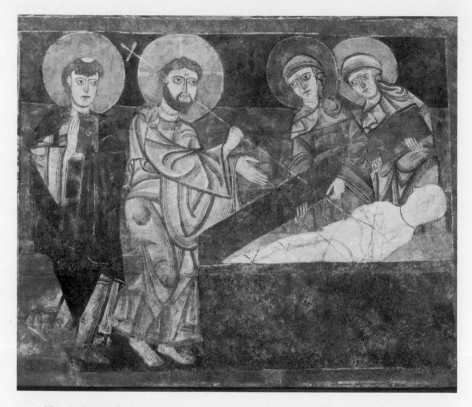

39 The Raising of Lazarus. Fresco transferred to canvas, from San Baudelio de Berlanga, twelfth century. Courtesy of The Metropolitan Museum of Art, gift of J. Pierpont Morgan, 1917.

40   The Raising of Lazarus. Lectionary from Reichenau, eleventh century. Utrecht, Aartsbisschoppelijk Museum, MS 3, fol. 68ʳ. Courtesy of Aartsbisschoppelijk Musea.

41 The Raising of Lazarus. "Gospel Book of Lazarus," Byzantine, eleventh, twelfth, or thirteenth century. Berlin, Staatsbibliothek Preussischer Kulturbesitz, MS graec. 66, fol. 307ᵛ.

The Raising of Lazarus

Resuscitatio Lazari

TONE AND QUALITY

ONE'S first impression is that *The Raising of Lazarus,* certainly composed for production, would never succeed with a modern audience. The seemingly insuperable obstacle is that nearly the entire play is sung to a single basic melody, repeated fifty times. The monotony, one suspects, would be intolerable. Even the longest folk-ballads that hold an audience today do not have nearly so many repetitions of their (generally comparable) melodies. A medieval audience, accustomed to listening to a *chanson de geste* by the hour, would have had no difficulty with a mere fifty repetitions of a tune, but modern listeners would shortly feel somewhat imposed upon. Or so one's initial anxieties run. Better, we may feel, to leave this play as a dramatic poem, to be read, not sung; leave it in the closet with Hilary's on the same subject.

Before dismissing the idea of producing such an obvious flop (even in a church, where a certain amount of tedium is to be expected), there are several aspects of the play that in all fairness should be considered. In the first place, we are not dealing with a ballad but with a play, an interesting story dramatized by actors in visual action. The Lazarus story depicts an action that parallels the great Easter stories. Christ is moved to perform perhaps his most outstanding miracle, in a context of warmly human relationships with friends who are outside the disciple group.

The story is staged in a way that permits a maximum of action and tension. The triple set, specified by the stage directions, represents the form of the drama and at the same time permits frequent movement between the two side sets and the climax at the center set. The details of this visual structuring of the play are presented under the proper headings below. All that need be said here is that except for the intense focus of *The Lament of Mary* on the cross, the organization of *Lazarus* is more theatrical, more controlled and less diffuse, than that of any other play in the repertory.

I do not mean to imply that the playwright worked harder at the structure of his play because he was stuck with its monotonous music. He certainly did not consider the music monotonous; he was more inclined to think of the fifty repetitions of the melody as water that turned the mill wheel, in the subtle image of a contemporary composer, Foquet de Marseille. One would never claim that the mill stream was as interesting to watch as the turning wheel, but one would acknowledge that without the water the wheel would not turn, or the poem move. If one reads or hears the melody composed by the playwright for the *Lazarus*, one notices that it is not a simple little tune. I quote a sample of it here, so that its complex beauty may be observed.[1] There are two sections of the

melody, each as long as the usual ballad tune, and the effect in ballad form would be like the alternation of two interacting melodies. In other words, one does not return to the beginning of the melodic material for the length of two tunes, and this length and the variety of the melody are powerful deterrents to a sense of monotony. It is so long and complex that one wonders if more than a few in a modern audience would be able to reproduce it after hearing it, submerged in the play, so many times. If the melody were played instrumentally, without the constant flux of dialogue and flash of movement in the play, the melody and we would be exhausted long before the fiftieth repetition. In the context of the play,

---

[1] To do justice to the composer I should have to quote all fifty-one forms of this melody. Its small but effective variations are like those in the St. Nicholas plays, but smaller than those of the Beauvais *Pilgrim* or the Limoges *Procession of the Prophets.*

and with its frequent but minute, almost subliminal variations, there is no difficulty, perhaps even added pleasure, for all in the audience except those few musicians who hardly watch a play for listening to the music—which was not what the playwright intended.

There is, moreover, a certain pleasure in the recognition of repetition in any art form. If this were not true, poetry would never have been written in stanza form—which in earlier times derived from its being sung to a repeated melody—or ballads sung to one tune, or Greek choruses sung and danced in strophe and antistrophe. Such repetitive elements in the performing arts act as a kind of measure or pulse. Eugene O'Neill's use of the tom-tom in *The Emperor Jones* is a good, if extreme, example of modern dramatic use of monotonous repetition, varied by its subliminal increases in tempo. Repeated modern performances of *Lazarus,* and of *The Three Daughters* with a similar amount of melodic repetition, were consistently pleasing to a variety of audiences in 1969 and 1971.

What is usually ignored in contemplating the fifty repetitions of the basic melody is that there are also two liturgical melodies in the play. The first is one of two hymns, *In sapientia disponens omnia* or *Mane prima sabbati,* according to the first stage direction. Young felt that "neither composition is very appropriate here, for in surveying certain events in the life of Christ neither mentions the occurences that follow in the dramatic text." [2] But the *Mane prima sabbati* is used in many versions of *The Visit to the Sepulcher,* and is thus associated directly with the theme of resurrection. Furthermore, its stanzas 1–9 and 14–16 are in praise of Christ's resurrection and of Mary Magdalene, who is to be a leading character in the *Lazarus.* Rather than flatly anticipate "the occurences that follow in the dramatic text" the playwright artistically sets up a relation between the events of Christ's resurrection, with Mary Magdalene's part in them, and the resurrection of Lazarus which historically prefigured that action. The second service-book melody is the usual *Te Deum* which appropriately closes this play, sung by the entire cast as a recessional.

Two lines of dialogue, curiously imbedded in manuscript stage directions and therefore without musical notation, pose a more than academic question about the playwright's intent. The first is Simon's "Si hic homo esset a Deo" (If this man be from God); the second is Martha's stage whisper to Mary Magdalene, "Magister te vocat" (The Master calls for you). One obvious but I think unsatisfactory answer is that the verbal and

[2] Young, II, 471.

musical scribes were not furnished with sufficient material at these points in their copying, and fudged the matter by tucking what they had into the rubrics. Another answer is that the verbal scribe, usually the first to work on the playscript, is indicating how to complete Simon's line: " 'Si hic homo esset a Deo' et cetera. Require in Evangelio" ('If this man be from God' et cetera. Look this up in the Gospel).[3] He might also have assumed that anyone would know how to look up in the musical Evangelary a passage which had "Magister te vocat" as an incipit, and so did not bother to refer this passage to the Evangelary.

The difficulty with the first rationalization is that there are two very similar fudges in an otherwise adequately drafted script. One of these evasions might be attributed to laziness, but not two at such similar moments of dramatic tension: Simon indignant at the whore in his house, Martha running to whisper in her sister's ear. The second rationalization has more holes in it. While there might have been a musical service-book paraphrase of the Vulgate's "Hic si esset propheta," Martha's "Magister te vocat" cannot be service-book paraphrase of her words in John 11:20; there is no dialogue at this point in the narrative, which merely reports that "Martha ergo ut audivit quia Jesus venit, occurrit illi" (Then Martha, as soon as she heard that Jesus was coming, went out and met him). Neither speech is a ten-syllable line, typical of the musico-poetic pattern of the play. Simon's lacks three syllables; Martha's lacks four, and is not in the right meter, the stress in "Magister" being regularly on the second syllable. Taken together, these facts seem to dispose of the possibility that the scribes had to cope with insufficient material. Indeed, the interaction of the two scribes on the script, one responsible for words and staff lines, the other for musical notation, served to double-check such discrepancies.

Let us suppose that the Simon speech may be explained as the incipit of an Evangelary piece; we know that most of the Gospels were and are sung in a free-rhythm recitative. Preceding his speech is the opening antiphon, probably *Mane prima sabbati,* followed by a complete double stanza of versified and mensuralized dialogue by Simon, "Tu dignare . . . subintrare," and a similar double stanza by Jesus, "Audit, fratres . . . compleatur." At this early point of the play one can hardly believe that a playwright with the dramatic sense of the author of the *Lazarus* would revert to another liturgical piece, one which was at best only a humdrum Evangelary recitative. Furthermore, this play is not, like some liturgical

---

[3] Luke 7:39.

plays, a patchwork of antiphons. There are no other service-book pieces in the *Lazarus* after the initial *Mane prima sabbati* until the traditional *Te Deum* at the end. The entire dramatic work, between the framing antiphons, is in the form of stanzas set to a steadily repeated double melody.

If neither the scribes nor the playwright were nodding in the Simon speech, we should have to conclude that the playwright intended this speech to be spoken. This conclusion is fortified by the similar conditions surrounding Martha's later speech, for which, as we have seen, there is no basis for a musical setting. Young rather offhandedly comments, "This speech has, of course, no music." [4] But if we agree that these two lines were spoken, we acknowledge that the playwright of the *Lazarus* here deliberately committed a major aesthetic heresy by introducing spoken lines into the midst of an exclusively sung form. I know of no other moment in the entire repertory of medieval church music-dramas when this definitely happens, not even where it might more easily have occurred and been accepted, as in the Peregrinus's single-note question, "Quae?" to the Disciples on the road.[5]

Appraising the playwright's extraordinary derring-do, one can accept his invented stage whisper line for Martha, because it dramatizes what in the Vulgate and in the Hilarius version of the play are merely narrative reports. One is less respectful of his intent in the Simon line, which comes too early in the play to serve as a dramatic jolt, and merely confuses the audience, like an unmotivated change of key. Perhaps the mixed reception of these two experimental lines explains why other composers of music-drama did not pursue his suggestion for occasional naturalistic dialogue.

DETERMINATION OF MAJOR EPISODES

The art works of the period naturally concentrate on the moment of Lazarus's resurrection, though they show some other scenes as well. The earliest illustration of the resurrection scene dates from the second century,[6] and we have a constant stream of illustrative art on the Lazarus subject through the thousand years preceding the composition of the

[4] Young, II, 207, note 2.
[5] Smoldon, *Peregrinus*, p. 4, Item 4. The only other possible instance of spoken dialogue is in the Fleury *Herod*. See above, p. 140.
[6] Lowrie, p. 40; see also his plate 8c.

Fleury *Lazarus* play.[7] This parade, which continues through the twelfth and thirteenth centuries, bears witness to the lasting popularity of the Lazarus story, as compared to that of *The Pilgrim,* on which there is a paucity of material before the twelfth century. The playwright must have written with some sense of how often and for how long the Lazarus theme, in liturgy, legend, and art, had been treated by other artists. His challenge and opportunity were to interpret it freshly by recreating it in dramatic form. We have no record of earlier plays on this extraordinarily popular theme, and one may speculate on the playwright's awareness of his responsibility as one of the first to portray Lazarus "on the stage," particularly in view of the quantity of visual representations of it within his ken.

The major episode of the Lazarus reappearance is exemplified in plates 39, 40, and 41. The other episodes are easily identified, and are treated in sections below.

CHARACTERIZATION

The key to the characterization of all the persons of this play, even of the Jews, who fare rather badly in some plays of the repertory, is the mutual friendliness of all the characters. Two sisters and a brother were never more genuinely devoted to each other than Mary Magdalene, Martha, and Lazarus. The attachment of Mary Magdalene to Jesus we have noted before, in *The Lament of Mary* and *The Visit to the Sepulcher,* although these plays are chronologically later. Jesus apparently regards Lazarus as his dearest friend outside the circle of disciples, and thus he must also have had some knowledge of Lazarus's sisters, Mary Magdalene and Martha. Although Young felt that the opening scene is "obviously unessential,"[8] its dramatic purpose is to set up a comparison between the well-to-do Simon's pleasant hospitality to Jesus and his disciples (which nevertheless costs him more than his meat and his manners) and the extraordinary devotion to Jesus of a common prostitute, Mary Magdalene. The contrast between Pharisee Simon's sumptuous table and the tattered

[7] In a volume published by the Aartsbisschoppelijk Museum, Utrecht, *Het Wonder: Miracula Christi* (Utrecht, 1962), there are reproduced in color some 35 plates of Lazarus scenes, from the fifth century to the present. One of these is my plate 40, reproduced directly from a manuscript in the Aartsbisschoppelijk Museum.

[8] Young, II, 209. The *Carmina Burana* version, though in a vastly different theatrical context, also includes this "unessential" scene. See Young, I, 523–24.

whore's dress ("habitu meritricio") of Mary Magdalene is that of the playwright, who appears to be stating as his underlying theme the variety and comparative depths of people's love for each other. Almost every action in the play is an act of friendship; the only unfriendly people are lurking off stage, ready to stone Jesus again if he appears in public. The only unfriendly act in the play is that of Simon toward Mary Magdalene, and he thought he was merely preserving the amenities by stopping such a woman from bothering his guest. Jesus' reproof of Simon makes the same ironic point about friendship: "To whom little is forgiven, the same loveth little." ("Cui autem minus dimittitur, minus diligit"), and the point is expounded in the play.[9]

The friends of Simon, apparently moved by what they have witnessed at his house, return to console Martha and Mary Magdalene when the women's moaning becomes audible. There is a scene of some depth in which these men try earnestly to counter the sisters' sense of irrevocable loss. None of this scene is in Luke, yet it occupies a considerable and touching portion of the play, similar to the consolation scenes in *The Slaughter of the Innocents* and *The Son of Getron*.

What remains to be said about the characters of this play may be noted opposite each role, in order of appearance.

SIMON. As a Pharisee he was taking some risk in being hospitable to Jesus and his disciples. There is a fine irony in his then being reproved for not accepting Mary Magdalene. He is man enough to acknowledge the validity of Christ's parable about the debtors and its application to him. Simon is far from being a stuffy old snob. He is able to learn.

FOUR PHARISEES. These four are called Jews in the three versions of the play, but if they are friends of Simon they are likely to be Pharisees. Their later comfort of the sisters on the death of Lazarus is even more telling if they are of a class that would not normally do anything about a death in a lower-class family. What makes the difference is that they were present in Simon's house when Mary Magdalene washed Jesus' feet, and with Simon they learned something about the responsibilities of love. And so they follow through to the end of the play, even assisting in the opening of the tomb, to judge from some illustrations. The only reason for four is that four makes a social group. The Fleury playwright, or his scribe, does not specify the number of them, nor does the Gospel account.

[9] Luke 7:47.

He merely writes, "Simon cum quibusdam Iudeorum," while Hilarius, for his own reasons, needing to divide them into twosomes, specifies "quatuor Iudeorum."

JESUS. The intimate quality of the play, and of the Biblical narrative behind it, is reflected in the Christus being called by his first name throughout the play. Simon and his friends are the only ones in the cast who are not so familiar with him; Simon addresses him as "doctor care" and "Magister." Even the Messenger, sent by Mary Magdalene to give Jesus an urgent message, rushes over to the Galilee set and says, "Ave, Ihesu, Redemptor omnium!" (Hail, Jesus, savior of all!). The awesome Christus of the Easter plays is here replaced by a friend who can help, and help more than the four well-meaning Pharisee friends. His meeting with Martha on the way to her house is in tender, humble dialogue, firm without pontificating about his powers, not even entirely sure he can bring off the resurrection of Lazarus, and able to bring it off only with the help of God to whom he prays before he calls Lazarus to come forth. The intent of the playwright about the character of Jesus in this play is shown in his omission of any paraphrase of the famous words of Jesus to Martha: "he that believeth in me, though he were dead, yet shall he live: And whosoever liveth and believeth in me shall never die." Also omitted is his didactic verse to the disciples before they leave for Bethany, "And I am glad for your sakes that I was not there [before Lazarus died] to the intent ye may believe."

THE DISCIPLES. Thomas "called Didymus," the intellectual doubter and aristocratic young man who has a crucial role in *The Pilgrim,* is named in John as one of those in the group with whom Jesus consulted at Galilee before returning to Bethany. The playwright's paraphrase of Thomas's speech in John 11:16 is no longer ambiguous, as it is in the Gospel, where the pronominal reference is not clear (or does Thomas intend an ambiguity?). When Jesus tells him and the others in the play, not in the didactic words quoted above, that they should not argue with him, that God's virtue must be made manifest in Judea, Thomas agrees that they should go back "et ibi vivere desistamus" (and no longer live here), but in John, Thomas says, "that we may die with him," the "him" being either Lazarus or Jesus, who with the disciples would risk stoning or catching the plague from Lazarus, or both. In either version, Thomas doubts that any of them will survive the adventure.

Another of the disciples participating in the Lazarus story is Peter, who is identifiable in illustrations of the subject such as plates 40 and 41. Peter's traditional character has been described in the characterizations of *The Visit to the Sepulcher.*

The other two disciples may as well remain anybody's guess. John reports the story, supposedly as an eye witness. Aside from Thomas's specified speech, the group of four has only one stanza to sing. The other three, including Peter, can divide these six lines among themselves.

Hilarius, probably without production in mind, lists among the necessary persons of his drama "duodecim Apostolorum, vel vi ad minus" (twelve Apostles, or six at the least). Like the group of Pharisees, and balancing them in the first and last scenes, four disciples are ample to make a group of followers of Jesus to Bethany, to Galilee, and back to Bethany, with as little dialogue as they have.

MARY MAGDALENE has been discussed at length in characterizations of *The Visit to the Sepulcher,* and needs no further introduction here, except to note that the playwright does not fudge her occupation. The Vulgate identifies her as a "peccatrix," which the King James Version translates as "a sinner." There are many ways a woman, or a man, can be a sinner. By describing her costume as a whore's, the playwright makes clear what her sin is, and the dramatic result is stronger. Something of her voluptuous sexuality is expressed in the washing of Christ's feet with her tears and her long hair; this quality is also evoked by her posture in the Saint-Gilles sculpture of the postcrucifixion scene (plate 2).

Her identification as Mary Magdalene seems to have been positive in the Middle Ages, even though the playwright, following the narrative in John, casts her only as Mary. In a sequel to the Lazarus miracle (John 12) she again washes Jesus' feet, this time in costly spikenard ointment. When Judas questions the expense, Jesus rebuffs him with, "Let her alone: against the day of my burying hath she kept this (spikenard)." There would thus have been nothing unorthodox in associating the nameless woman of Luke (7:37) at Simon's house with the Mary Magdalene of the Lazarus miracle and the visit to the sepulcher, and no present necessity to document the tradition.[10] We should, however, be aware of her past and her future in relation to Lazarus's resurrection. This consideration further justifies the Fleury playwright's inclusion of an opening scene at Simon's house, and distinguishes his intent from that of Hilarius, whose play begins with Lazarus dying at Bethany.

[10] Young comments on this tradition, I, 534.

MARTHA. Many of the stanzas of lament over Lazarus are prescribed for joint singing by Mary Magdalene and Martha. As in *The Lament of Mary,* an alternation of voices for these stanzas, or even half stanzas, individualizes the expression and may well have been the way these lines were delivered. There seems to have been no intention to play up Mary Magdalene over Martha. It was a Biblical arrangement, not the invention of the playwright, that Martha first runs to meet Jesus, but it serves the purpose of balancing the importance of the two roles. If the scene with Jesus on the road had been Mary Magdalene's, Martha would have seemed just a sister, for Mary Magdalene has the first scene with Jesus all to herself. She does, of course, later run to meet Jesus as Martha did, and as she had in the opening scene, throws herself at his feet. These parallel actions of Martha and Mary Magdalene again emphasize the equality of their roles, both in the Gospel and in the play, though more vividly in the latter.

The only distinction between the two is the suggestion that Martha is the more practical. Though Mary Magdalene sent the Messenger, Martha is the one who runs to meet Jesus while Mary Magdalene stays at home. It is likewise Martha who has qualms about the practicality of disinterring Lazarus. "Do you really think you should?" she implies when Jesus orders the tomb opened. "Lazarus has been dead four days and the smell will be putrid." In the play Jesus does not, as in the Gospel account, reprove Martha for her lack of faith in bringing up such mundane matters, and the playwright's emendation here is dramatically right, for there is no time at the climax of the play to judge Martha for her very natural remark. She was not skeptical of Jesus' powers, but merely squeamish at the prospect of smelling her brother's corpse and of the indignity to him. Plate 41 catches something of her expression at this moment, though the actor no doubt projected his expression more fully.

LAZARUS. The character in the title role is seen in the play only at the opening of the first scene at Bethany, when he is dying, and after his resurrection. The stage direction suggests that he begins to be sick ("tunc incipiat infirmari") only after he comes on to the set to take his place with Martha. Does this mean that, as any medieval person would suspect, he is stricken with the plague? If when the scene opens he were already sick in bed, we might assume that he had been ailing a long time and was now only taking a turn for the worse, which would be less shocking, less stimulating to the laments of the sisters. Sudden death from the plague is more moving, to us as well as to the sisters, than wasting away, and creates more sympathy for Lazarus. The Gospel merely says, "Now a certain man was sick ('languens' = languishing)." But from the Vulgate we get one other important fact that the playwright probably assumed his audience would know (which incidentally is not made explicit in the King James translation). Lazarus, in contrast to Simon's wealth, does not even own the Bethany house; it is "castello Mariae et Marthae sororis eius" (the house of his sisters, Mary and Martha).

He lives with them, is suddenly taken ill, and knows he is dying. This is the opening of the scene, and the preparation for his two stanzas, beginning "Cara soror." The first stanza, or part of it, is directed to be sung to Martha, but Mary Magdalene is directed to remain on the set while the Simon set is being remodeled, and one assumes that she soon becomes aware of Lazarus's trouble and crosses to join Martha beside him, for it is Mary Magdalene who replies to him. Martha, incidentally, should probably be given the second stanza of this reply, beginning "Quamvis eum." Lazarus's two stanzas would have been delivered with strong manly conviction and a genuine belief in God. After all, this is the title role, and these stanzas set him up for his next appearance at the climax of the play. At that last moment, Lazarus is truly alive again, yet he still wears his grisly graveclothes and, to judge from many of the illustrations, smells as foul as Martha had predicted he would (e.g., plates 40, 41). One may wish that the Fleury playwright, like Hilarius, had invented a stanza for Lazarus to sing after his raising, though modern performances have revealed that a stanza from Lazarus at this point might upset the timing of the catastrophe. Hilarius's version has no music, and his stanza form does not fit the Fleury melody.

MESSENGER. The Fleury playwright, unlike Hilarius, could not use Pharisees as messengers because they could not yet have arrived to console the sisters. While both scripts specify more than one, a single messenger is more credible for Fleury's Mary Magdalene to find in a hurry, and probably more effective in dialogue and action. The stage direction does not say where Mary Magdalene found even one messenger in this emergency. Certainly he (or she) was not in Magdalene's house, waiting to run errands, but must have been a passer-by or a neighbor. Theatrically, with the kind of staging I infer from the stage directions, the Messenger would be walking down the street, to one side of the Bethany set, and would be the first person Mary Magdalene encounters when she rushes out. Whether the character is a boy or a woman is not settled by the stage direction "quidam ex Nunciis" (one of the messengers), but the actor of this role was probably a choir boy. The *tessitura* of a boy soprano for his two-stanza speech to Jesus and his report to Martha would be appealing and another source of variety.

MOVEMENT AND GESTURE

Some of the details of movement have already been mentioned in the discussion of characterizations. Others can be more clearly explained in connection with the staging as it is outlined below. Further details are evident in plates 40 and 41; especially notable are the gestures of Jesus at the tomb, the postures of the prostrate sisters on the road and of Mary Magdalene at Simon's house, and the gestures of the Pharisees—and perhaps the Messenger—at the odor coming from the risen Lazarus. The grouping for this last scene is suggested best in these same plates. It is of course a grande finale, with thirteen of the cast grouped around the elevated anastasis-tomb.

Jesus' gesture just before he performs the miracle is a traditional and dramatically effective one known as the *orant* gesture. It is surveyed by Lowrie, who notes that fresco examples from as early as the third and fourth centuries show the same gesture as that of a modern Catholic priest at the altar (Lowrie's plates 12b, 18b, and 93b). The *orant* gesture seems to derive from the attitude of the arms of Christ crucified, but the elbows are nearly at waist level, the forearms stretched upward at about 45 degrees, the palms out.

The first stage direction is fairly explicit as to how the play opens: "In primis adducatur Simon cum quibusdam Iudeorum, et resideat in domu sua" (To begin the play let Simon with some of the Jews be brought out, and let him take his place in his house). Whether "adducatur" means "let Simon get himself out there and on stage," or "let him be led in a short procession from the sacristy to his house" is not entirely clear, though the latter is preferable. The next sentence in the same opening stage direction reads: "Post haec veniat Ihesus in plateam, cum Discipulis cantantibus. . . . (*Mane prima sabbati*)." This hymn is long enough to have paced a procession from the rear of the church to the crossing, where Simon came from his house to meet Jesus.

One possibly vexing matter of blocking: How and when was the dead Lazarus removed from the Bethany set? The body could not remain on its pallet, for Lazarus had to reappear in the tomb set in another costume at the end of the play, and there were no intermissions. The best moment seems to be during the scene at Galilee, the set for which is at the opposite side ("ex adverso") of the stage area from the Bethany set. At this time Lazarus could have been carried out by the Pharisees in character, Martha and Mary Magdalene remaining on the set, also in character, and later leaving it to meet Jesus on the road.

As an indication of how active and theatrical this play is, attention might be called to the number of times the stage area between Bethany and Galilee is crossed. Jesus and the Disciples go from Galilee to Simon's house (later the location of the Bethany house), and back. The Messenger runs from Bethany to Galilee, and returns to Bethany. Jesus and the Disciples go toward Bethany. Martha goes toward Galilee and meets Jesus on the way. Martha goes back to Bethany to tell Mary Magdalene to come. Martha and Mary Magdalene, accompanied by the Pharisees, go to Jesus at the tomb. This amounts to four complete crossings and four half-crossings, involving every one in the cast except Lazarus.

On the basis of many of the illustrations of the period, which show Lazarus standing in the vertical archway of the tomb, I posit the use of the anastasis-tomb structure. Some illustrations, however, show Lazarus beginning to sit up inside a horizontal sarcophagus sepulcher as in plates 39 and 41. If one recalls that in *The Visit to the Sepulcher* scene the sepulcher is inside the tomb, these two views of Lazarus' resurrection can be reconciled, the picture of the sepulcher being a close-up inside the tomb. Furthermore, the illustrations are of two different points in the action, the first a consequence of Jesus' order to the Disciples to take away the stone from the cave (i.e., the lid from the sarcophagus), the second (again at Jesus' command) a result of Lazarus's release from the ropes that prevented him from rising, and being thus able to step out of the sarcophagus to the door of the anastasis.

STAGING AND THE DEFINITION OF ACTING AREAS

Young, in his consideration of the staging of the play, writes: "For the staging of the performance are required four *sedes,* or *loca*—representing the house at Bethany, Galilee, Jerusalem, and the tomb—arranged in the choir or some other part of the church. A single *sedes* appears to have served both as the house of Simon and that of Lazarus and his sisters. For the tomb may have been used the Easter sepulcher, for as we have already observed, this structure at Fleury was sufficiently large to allow a person to enter." [11] Not looking at the play through the eyes of a producer, Young was misled by the Fleury stage direction, "Postea recedant Iudei in quendam alium locum quasi in Ierusalem, ut inde in competenti loci veniant consolari duas Sorores" (after this [the supper at Simon's] the Jews [Pharisees] retire to some other place as if having gone to Jerusalem). He supposed that the Jerusalem location had to be shown on stage, when there is no later scene to be played in such a location, and the obvious intention of the medieval playwright-producer was to take the Pharisees off stage. They would logically walk beyond the Bethany house (stage right), and go out the north transept door or otherwise out of sight, to return to the Bethany set later by the same way, talking as they walk ("in itinere dicant"). There are thus only the usual three sets or *sedes* required.

By the process of elimination, one arrives at the only possible arrangement of the three *sedes*. The anastasis-tomb was placed in the same position as for *The Visit to the Sepulcher,* a little stage right of center and east of the front steps of the choir. This structure was probably not centered, in order to permit masked access to its interior from stage right in the choir; this was particularly necessary for concealing Lazarus in his graveclothes. The use of a single set for Simon's house and the Bethany house is, from the stage directions (particularly "Domus vero ipsius Simonis . . . efficiatur quasi Bethania," Let the house of Simon be efficiently changed to resemble the Bethany house) and from an analysis of production requirements, a thoroughly practical means of keeping the quantity of sets to an efficacious ("efficiatur") minimum. The third set, Galilee, was "ex adverso preparatus" (prepared at the opposite side of the stage area) from the Simon-Bethany set, probably farther from the anastasis set than it was from Bethany. We thus have a clean design for the staging: the anastasis-tomb at nearly the focal center, flanked by the Simon-Bethany and the Galilee sets, and an unfurnished street or road area in front of all three.

The tomb set has already been described, so we may confine our attention here to the side sets. The size of the Simon-Bethany set was determined by the fact that it must contain, and not merely back, the eleven persons who are in Simon's house for supper. There seems to be no need for a front curtain for this set; the shift of furnishings for the transformation from Simon's to Bethany can be made in full view of the

[11] Young, II, 210. (His footnote refers to I, 395, an error for I, 397.)

audience, since their attention is at that time on the scene at Galilee, at the other end of the street. The Simon-Bethany set would, however, need a back curtain, split in the center.

The Galilee set would have been somewhat smaller than the Bethany set, for it had to contain only Christ, the four Disciples, and possibly the Messenger. I see no great need for furnishings on this set, though a couple of benches would provide for more interesting tableaux during the time Christ and his Disciples are there and scenes are being played at Bethany.

The *platea* mentioned in the opening stage direction is apparently the street that connects all three sets, and is of course in front of it. This area, as we have seen, is used a great deal during the play, and has a function that is curiously like that of the traditional set for Roman comedy: two houses at opposite ends of the stage, and a street between with much movement on the street back and forth between the two houses. Because there is so much action on the *platea,* my inference is that it was not in the width of the choir, as Young suggests, but in front and to the sides of that area, including the crossing and both transepts.

There is nothing in the stage directions to indicate that either of the side sets was elevated. When platforms were required in plays of the repertory, directions for entrances and exits from a set used such verbs as "ascendere" and "descendere." For example, in the *Annunciation* "Maria descendat de loco suo et vadat ad locum Helisabeth et Ioachin" (Mary descends from her platform and goes to the platform of Elizabeth and Joachim). Practically, platforms for the side sets of *Lazarus* would have been awkward, with the need for so much hasty running back and forth.

8. The Conversion of St. Paul

42 Events in the Life of St. Paul. The Gumpert Bible, before 1195. Erlangen, Universitätsbibliothek, MS 1, fol. 387ᵛ.

43 St. Paul on the Road to Damascus. Enamel plaque, English (?), late twelfth century. Courtesy of Musée de Lyons.

44 St. Paul on the Road to Damascus. Psalter, ca. 1104. Oxford, Bodleian Library, MS Auct. D.2.6, fol. 170ᵛ. Courtesy of the Bodleian Library.

173

45 St. Paul Escaping from Prison. Enamel plaque, English (?), late twelfth century.
Courtesy of Victoria and Albert Museum, Crown copyright.

The Conversion of St. Paul

Conversio Beati Pauli

TONE AND QUALITY

IF THE initial stage direction for *The Conversion of St. Paul* were not
so detailed about the four platforms and the couch for Ananias, and
who is on each platform, one might doubt that the unique manuscript
of this work actually contains a play. After the generosity of this opening
stage direction, the ones that follow leave many questions unanswered.
The outline of the story is clear enough; it follows the account in Acts 9
very closely. The missing links are all of theatrical import, concerned
with how the story is to be shown on the stage.

Even when the gaps are filled in by surmise and deduction, one has
the feeling that the stage structures are too big for the size of the play. For
example, the house of the High Priest of Damascus is necessary, but all
that is shown there is the High Priest somehow overhearing Paul's loud
conversation next door and, in one stanza of four lines, ordering his armed
men to go and arrest Paul. Presumably they go, and that is the last we
see of the High Priest and his house; we even have to infer that the armed
men go to Judas's house next door and wait at the gate for Paul. Similarly,
there is only one brief use made of the High Priest of Jerusalem and his
house at the other end of the staging area; he and Paul have an exchange
of dialogue there which totals two stanzas.

The whole play is brief; there are only twenty four-line stanzas in all
with ten scenes in six separate locations (four or five of them interiors),
and a cast of about fifteen. Even with the setting of the guard, the march
toward Damascus, the blinding of Paul, the lowering of Paul in a basket,
and some other bits of pantomime, the running time of the play can
hardly exceed twelve minutes without the *Te Deum* as epilogue.

By anybody's standard, this is not an artistic way to construct a play.
There is too much brief and scattered action, and no imaginative shaping
of the dramatic materials of the story. The bones of it are the three
experiences of Paul: arrogant against the Christians; struck blind on the
road to Damascus; converted and joining the Apostles. In the play each

of these events seems simply to happen at random; they are not caused by anyone's struggle for or against anyone else, and so make little more impression than a perfunctory Sunday-school pageant on an assigned subject. Compared with any of the plays considered above, it is the work of a beginner. The variety of melodies, and their expansions, are far more interesting than the dramaturgy, and one wonders if the composer may have been an old hand at lyric works who had never before tried a play.

The subject matter of the story was frequently used in twelfth- and thirteenth-century art, but we have no record of other twelfth-century efforts to make a play of it. Perhaps this was the playwright's difficulty. The story was new to church drama, and the playwright did not know from others' experience how to expand and shape this Biblical narrative. It is a good story but it needs dramatic transformation to become a play, and the playwright merely followed Acts 9. He passed over such important dramatic possibilities as the verse about the Apostles being afraid of Paul at his approach (Acts 9:26); they do not utter a word until the *Te Deum,* and are not even named as speakers of the last stanza of the play.[1] Other missed opportunities from the Vulgate are Ananias's baptism of Paul and the restoration of his sight. The visual artists did not miss them.

DETERMINATION OF MAJOR EPISODES

The artists of the period saw several major episodes in the story: Paul receiving letters of authority, Paul stricken on the road to Damascus, Ananias receiving instructions, Paul let down in the basket, Ananias giving the message to Paul (plates 42–45). Roughly five of the playwright's ten scenes are frequently illustrated, but so little does he do with any of the ten that the emphases suggested by the pictorial artists are of little use to students of the play.

CHARACTERIZATION

The artists have great admiration for Paul; they show him either as taller than those around him, or with a larger head. Of the play's twenty

---

[1] Young points this out, II, 223.

stanzas, Paul sings only seven, and this compares rather unfavorably with the proportions of the Virgin Mary's role in *The Lament of Mary* or Mary Magdalene's in *The Visit to the Sepulcher.* As a consequence we do not see enough of Paul to know who he is. The playwright describes him in the initial stage direction as young.

The other fourteen or fifteen characters in the play are even less firmly characterized. Ananias, usually drawn by the visual artists as an old man who reluctantly accepted his role, is the most promising of the group, and we do see him trying to do his duty in two scenes, and trudging along the street between the scenes.

Perhaps the best one can do is to list the *dramatis personae,* those who sing and those who do not:

Singing roles	*Nonsinging roles*
Paul	Three soldiers (Paul's)
High Priest of Jerusalem	Two Christian Captives
The Lord ("Dominus")	Two Armed Men (Damascus High Priest's)
Ananias	Other Apostles (Judas? Two others?)
High Priest of Damascus	
Barnabus	

The three soldiers of Paul apparently follow along with him to Judas's house, and change their clothes when Paul changes his (plates 43, 45). Plate 44 shows only two soldiers, perhaps for want of space in the miniature. The two Christian Captives may not be worth bringing on stage in costume. The Damascus High Priest can hardly send fewer than two Armed Men ("suis armatis") to arrest Paul. The number of Apostles needed to make a group may be inferred from the fact that three are required in *The Pilgrim,* three or four in *Lazarus.* Three of the ten scenes occur in Judas's house, and though we never meet him, he deserves to be one of the Apostle group at the finish.

The High Priests of Jerusalem and Damascus are indistinguishable. What they say does not individualize or even characterize them as more than stock authoritarian figures. The Damascus twin does have an opportunity for villainous pantomiming while he listens to Paul's conversation next door, though the stage direction merely describes this miming as "Haec audiens" (hand to ear, no doubt).

The Lord ("Dominus") of the play is a mysterious character, about whose identity the playwright is silent. The artists had several interpretations of the Vulgate's "in visu, Dominus" (The Lord, in a vision). Plate 42 materializes the vision as an Angel. Plate 44 shows a nimbed figure who could also be an angel, but may well be the Christus, because in the Vulgate "The Lord said, 'I am Jesus whom thou persecutest,'" and Ananias says that "the Lord, even Jesus," appeared to him.

Barnabus has little character. One does not know whether he encounters Paul on the street boldly, or while trying to run away from him, like the other apostles.

MOVEMENT AND GESTURE

The business of Paul and the basket is the most complicated movement in the play. The stage direction reads: "Quo comperto, Saulus cum Discipulis suis in sporta ab aliquo alto loco, quasi a muro ad terram dimittatur" (When they learn this, let Paul and his Disciples lower him to the ground in a basket, from some high place, as if from a wall). As with everything else about this play, the stage direction is not theatrically viable, and suggests a literary statement that has not gone through the test of staging. The vagueness of the phrase "quasi a muro" is in contrast to the pictorial definition of the twelfth-century English plaque (plate 45), which shows a tower at extreme left, a Disciple in the tower holding the slack ropes to the grounded basket at center, and Paul about to disembark with the aid of two other Disciples. If the plaque reflects the actual performance of a superior version of the play, the contrivance would probably have called for the basket and Paul to have been concealed behind the tower platform while the Disciple above pretended to pay out the ropes. When the ropes went slack, the other two Disciples could have pulled Paul and the basket to stage left of the platform and into view. The audience would have been watching the efforts of the Disciple on the parapet, the slackening of the ropes, and the mimed encouragement of the other two Disciples to the rope-handler, and would be relieved when the basket and Paul were dragged into view.

Other movements and gestures may be derived from plates 42 through 45. The striking down of Paul on the Damascus road might have been an effective scene of violent action. There is no indication of how these movements might be handled on the stage, though we do gather from the Vulgate and the contemporary artists that what struck Paul down was not lightning but a blaze of light. The Vulgate says, "et subito circumfulsit eum lux de caelo" (and suddenly there shined round about him a light from heaven). The pictorial artists visualize this effect, if at all, as sun-rays (plates 42, 44). It is not an effect that either artist or playwright could manage in the Middle Ages. The difficulty about getting the audience to imagine for itself the brilliance of this light is that the playwright does not give Paul an opportunity to mention the light until the end of the second line of his answer to Dominus's voice from the heavens. By this time, the audience will have already made up its mind that something happened—a vision, a voice, or whatever—but nothing vivid enough to be a shining light from heaven.

COSTUMES

There are no problems of costume that are not explored in relation to the other plays, unless one takes the costume of the High Priests as something new. Plate 42 suggests that a High Priest wore an Arabian kind of veil on his head, probably to distinguish him from a Christian ecclesiastic.

PROPERTIES AND FURNISHINGS

The furnishings for the four "houses" specified for the play are not even hinted at in the dialogue and action of the play. How can we know what is in Judas's house, for instance, when we are never confronted with him? The only property other than the basket and ropes, which are visualized in plate 45, is the correspondence given by the High Priest of Jerusalem to Paul. Both characters mention more than one letter, and plate 42 shows a long scroll being handed to Paul. Although in the Vulgate narrative the High Priest has time to compose several letters, in the play he has neither time nor cover to write even one, as the stage direction implies: "aliquid breve sigillatum" (some brief scribble). Apparently the playwright accepted the incident without knowing how to handle it dramatically.

STAGING AND THE DEFINITION OF ACTING AREAS

The staging suggested in the opening stage direction is much more ambitious and on the whole more practical theatrically than the dialogue and action to be played upon it. The positions of the four platforms are not defined as to stage left or right, but one usually assumes a left-to-right progression of scenes, in art or on the stage, and hence the four structures can be placed with some confidence. The two buildings at Jerusalem are stage right, the two at Damascus stage left, and there is a considerable open space (*platea*) at center between the two groups. The stage direction specifies this open area. "Ex alia vero parte, aliquantulum longe ab his sedibus" (On the other side, in fact, somewhat distant from those platforms). The two Jerusalem buildings may adjoin; there is no dramatic reason for their being separated unless for symmetry of the total scenic composition. Between the two Damascus buildings, which must be close enough to allow the High Priest to overhear Paul's loud ("alta voce") expression of conversion in Judas's house, there is specified a *lectus* (couch) for Ananias. Possibly there are steps from the two buildings converging in such a way as to allow space under a landing for Ananias and his couch. The stage direction locates this couch "inter has duas sedes" (between these buildings). All sets may have been designed in the style of those shown in plate 45. Compared to the functional design of the *Lazarus sedes,* the sets for the present play ask for a lot more theater than is going to happen in them, and are another indication that the playwright was a beginner who did not understand the relation of his means to his ends, and overcompensated in his staging for what is lacking in the play itself. No other play of the repertory makes such exorbitant scenic demands; even the spectacular *Daniel* works out the scene design satisfactorily in terms of the usual three locations.

MAKEUP: BEARDS AND HAIRSTYLES

All the characters in *The Conversion of St. Paul* are male, and Paul in particular always has a beard (plates 42–45). Ananias, as an old man, presumably has a white beard (plate 42). Other beards are optional.

LIGHTING

Aside from the "lux de caelo" discussed above, of which a modern producer might make more than his medieval counterpart could, no special lighting is required for this play. There are four, possibly five, interiors to be adequately lighted. Having examined the play from nine basic production angles, I wonder whether it was included in the Fleury playbook, along with all those beautifully constructed plays, only because someone (possibly the author himself) wished to salvage a script that had been found unproduceable although it contained some fine melodies. An effort to produce this script would have necessitated major revisions.

SOUND EFFECTS

A thunder of drums might have accompanied the "lux de caelo."

9. The Wise and Foolish Maidens

46 The Wise Maidens, with Christ as Bridegroom (top) and the Foolish Maidens, with
the Tempter, who figures in some versions of the story (bottom). South Portal of
west façade, Strasbourg Cathedral, second half of thirteenth century.

47 The Wise and Foolish Maidens (left) and Ecclesia (right). *Speculum Humanis Salvationis,* Alsatian, fourteenth century. Munich, Bayerische Staatsbibliothek, MS Clm. 146, fol. 43ʳ. Courtesy of Bayerische Staatsbibliothek.

48 The Maidens and the Oil Merchant (top) and the Celestial Banquet, with the Christus and Ecclesia (bottom). Miniature, Abbey of Bury St. Edmunds, twelfth century. New York, The Pierpont Morgan Library, MS 521ᵛ, no. 13, A and B.

49 The Harrowing of Hell, showing Hellmouth. English Gospel Book, early twelfth century. Cambridge, Library of Pembroke College, MS 120, fol. 4ᵛ. Courtesy of the Masters and Fellows of Pembroke College, Cambridge.

50   Demon, caught by an Angel. Capital, Ste. Madeleine, Vézélay, ca. 1140. Photo
Jean Roubier.

The Wise and Foolish Maidens

Sponsus

TONE AND QUALITY

THE unique version of *The Wise and Foolish Maidens* appears in a manuscript from Limoges—with a clear Aquitanian musical score, a mélange of Latin and northern French verse, and an incomplete identification of roles. To read the hypotheses and emendations of the several scholars who have overhauled the literary text [1] is to be overimpressed by the confusion of the manuscript, and to doubt the artistic merit of the play. The neglected fact is that the playscript is eminently produceable without much recourse to the hypothetical reconstructions. Most of these are concerned with origins (there was possibly an all-Latin form of the play, twice revised by other French playwrights in the last years of the 11th century), and very little with how well the existing playscript may have been performed with a minimum of emendation and fill-in. In sharp contrast to the explicit manuscript of *The Conversion of St. Paul,* which nevertheless yields a poor play, the theatrically reticent manuscript of *The Wise and Foolish Maidens* reveals a dramatic work of the highest quality. Had as much intelligent effort been put into producing the play as has been lavished on editing it within an inch of its life, its great art would be more generally apparent. [2]

The action of the play follows, enlarging as it dramatizes, the parable of the wise and foolish virgins [3] in Matthew 25:1–13. The Foolish

[1] Young, II, 367–68; Coussemaker, pp. 1–10 and 311–18; L.-P. Thomas, *Le "Sponsus"* (*Mystère des Vierges sages et des Vierges folles*), (Presses Universitaires de France, 1951), in which are summarized the views of W. Cloetta, H. Morf, and F. Liuzzi.

[2] Cohen notes in the introduction to his second edition of *Histoire de la Mise en Scène,* p. x, that L.-P. Thomas was preparing a new edition of *The Wise and Foolish Maidens* "après avoir d'abord tenté à Bruxelles, le 2 juin 1925, une restitution scènique de ce vieux 'mélodrame.'" Another revival was by a cast of students and faculty of Mary Baldwin College at the Folger Shakespeare Library December 12, 13, and 14, 1969, the score being based on my transcription of music and words, and the production on the materials of the present study. Wendell Margrave reviewed the latter production in "Music Dramas Full of Delight," *The Evening Star* (Washington D.C.), 13 December 1969.

[3] Until very recently in Western society, women who were not married were presumed to be virgins, and were so titled. I have ventured to translate "virgines" as "maidens" to

Maidens have not brought enough oil to provide light in their torches for the midnight arrival of the Bridegroom, and they are also very sleepy. The Angel Gabriel, the customary annunciator in medieval church music-dramas, arrives to emphasize to the ten maidens the importance of being ready for the imminent Second Coming of Christ. The Foolish, rallying, try to borrow oil from the Wise, who regret that they are unable to lend it and who suggest that the Foolish could go and buy some. The Oil Merchants explain that they cannot sell oil at that hour. As the Foolish Maidens return to the Wise, the Bridegroom appears and, ignoring their apology for having no light, summons grotesque Demons to toss the Foolish Maidens into Hellmouth. The Christus then presumably escorts the Wise Maidens into the banquet room, and seats them at the celestial banquet table with his bride, Ecclesia (the Church).

The severe punishment fits the crime only if we, like its medieval audiences at Limoges, recognize the play as the parable that it is. According to such eminent theologians as Hugh of St. Victor (1096–1141) and Gregory the Great, the ten maidens represent all mankind, waiting for the predicted Second Coming, which is also the Last Judgment.[4] The wise five are those who are "in love and charity with their neighbors" without expecting neighborly recognition or reward. The foolish five represent those who do good works only out of pride and for the sake of earthly reputation. The oil burning in the wise maidens' torches is this same love and charity, which not only must be plentiful enough never to burn out, but which also cannot be borrowed or bought as the wise maidens realize. Nor can the grubby oil merchants provide at the last moment for a longstanding deficiency. The foolish maidens, whose torches seemed so bright to mankind and therefore to themselves, now—much too late—find the worldly flames sputtering out when a spiritual judgment is about to be made.

Visually and musically the play is attractive. The two groups of five maidens act as groups without being merely choruses in a musical play. They are individualized within the groups, as the pictorial evidence often shows, and as I believe is indicated by such arrangements as the provision of five stanzas in the second item. There is interplay between the two groups, and a final separation of sheep from goats when the Bridegroom

---

avoid the tasteless modern misinterpretation of "foolish virgins," and to forestall a distortion of the medieval intention toward the ten girls in the play. Their chastity was not in question. Other possible translations of "virgines" are "bridesmaids" and "girls." Their youth and beauty are obviously important to the play.

[4] Hugh of St. Victor, in J. P. Migne ed., *Patrologiae Cursus Completus: Patrologia Latina*, CLXXV, cols. 799–800.

condemns one group and welcomes the other. The melodies for the characters are well differentiated without being unrelated. There is a majestic yet simple dignity in the melody of the opening item, "Adest Sponsus," and this melody should be recapitulated as the next to last, *Amen dico* item.[5] Gabriel's melody is as much in contrast with this opening as are his remarks in the vernacular. The related melodies for the two groups of girls are strongly declarative for the Wise Maidens, less confident for the lethargic Foolish Maidens, particularly in the "Dolentas" refrain of the latter. In sight and sound, choreographically and musically, the play is a charming piece of theater, brief but intense, moral without being narrowly didactic.

In this last connection I do not agree with Young that the Demons are "employed not comically, but with grim seriousness."[6] What he did not see, because he did not take the music into account, is that after the Bridegroom sings the majestic "Amen dico," he closes the play with the vernacular stanza, "Alet, chaitivas," presumably sung to the sprightly melody of the Wise Maidens, and that meanwhile the Demons dance in and back out with the Foolish Maidens. The playwright suggests, I think, that having made the serious point of the play in the first half of the Bridegroom's speech, he and the Bridegroom and the audience may relax in the comparative lightness, even gaiety, of the second and closing half of the speech and its consequences. Chambers was of the opinion that the Demons in this play reflect the influence of folk plays of the period, and Allardyce Nicoll, in his study of late medieval devils in *Masks, Mimes, and Miracles,* concludes that "Obviously the devils were dear to the medieval imagination, and dear not because of their evil, but because of their comic irresponsibility, their posturings, their extravagance."[7]

DETERMINATION OF MAJOR EPISODES

There are no extensive travel or transitional scenes. This play has a solid, compact structure, based on the Bible and on the traditional por-

---

[5] The last two items, incorporating the speech of the Sponsus, are without notation in the Limoges manuscript, although space was left for the music. Thomas, Le *"Sponsus,"* also makes this suggestion of repetition. He does not agree, as seems equally obvious, that the last item, "Alet chaitivas," should repeat the melody of lines 46–49 (Young, II, 364). Instead, he considers the possibility of using Gabriel's theme, which is less well fitted to the verse.

[6] Young, II, 367.   [7] Nicoll, p. 188, and Chambers, II, 91.

trayals of the story in art. Visual representations of the Biblical parable generally show three, occasionally four, episodes. The first is the tableau of the maidens, with an evident contrast between hope and dejection (plates 46, 47). The second shows the moment when the Bridegroom, having shut the door against the Foolish Maidens, who try futilely to open it, beckons the Wise Maidens to come to the banquet table.[8] The third, comparatively rare, is the scene at the banquet table, with Christ the Bridegroom at the center, flanked by the Wise Maidens on his right, Ecclesia (as the Bride) and two servitors on his left, and the five Foolish Maidens, uncrowned and disconsolate, outside the door (plate 48). The fourth is the scene of the Wise and Foolish Maidens with the Oil Merchants (plate 48).[9]

Portrayals of the Maidens are found as early as the fourth century, and continue unabated through the fourteenth. Illustrations of the waiting scene and the last scene at the door are plentiful in the period, and reflect the theatrical content of the play. The scene with the Oil Merchants, like that of Ecclesia at the banquet, is depicted rarely, yet the manuscript of the play identifies the Merchants as characters.[10]

CHARACTERIZATION

The Wise Maidens are the more difficult to characterize. They could so easily look and act smug about their prudence and their refusal to lend oil to the others. If their prudence was expressed as a strongly joyful anticipation of the coming of the Bridegroom, because they had made preparations and because they were as gay as any bridesmaids at a wedding, the danger of self-righteousness may have been avoided. There is a difference between smugness and security. The Wise Maidens' refusal to lend to the Foolish is another matter. The Wise Maidens must have been able to show their reluctance to refuse the Foolish, while indicating that their oil could not be borrowed. The suggestion that the Foolish Maidens hurry to the Oil Merchants would have also been delivered in a genuinely innocent

[8] Francovich, *Benedetto Antelami,* plates 325 and 327.

[9] Though he is not identified by oil drums or other marks of his trade, the face of the supposed Merchant in this illustration is different from that of the Christus in the picture immediately below it. The costumes of the two figures are also different; the supposed Merchant wears a knee-length tunic and an only slightly longer mantle, much too short, in this period, for the usual costume of the Christus at such moments.

[10] Thomas includes Ecclesia in the cast of characters of the play, and cites two examples in art of Ecclesia at such a banquet. The files of the Index of Christian Art contain a few more, notably my plate 48, bottom.

spirit, not a cynical one. At this point in the dialogue, incidentally, the "Dolentas" refrain after the Wise Maidens' speech to the Foolish would have been sung by the Foolish, not assigned—as most editors do—to the Wise Maidens as a judgment upon the others. After this speech [11] the Foolish Maidens continue to beg for the oil, in answer to which foolishness the Wise must have more bluntly refused and urgently repeated the suggestion that the Foolish go and buy from the Oil Merchants. At this point there seems dramatic reason to move the Wise Maidens' lines 66–70 to follow line 60, ahead of lines 61–65, in order to conclude the dialogue with the Foolish before the latter move on line 61 to the Merchants, who reply with lines 71–78.[12]

Despite the fact that the Foolish Maidens have twice as many lines as the Wise, I do not understand Young's reference to "the dramatic prominence of the foolish virgins," [13] unless he considers their final violent demise more important than the success of the Wise. The stage direction does not mention the action of the Wise Maidens at the end of the play, but their movement, to judge from the visual arts, is certainly a procession through the door, led by the Bridegroom. The final tableau, documented by the visual arts, includes the Wise Maidens.

The Foolish Maidens are pitiful, but we do not grieve for them. They are foolish, they are silly, but their laments are hardly to be taken "with grim seriousness." Indeed, they should not be labelled laments as if their grief were in a class with Mary's or Rachel's. Without condescension to the play, it may be considered as in some respects a religious game, its mood being that of a grown-up *London Bridge* or *Old Roger Is Dead.* The Foolish Maidens are not literally cremated in Hell, nor do the Wise Maidens fill their stomachs at the banquet table. The symbolic actions are taken, the dialogue is sung, the idea is expressed and lingers after the masque of the play is finished.

The Bridegroom is the customary Christus, whose character has already been discussed in relation to *The Visit to the Sepulcher, The Pilgrim,* and the *Lazarus.* The Oil Merchants—two are pointed out by the Wise Maidens in line 60—are the same hearty characters who sell spices in the St. Quentin and other versions of *The Visit to the Sepulcher.* The Oil Merchants do not bow and scrape to customers, they know as well as anyone what one's duty to God is, and they do not hesitate to say so. In

[11] Young, II, 363, lines 46–49 and 51–54.

[12] Coussemaker makes a somewhat similar transposition, lines 66–70 following line 56. Thomas does not accept such changes, though clearly the stanza of lines 66–70 is defective in the manuscript, lacking line 69.

[13] Young, II, 366.

production, these characters inevitably become comic, along with the Demons, and join the Shepherds' company of folk types.

The most comprehensive editor of the play, L.-P. Thomas, proposes that the play means to include the singing role of Ecclesia. Although the action of the play may well include a final banquet scene, with Ecclesia represented in tableau, her singing of or presence during the opening item, as Thomas wishes, is not dramatically appropriate in any case, for it raises an awkward theatrical question as to why she as the bride would have come ahead to alert the maidens and to tell them who the bride-groom is. The bridesmaids would know; the bride would not come un-accompanied to tell the bridesmaids to be vigilant. The fact that there is no representation in art of such a scene, and only a few of Ecclesia at the banquet, is further reason to consider her presence unlikely at the begin-ning of the play. M. Thomas hedges his point in suggesting that the role of Ecclesia was taken by the choir because the opening item is in the nature of a hymn.

The heading for the second item of the play is "Prudentes," which C. Magnin in 1835 amended to "Accedant Prudentes et dicat Gabriel." [14] The Archangel is obviously the speaker, for he so identifies himself in its fourth stanza. Magnin's only error was in assuming that the Wise Maidens would not enter until the conclusion of the first item. With the five Fool-ish Maidens, they may, I believe, be assumed to be the singers of its five paired stanzas. Gabriel appears to them, not they to him, just as he does in *The Shepherds, The Visit to the Sepulcher,* and *The Annunciation.* As in these plays, he is here individualized to the extent of having a melody of his own.

What may be inferred about the acting company for this play, in which ten of the cast are women? There are no more than three female roles in such plays as *The Lament of Mary* and *The Visit to the Sepulcher:* here are three times that many, all of them protagonists. Are we to assume that male members of the choir took these roles? There may have been enough countertenors and boy sopranos in the choir of St. Martial at Limoges, but other explanations are possible. Perhaps the play was first composed and performed at a nunnery, and the script somehow found its way to Limoges without identification, or ten members of a neighboring convent's choir were borrowed for the performance at Limoges. We have other records of such mixed casts. [15]

[14] *Journal général de l'Instruction publique,* IV (1835). Coussemaker and Young follow this emendation, which I take from them without having seen Magnin's article.

[15] See above, p. 65n.

In any event, a medieval playwright would hardly compose a play requiring ten good sopranos, altos, and countertenors without having them at hand. The odd circumstance is that in the Limoges manuscript the adjacent playscript, written for the same season of the year, has a reverse distribution of roles; a cast of thirteen men and one woman in *The Procession of the Prophets*. A further coincidence is that the total of singing roles in the companion piece is also fourteen, yet surely those who were qualified to perform the ten Maidens would not have been able to play the twelve adult Prophets. Perhaps the manuscript's juxtaposition of the two plays is the basic coincidence.

There is need for three or four Demons to herd the Foolish Maidens into Hellmouth effectively. They are elsewhere called devils, and as already remarked are grotesque, comic figures.

10. The Three Daughters

51 St. Nicholas, the Three Daughters, and the Father. English Missal, late fourteenth century. London, British Museum, MS Add. 29704, no. 91. Courtesy of the Trustees of the British Museum.

52 St. Nicholas, the Three Daughters, and the Father. "Prayer Book of Joanna of Naples," fourteenth century. Vienna, Österreichische Nationalbibliothek, MS 1921, fol. 214ʳ.

53   St. Nicholas, the Three Daughters, and the Father. Panel by Ambrogio Lorenzetti of Siena, Uffizi, Florence, ca. 1330. Photo Alinari.

54   The Three Daughters and the Father. "Queen Mary's Psalter," beginning of fourteenth century. London, British Museum, MS Royal 2 B. VII, fol. 315ᵛ. Courtesy
of the Trustees of the British Museum.

55   St. Nicholas, the Three Daughters, the Father, and the Suitor. Font, Winchester
Cathedral, ca. 1160–70. By permission of the Dean and Chapter, Winchester
Cathedral.

56 A Bishop's Crosier, head of gilded bronze. Limoges, early thirteenth century. Courtesy of the Metropolitan Museum of Art, the Michael Friedsam Collection, 1932.

The Three Daughters

Tres Filiae

TONE AND QUALITY

IF THE wit of the circular form and action of *The Three Daughters* is not caught by the audience by the time the second bag of gold comes through the window, the play is lost. Some scholars have failed to appreciate the play's form. Karl Young, for example, condemned the repetitions of action and of language as "drearily mechanical," regretted "the solemnity of the plodding author's intention," and resented "the absence of an unequivocal pecuniary provision for the father at the end." [1] The style of such objections suggests that the wit of the form and of the characterizations was missed, mainly because the work was not seen and heard as an intricate trefoil (plate 52).

The repetitive structure of the play requires the same kind of consideration, if not sympathy, that has already been given to the play of *Lazarus* above. The musical situation is even more extreme than in the former play. After the first two items of fifty-six measures each, the remainder of the drama is sung to a single melody, repeated with slight variations fifty-seven times.[2] This melody, while intricate and shapely, has

---

[1] Young, II, 322–23. Otto Schumann, however, defended the quality of the several versions of the play, in *Zeitschrifte für Romanische Philologie,* LXII (1942), 390: "Ich sah und sehe in alledem, im Gegenteil: es ist bewuszte Kunste, gewollte Schlichtheit und strenge Beschränkung auf des unbedingt Wesenliche."

[2] The structure of the opening melody clears up a matter of difficulty in the arrangement of the lines of the stanzas to which it is sung. Rather than attempt to describe the necessary rearrangements, which have puzzled editors of the play (Otto E. Albrecht, *Four Latin Plays of St. Nicholas* [Philadelphia, 1935]; and Young, II, 316 and note 3), I quote the stanzas in their entirety as the melody defines them:

> *Pater:* In lamentum et merorem
> Versa est laetitia
> Quam praebebat olim nobis
> Rerum habundancia.
>   O rerum inopia!
>   Heu! heu! perierunt
>   Huius vitae gaudia.
> Forma genus, morum splendor,
> Inventutis gloria,

only one section and thus only half the melodic content of the *Lazarus*. Within its twelve measures, the opening two-measure phrase:

is usually repeated twice, appears again in the refrain, and is imitated once. In other words, more than half the contents of the repeated melody is itself repetitive; roughly speaking, the two-measure phrase of six notes is heard during the play about 350 times, or perhaps fourteen times a minute. Annoyed as Young was by the repetitious action and language, he would have been appalled by these statistics.

In the swirling blend of action, language, and music, there can be no doubt that this amount of repetition was the deliberate design of the playwright. Had he thought it was too much he would have done something to reduce it. He could, for example, have cut the musical repetitions in half by adding another section to the main melody; he could have written different verses for some of the seven Suitor-Father-Daughter items which are now twice repeated; and he could have had the three daughters dowered simultaneously and the suitors entered as a group of three. That he took none of these obvious steps to reduce the repetitiousness suggests that he intended it—and that the medieval audience was

---

            Cumprobatur nichil esse,
            Dum desit pecunia.
                O rerum inopia!
                Heu! heu! perierunt
                Huius vitae gaudia.
Filiae: Finis opum, dum recedunt,
            Luctus et suspiria.
            Eia! Pater ipse lugens
            Opes lapsas, praedia.
                O rerum inopia!
            Adeamus, audiamus
            Que cepit consilia.

This emendation omits two *Filiae* lines which previous editors have found defective ("Tractat secum . . . socia" and the further repetition of "Heu! heu! . . . gaudia"), replacing the latter with the "Adeamus, audiamus . . . consilia" as the appropriate end of the last refrain. The melodic pattern of the stanza and refrain, established and repeated by *Pater,* may thus be exactly reproduced by the *Filiae* without awkward repetitions of melodic phrases and violation of the stanza form. The last line ("Que cepit consilia") then serves as the end of the refrain, with a conclusive cadence on "consilia." These emendations require no transfers of lines to other melodic phrases, and are accomplished solely by the omission of the four offending lines and their manuscript settings.

pleasantly affected by it. Tastes in theater have not changed so much that we find less pleasure when this work is properly produced.[3]

In fact when one examines the convolutions of the structure, one sees that the extent of the repetitions creates an intriguing design. Everything comes in threes: the daughters; the suitors; the bags of gold; the melodic repetitions and the triple rhythm of the score; the triple use of seven speeches, in which half of each verse line is dactyllic. What evoked the triplet in language and music was the triples of characters and actions. Because no other known version of this story, as literary legend, play, or pictorial narration, has more than one suitor, and most have none at all, we may legitimately speculate that the playwright of the present version began by positing three suitors, who would say and do exactly the same things, and then played out this gambit.[4] The medieval mind was Platonically in love with the number three, partly because it represented the Trinity, but equally because it was a perfect number—its first ten multiples not repeating the number; its horizontal balance being left, right, and center; its vertical symmetry being above, below, and on (heaven, hell, and earth); its sexual manifestations being outwardly male and inwardly female. There was even a theoretical disposition to believe that music should be composed only in triple rhythm, never duple, though in practice the music of the play repertory seems to have produced some melodies in duple. With this symbolic background of triplicity, the playwright may even have been motivated to see how far he could expand the concept, how many three's in character, action, language, and music he could blend. From the high quality of his language and music one accepts him as a sophisticated poet and musician. His dramatic complex in three's must therefore have been intended as sportive, not "drearily mechanical." The staging of the play, with its opportunities for visual emphasis of triples in setting and in movement, clearly demonstrates the frolicsome quality of the playwright's work. If one demeans the play, as some scholars do, by calling it a mere schoolboy exercise, one will also have to belittle many of the most fascinating experiments of Bach and Hindemith, or of Giraudoux and Ionesco.

[3] For indications of the success of this play with a modern audience, see two reviews of the performance staged by Mary Baldwin College students and faculty at the Folger Shakespeare Library 12–14 December 1969: Wendell Margrave, "Music Dramas Full of Delight," *The Evening Star* (Washington, D.C.), 13 December 1969; and Joan Reinthaler, "Medieval Drama on the Folger Stage," *The Washington Post,* same date.

[4] Young prints a prose version of the legend, II, 488–90. The Hildesheim version of the play (Young, II, 312–14), while having in common with the Fleury text fifteen stanzas, has no suitors. The standard form of the narrative merely implies their existence.

DETERMINATION OF MAJOR EPISODES

The visual arts do not follow the triple design of the play, though one may wish that the multiple effects of such modern paintings as "Nude Descending a Staircase" had been explored in the twelfth century. The marble font at Winchester Cathedral summarizes the action of the story by showing (left to right) a suitor, with a falcon in his hand; three daughters, two with bags of gold; the kneeling father, passing on the second bag of gold; and St. Nicholas bestowing the third upon the father (plate 55). Other illustrations of the story are content with an earlier moment, the first appearance of St. Nicholas at the window, the bag of gold being tossed in (plates 51–53). Still another illustration depicts the opening of the story, the three daughters and the father lamenting their poverty, with St. Nicholas nowhere to be seen (plate 54). Whether the presence of the suitor in the Winchester portrayal is an indication of influence either upon or from the playwright cannot be determined.[5]

CHARACTERIZATION

Following the order of the characters in the Winchester font, we come first to the Suitor(s). On the font he is a handsome young fellow, his hair fastidiously set, his moustache and beard dapper, his falcon held stylishly on his wrist. Clearly the eldest daughter will be well matched. In the play, the Father describes the Suitor(s) as "iuveni, venusto corpore, Et nobili" (young, of charming appearance, and noble). Whether the Suitor is interested only in the dowry the artist of the font does not reveal, and one cannot be sure that the medieval mind would be much concerned with this question. No respectable woman could or would marry without a dowry. All that the illustration and the play are saying at this point is that the way is now clear for the eldest daughter to marry, the inference being that she and the suitor had both been waiting for this happy moment, and that now she can marry her favorite suitor instead of turning prostitute to get the needed money, and thus losing the

[5] If the attachment of the play to Fleury in the twelfth century were at present more established (see above, pp. 33–34) one might find some significance in the fact of the known contacts between Winchester and Fleury from the tenth century on, including the expressed debt of the *Regularis Concordia* to monastic customs at Fleury.

suitor. The speed with which the Suitor of the play follows the appearance of the bag of gold is not evident in the Winchester font, but I do not think that his arrival is immediate. There are two stanzas, or about a minute and a half of playing time, between the arrivals of gold bags and the arrivals of the first two Suitors, and the same amount is allotted for St. Nicholas to go and get the Third Suitor.

One could either play the Suitors as rubber stamps of one another, or individualize them as much as the three Daughters. The only difficulty with the latter interpretation is that the three Suitors have identical speeches, which suggests that the playwright intended a multiple character, not three individuals. There is a gentle humor in the triple appearance even if the Suitors are played as stock romantic figures, not as farce gigolos. And this brand of humor is more appropriate to the tone of the play, which is romantic, in the vein of Marlowe's *Edward II* or Shakespeare's *As You Like It,* rather than farcical in the manner of a medieval *fabliau.*

The roles of the three Daughters are crucial to the play. They should be interpreted almost as romantically as the Suitors, but not as stock characters, not as units of a multiple character. They are not caught up in a grim story of abject poverty, nor are they Foolish Maidens. The intent of the playwright for them is something like that of Shakespeare for Rosalind and Celia, who are in equally desperate straits in the forest, yet are more charming than pitiful or lamentable. The predicament in both plays is that of women trying to make their way alone in an alien world. The women in *Twelfth Night* and the lovers in *A Midsummer Night's Dream* may provide further suggestions for interpretation of the three Daughters.

The illustrations in art make clear the social status of the Daughters. Their clothes are elegantly trimmed, they wear fillets around their heads (plates 53 and 55) or a stylish veil (plate 54). It is evident that their father has been a man of some wealth. The Suitors are fashionable fellows (plate 55), not indigent young social climbers, and the Daughters are in the proper social bracket to marry them. The young ladies are charming and bright, and even when they lament they do it prettily. They know how to curtsey and otherwise to show respect to their poor old father. When the first two leave with their Suitors, there is no suggestion that great passion will follow; but one feels that they now have their men and are going to live happily ever after.

The character of the Father is considerably defined by the same illustrations. In three of the five examples (plates 51, 52, 54) the father is reclining on a couch or propped up in bed, and is obviously in poor health as well as poor spirits. From these portraits of him comes the suggestion that he has not much longer to live. To play him this way is to satisfy those critics who feel that his future is uncertain because he kept none of St. Nicholas's gold; he will shortly be beyond the need of it. In the acting of the role, the business with the bag of gold demonstrates the father's noble sacrifice of himself to his daughters. Because each time he is the first to speak after the stage direction for tossing in the gold, we may assume either that he picks it up and presents it to a Daughter (an unlikely action), or if he remains on couch or bed that his gestures and blessing will make plain that the eldest Daughter is to have the gold as a dowry.

His noble behavior, moreover, stands a good chance of being rewarded, for after the usual exchanges between Father, Third Daughter, and Third Suitor, the play is over, except for the processional epilogue by the choir, and there is no dramatic compulsion for the Third Daughter and her Suitor then to rush off stage. The two young people remain and demonstrate that they intend to take care of the Father by taking his arms as St. Nicholas intones the beginning of the epilogue, *O Christi pietas*.[6] The

[6] The following transcription of the *O Christi pietas* is not found in modern service books but is included in a facsimile edition of a Sarum antiphonary, as edited by W. H. Frere, *Antiphonale Sarisburiense* (Cambridge, 1901) II, 361–62. The antiphon has been transcribed by my colleague and co-worker in these vineyards, Professor Gordon C. Page, through whose courtesy I reproduce it.

four characters may then lead out the choir, possibly joined at the rear of the procession by the other two couples. This kind of final movement is eminently dramatic, eliminating the need for ratiocination on the part of the audience. Most playscripts in the repertory are reticent about such matters probably because so significant a final action was memorable enough in the experience of the playwright and the actors not to need recording. Unlike the carefully specified moment at which the bags of gold are thrown in, this final action could only take place after the last speech, and so needed no prompting.

The character of St. Nicholas is identical in each of the four plays concerned with his miracles. He is a humble saint who inconspicuously rescues the unfortunate in their moment of crisis. In *The Three Daughters* he would have been content to remain in hiding, and only allows himself to be caught by the Father in order to explain that the thanks for the rescue should go only to God. He appears in all four plays in the dress of a contemporary bishop, equipped with mitre and crosier (plates 51, 55). His bearing, therefore, is episcopal and authoritative, modest but firm. He is a historical character, appointed Bishop of Myra, in Lycia, in 325. In a study of the St. Nicholas liturgy, C. W. Jones concludes that in this liturgy, as in the plays, "Nicholas of Myra is developed as the image of the ideal prelate." He was noted for his benevolent acts on behalf of those in poverty, sickness, and danger at sea, and in the middle ages he was "the most popular saint in Christendom." [7] His connection with the more modern version of Santa Claus is through his reputation for good-humored benevolence.

One may suppose that the role of St. Nicholas in *The Three Daughters* was acted genially and that he communicated to the audience his pleasure as he slyly tossed the bags of gold through the window behind the characters and then stepped back out of their view but probably not out of the audience's. Another possibility for his activity on their behalf is his notifying the Suitors and escorting them to the house. In theatrical terms this action would mean his leaving the scene at the exact place where the Suitor is waiting off stage, so that when he returns shortly thereafter with the Suitor, the audience will make a causal connection. As had been remarked above, there is about a minute and a half for such a dramatic action, however the director arranged it, and it would enhance the characterization of both parties to the scheme. When St. Nicholas returns with the first two Suitors, he watches from the doorway to be sure that the

[7] C. W. Jones, *The Saint Nicholas Liturgy*, pp. 1–4, 116.

matches are made. When he brings in the Third Suitor he remains and allows himself to be caught onstage and to be venerated by the Father.

While St. Nicholas has no reputation elsewhere as a matchmaker, such activity would be very much in keeping with his other benevolences. In any event, the actor of the St. Nicholas role must have made it plain to the audience that he enjoyed his work as a rather busy *deus ex machina.*

MOVEMENT AND GESTURE

While only two areas are required for *The Three Daughters,* and technically only one location (*sedes*) — in and outside the room — the chief acting areas are three: the couch or bed, the window, and the exterior. One frequently illustrated pattern of blocking for the first episode of the play is to place the bed, the Father propped up in it, a little left or right of center, with a threadbare cloth pulled up over his loins and his torso bare (plates 51, 52). He has had to sell the shirt off his back, and is therefore not exaggerating when in his first lines he says that he has lost everything. The three Daughters are across the room from the Father, and make their lament as they move to stand near him, one at the foot of the bed and two at the upstage side, in postures of despair. Plates 51 through 54 are explicit as to the postures and gestures.

Shortly to be framed in the small window at the side is St. Nicholas. After the laments of the Father and Daughters, St. Nicholas tosses the first bag of gold to the floor behind the First Daughter. She turns, picks it up, and gives it to her father, who returns it to her joyfully. As soon as St. Nicholas sees these actions completed, he withdraws from the window and goes to get the First Suitor, who arrives just in time for his first speech. The Father bestows the purse and his blessing on the happy couple, there are embraces all around, and the first couple leaves. The Second and Third Daughters wave rapturously until it strikes them that they are now right back where they and the play started. This modulation from rapture to despair, repeated by the Third Daughter when the Second leaves with *her* Suitor, is basic to the interpretation of the form of the dramatic narrative, and is both touching and amusing. After this business, the next Daughter moves to the foot of the bed, in order to maintain the screen against the Father's view of the window.

The Father need not leave his bed until after the third bag of gold has been thrown out on the floor, and the Third Daughter has moved to pick it up. St. Nicholas, admiring his work, remains visible at the window, and at this moment the Father sees him, there being no longer a daughter in position to screen him. The Father sings to St. Nicholas, "Siste gradum, quisque es, Domine," rises with the aid of the Third Daughter, and by "Me beatum!" has moved into position to fall at the Saint's feet. The Father rises from his kneeling position after St. Nicholas' first speech, and goes in the opposite direction ("adversus") toward the Daughter, his back to St. Nicholas. The Saint then slips out to fetch the Third Suitor, and returns with him at the conclusion of the Daughter's reply to the Father, "Care pater." This blocking for St. Nicholas and the Suitor allows exactly the same amount of time for the business of getting the Third Suitor as for the First and Second, during the exchange between Father and Daughter. The remainder of the blocking has been described in discussion of the characterizations of the Suitors and the Father, above.

If the business with St. Nicholas and the Suitors may be regarded as a legitimate expansion of the action, the play would be rather consistently lively. The opening of the play tends to be slow, but with three daughters to share in the first speech, and four characters to give the audience the necessary exposition of the situation, those items are efficiently handled by the playwright and could also have been by the actors.

11. The Three Clerks

57 The Innkeeper and the Three Clerks (top) and the
Murder of the Clerks (bottom). Stained glass window,
St. Severus Chapel, Cathedral of Notre Dame, Rouen,
thirteenth century. Caisse Nationale des Monuments
Historiques.

58 The Innkeeper Murdering the Three Clerks (left), St. Nicholas Restoring the
    Clerks (center), the Penitent Innkeeper and His Wife (right). Font, Zedelghem
    Church, second half of twelfth century.

59 The Restoration of the Clerks. "Queen Mary's Psalter," beginning of fourteenth
    century. London, British Museum, MS Royal 2 B. VII, fol. 317ᵛ. Courtesy of the
    Trustees of the British Museum.

The Three Clerks
Tres Clerici

TONE AND QUALITY

IN CONTRAST to *The Three Daughters, The Three Clerks* is a medieval shocker, in which three innocent students are murdered by an innkeeper and his wife. The interest in the play is hardly romantic or witty, as in *The Three Daughters*. This is the story of a murder perhaps more horrible than the slaughter of the Innocents, because there are only three clerks, who are therefore more individualized than a larger group of children in an equally short play can be. The murder of the students, moreover, is plotted by the killers themselves, not by a Herod whose orders are executed by others, and the killers' motive is sordid and mercenary. The story is a fairy-tale on the order of *Little Red Riding Hood*, resembling a bad dream that eventually turns out happily for all but the evildoers.

The question of repetition of melodic content is relevant also to this play. It is short, not more than eleven minutes in the playing, during which time the melody for all but the final stanza is repeated seventeen times, with slight variations. This is nothing like the amount of melodic repetition encountered in the *Lazarus* and in *The Three Daughters,* but the reduction is fortunate, the narrative content and the theme of *The Three Clerks* being comparatively slight.

While the play lacks depth and complication, the dramatic narrative moves rapidly in literate dialogue to a sufficiently sophisticated melody, and is probably worth the time it takes to produce. We may reasonably assume that the original audience was in an abbey like that of Fleury, and thus was largely composed of students, goliardic or indigenous. Such an audience had a special, parochial interest in St. Nicholas as the patron saint of students. The Three Clerks introduce themselves as goliards, wandering scholars, and the student audience knew immediately that it was seeing a play about their own kind, a modern story rather than a dramatized story from the Bible. The play in some ways resembles a documentary, which makes it unique in this repertory. The lack of pictorial evidence for the legend before the twelfth century, combined with its late appearance in literary and dramatic forms, reinforces our sense that the play is not indebted to traditional narrative. Like a broadside ballad, the story may have been based on actual incidents between innkeepers and itinerant goliards; it was certainly presented from the goliards' point of view, if not in fact composed by a clerk.

Any play which is chiefly a satire on contemporary life suffers by comparison with those which, while fully aware of contemporary problems and issues, customarily take their narrative material from another time. Shakespeare is superior to Jonson in this respect, as Shakespeare and the Greeks are to Shaw, Molière, and other satirists. One of the great virtues of most of the plays in the medieval repertory is that their narratives were seasoned and deepened by generations of telling and pondering and believing, before they were ready to be fully dramatized. Perhaps this is why *The Three Clerks* is only a mediocre play.

DETERMINATION OF MAJOR EPISODES

The visual arts identify three major episodes in the story: the students asking the innkeeper for lodging (plate 57, upper section); the murder of the students (plates 57, lower section, and 58); and the rescue by St. Nicholas (plates 58, 59). The only episode in the play not covered by the pictorial artists is the dialogue between St. Nicholas and the innkeepers, but this lack is compensated, pictorially, by the fact that the innkeepers are shown as onlookers at the restoration of the students by St. Nicholas.

The playwright organized his materials differently because he obviously could not show the butchering and the piecemeal restoration scenes. While the stage directions are laconic, one infers that the following actions take place in the course of the play:

The three students discuss their problem of lodging, in front of the door to the Inn (ll. 1–12).[1] The Innkeeper appears at the door in response to their ringing the bell, and the Students ask for lodging. He bluntly refuses them (ll. 13–20). The students move into the Inn and grossly flatter the Old Woman by telling her that God may give her a baby if she helps them. She persuades her husband to give the Students lodging, and the Innkeeper shows them to their cubicle off stage (ll. 21–32). The Innkeeper proposes stealing the Students' wallets. His wife, now aware that she has been cozened, proposes murdering them as well. The evil pair goes offstage to rob and kill (ll. 33–44). Interrupting the sounds

[1] Young, II, 330.

of butchering, St. Nicholas rings the doorbell, and is admitted because the Innkeeper and his wife agree he is worthy—and perhaps wealthy. The Innkeeper offers to bring food. St. Nicholas sits at table and asks for fresh meat, which the Innkeeper says he does not have (ll. 45–60). St. Nicholas calls them liars, and accuses them of murder. They confess their crime and ask for pardon. He tells them to be heartily contrite, and offers to God a prayer for the Students' restoration to life (ll. 61–76).

There are only three explicit stage directions for the actions described above; these indicate that the Students sleep, that St. Nicholas sits at the dining table, and that he prays. All the rest must be read between the lines of the dialogue with a sense of what would be dramatically viable on a medieval stage. The playscript leaves the ending of the play up in the air, merely stating that after St. Nicholas's prayer the choir sings *Te Deum Laudamus.* Might not this conclusion be used to display the restored Students by having each enter singing a melodic phrase of the *Te Deum?* St. Nicholas as cantor would be expected to intone the first phrase, "Te Deum laudamus," and then:

First Student (entering): Te Dominum confitemur.

(We acknowledge Thee to be the Lord.)

Second Student (entering): Te aeternum patrem,

(Thee, Father everlasting,)

Third Student (entering): Omnis terra veneratur!

(All the earth doth worship.)

Choir and Students: Tibi omnes angeli, tibi caeli . . .

(To Thee all angels, to Thee the heavens . . .)

The Students fall in behind St. Nicholas and are followed by the Innkeeper and the Old Wife, the entire company singing the remainder of the recessional as they leave.

The Hildesheim version of the play, related to the Fleury but less adroit, brings in an angel after the play is over to announce that the Students are alive and well again. The Einsiedeln version has St. Nicholas inexplicably restore the Students in his final speech, with no antiphon or hymn thereafter.

CHARACTERIZATION

The Three Students are stock goliard characters, wandering scholars, and no doubt were acted and recognizable as such to the original academic audience. Young remarks that "the Fleury writer, indeed, creates a certain literary tone of his own through introducing into a Christian play the pagan suggestiveness of such lines as the following (5–6): 'Iam sol equos tenet in litore,/ quos ad praesens merget sub aequore' " (Now the sun reins in his steeds at the shoreline,/ And presently will plunge them into the sea).[2] The tone the playwright was creating is not so much his own as the Students'; it characterizes them as very young intellectuals, who must talk in such hyperbole rather than merely state that the sun is setting. This intellectuality is a key to interpretation of the Students' roles.

The old Innkeeper—he is called "Senex" in the manuscript—is surely being satirized by the playwright. The Students' polite request for lodging is met by his surly refusal, in blunt words that contrast with the poly-syllabics of the students:

> Nam non dabo vobis hospitium,
> Nam nec mea in hoc utilitas,
> Nec est ad hoc nunc opportunitas.
> (So I won't give you any hospitality;
> It wouldn't do me any good;
> I'd get nothing out of it.)

We are not sure whether he is grouchy because he is tired, or the reverse. In any event, he is like the occasional modern shopkeeper who hates to be bothered with customers. In the Fleury version and in the Einsiedeln the Innkeeper's chief trouble is that he is henpecked.

The Old Woman ("Vetulam") is more vigorous than her husband, and while she persuades him to take the Students in, she soon has in mind their wallets rather than their welfare. She must know that the Students' talk of her bearing a son is flattery or jest. Perhaps this motivates her response to the Innkeeper's suggestion that they rob the sleeping Students: she wants to murder them too. Some illustrations show her holding the basket or bowl for the choice cuts while the Innkeeper slashes away. On the Zedelghem font are two illustrations of her, urging him on to the kill like a Lady Macbeth (plate 58).

St. Nicholas is rather less jovial than in *The Three Daughters,* but his same quiet way is in evidence in this play also. Sherlock Holmes could have done no better in the dialogue about the fresh meat.

[2] Young, II, 334.

12. The Image of St. Nicholas

60 The Jew Entrusting His Treasure Chest to the Image of St. Nicholas. Stained glass window, St. Severus Chapel, Cathedral of Notre Dame, Rouen, thirteenth century. Caisse Nationale des Monuments Historiques.

61 The Sleeping Jew and the Robbers (bottom left), the Jew about to Beat the Image of St. Nicholas (bottom right), St. Nicholas Confronting the Robbers (top right). Ceiling fresco, St. Maria-Lyskirchen, Cologne, ca. 1270. Courtesy of the Rector, St. Maria-Lyskirchen.

The Image of Saint Nicholas
Iconia Sancti Nicolai

TONE AND QUALITY

WORKING with somewhat more seasoned material, extra-Biblical though it is, the playwright of *The Image of St. Nicholas* created a powerful music-drama for an all-male cast. Even without hearing its music or seeing it performed, scholars and editors have praised the play highly, chiefly for what Young calls the "psychological disclosures" of the protagonist and the Robbers. Because the music of the Fleury version has not been accessible, and has not been a practical criterion in their judgments, scholarly editors have preferred Hilarius's nonmusical version of the play, which also has the advantage of an identifiable author. When the Fleury version is judged as a music-drama, it comes off very far ahead, if only because Hilarius lacks the musical dimension. One cannot even justly compare the two, for the variety of the latter's verse suggests that the missing score for it must have been as inventive as that of the Fleury playwright, yet we cannot hear it as we can the Fleury. The effort is like attempting to judge a songwriter's verses without their music, or compare the verse of Campion with that of Donne.

The Image of St. Nicholas in its Fleury version is a finely wrought opera. For example, when the Jew comes home and finds his treasure stolen, his first word is "Vah!" while in the Hilarius version Barbarus' reaction is "Gravis sors et dura!" Hilarius's verse is more literary, but the audience for the Fleury version heard the Jew sing:

Vah!

This is an entirely different medium of dramatic expression.

In this play there is no problem of a melody being repeated scores of times. The musical pattern is rich, with ten mensuralized melodies for the thirty minutes of playing time. True, the first melodic item is repeated ten times, the second eight with some variation, and the later St. Nicholas item seven times. The remaining items are very little repeated, some not at all. There is even a successful attempt on the part of the playwright, as in *The Son of Getron,* to characterize the Jew and each of the three Robbers by means of melodies.[1] Rather curiously, St. Nicholas's only melody in this play is a variant of the first section of the chief melody of *The Three Daughters,* and can hardly represent the playwright's intention to individualize. The most brilliant item of the play is the Jew's lament for his lost treasure, an extended virtuoso composition both musically and dramatically. Because it is written in hexameters rather than in stanza form it is not subject to melodic repetition and is easily used by the actor for dynamic expression.

Why is it that two of the three plays in the repertory that have all-male casts (*The Image, The Pilgrim,* and *The Conversion of St. Paul*) also have more human drive, and are more humanistic and even psychological in nature, than all the others? A partial answer is that the emotional immaturity of the boy sopranos limited the amount of psychological expressiveness that the playwright could expect of them. Only with a mature cast of men could this kind of drive be given full sway. The laments of the Marys and of Rachel, on the other hand, are in a more lyrical, less psychological vein, and could have been handled satisfactorily by talented choirboys.

DETERMINATION OF MAJOR EPISODES

Several episodes of the play are illustrated in art works of the period. In the vaulted ceiling of the small south chapel of St. Maria-Lyskirchen in Cologne are three adjacent scenes: the theft (or return?) of the treasure chest while the Jew sleeps, the beating of the image of St. Nicholas by the Jew, and the penitence of the Robbers when accosted by St. Nicholas (plate 61).[2] A window in the Cathedral at Rouen shows the Jew putting his treasure chest into the care of the image (plate 60). These scenes appear to have been central to the story, and are likewise the chief scenes of the play. All that is omitted in the illustrations is the finale, in which the Jew rejoices in the return of his treasure, and urges the audience to praise

[1] For further comment on the musical resourcefulness of the playwright, see W. L. Smoldon in *New Oxford History of Music* (London and New York, 1954), II, 209.

[2] Next to these scenes, the Cologne artist has a painting of St. Nicholas after having put the dejected robbers in the stocks, by the legs. The Fleury playwright wisely discards this scene as impractical in his medium.

St. Nicholas—a sharp contrast to the preceding scene in which he vows to beat the image. The playwright cannot use the same kind of violence, his form being more immediate, and he cleverly avoids the beating while the visual arts revel in it.

CHARACTERIZATION

The cast is small, but the play is as long as any but the *Daniel* in the produceable repertory, with the happy result that all five members of the cast have time to register themselves as individuals. The Jew is of course the protagonist and dominates the play, singing nearly two-thirds of the lines. Like the Jews in the *Lazarus*, and unlike those excoriated in *The Lament of Mary*, this character is presented sympathetically in spite of his origins and his mistakes. The fact that he has long venerated an image of St. Nicholas in his house, even though he is apparently not a full-fledged Christian, was an initial mark in his favor with the medieval audience.

This background ingratiates him with us, also, because the latent theme of the play has to do with the basis of faith. The Jew has made a lot of money, and ascribes his success to the image, his rabbit's foot. But as he leaves his treasure to be guarded by the icon, not even locking the lid of the chest, he has qualms of doubt and warns the image to be careful or there will be trouble. He is not as trusting as those Christians, and has thereby made a serious, pragmatic mistake. He believes in the power of the image only as long as it helps produce and protect his money, and he is thus a philistine, lacking in spiritual values. When it fails to protect his material goods, he blames the image and the Christians who first led him to believe it was powerful. He has failed to understand what kind of power they meant. After St. Nicholas, without showing himself to the Jew, restores his treasure, the Jew recognizes that graven images are effective only if one believes in the subject of the image.

Christ is not mentioned, and there is no indication that the Jew will forwith become a Christian, as he does in the Hilarius version. The play is not a tract, and the Jew is not to be damned or even laughed at anymore or any less than Shakespeare intends us to laugh at Shylock. One may wish that the Fleury playwright had been able to find another name for this protagonist. Hilarius used Barbarus (foreigner, pagan) but the Fleury characterization would have been seriously marred by euphemizing the mercantile semitism of its protagonist.

The Three Robbers have two highly characterizing and amusing scenes.

The Third Robber is the most timorous, in the first scene and in the second. While one recognizes their similarity, in their comic aspect, to certain cartoon thugs, they have a serious aspect as the other philistines in the play. They think they can make money by stealing, which puts them almost in the same category as the Jew, but more despicable because they have not respected even the image. It takes St. Nicholas in person to put the fear of God into them, and even then two of the robbers argue that St. Nicholas's threats mean nothing, while the third is not so much afraid for his soul as for his neck. The Robbers learn nothing from their come-uppance; the Jew learns a basic truth.

St. Nicholas is the same patient, resourceful benefactor as in the other plays. He might easily have been annoyed with the Jew's attitude to his image, and unwilling to go and force the Robbers to return the treasure. A more severe man of God would have chosen to let the Jew suffer for his philistinism. For St. Nicholas, in this play as in the *The Three Clerks,* the proper consequence of crime is penitence, not punishment.

MOVEMENT AND GESTURE

The structure of the action in this play is strong. The Jew orders the image to watch over his treasure chest, and goes away. The Robbers come from their hide-out and steal the money. The Jew returns and laments the loss and his confidence in the image. St. Nicholas goes to the Robbers' hide-out, catches them in the act of dividing the loot, and threatens to turn them in if they do not make restitution immediately. After he leaves they debate the question and decide to return the pelf. The Jew, exhausted by his fury, puts off beating the image until the next day, and apparently falls asleep—or else faints. While he is unconscious the Robbers replace the loot. The Jew thereafter awakens, sees the treasure, and turns to the audience for the "Gaudeamus" item, while the Robbers lurk on the street (*platea*). St. Nicholas appears in the *platea,* between the two houses, to lead the choir in the introit, *Statuit ei Dominus,* and in the procession of all the characters.

These last movements are conjectural, there being no stage direction to support them, and are only possible if there is a valid dramatic point in the saint's reappearance, juxtaposed to his image. In the Hilarius version, when Barbarus prays to the image to forgive him for his rage against it, St. Nicholas appears in person and converts him to Christianity, so there could have been no theological difficulty with doubling the saint and his image. Pictorial representations of the scenes containing the image (plates 60, 61) do not suggest that the image is large enough to have permitted a theatrical device whereby the image came alive and stepped down from its niche, although the dimensions of the Rouen image are not entirely clear.

In the Fleury play there is every reason rather to have the displaced image, as in plate 61, restored to its niche by the Jew after the second or third "Gaudeamus" refrain. He had torn it out of its niche at some point (possibly at line 104) of his raging speech about the loss of his wealth. This hypothesis is encouraged by the fact that one of the Cologne illustrations (plate 61) shows the Jew beating the image that is leaning against the empty chest. This conjectured restoration of the image would be valid even if in the first episode the Jew had taken it down and placed it against the chest as a guard, as the other Cologne scene shows. It is remarkable, however, that the Robbers make no reference to the image in their business with the chest, and they surely would have been impeded in their work if the icon had been leaning against the chest. Further, the Rouen window (plate 60) shows the Jew, apparently at the end of the first episode, taking his leave of the icon in its niche, rather than raging at it or rejoicing at the finale, unless I misinterpret his gesture.

13. The Son of Getron

62 Three Episodes in the Story of Adeodatus, the Son of Getron. Lintel, right portal, west façade, St. Salvatore Church, Lucca, twelfth century. Photo Alinari.

63 Three Episodes in the Story of Adeodatus, the Son of Getron. Relief, architrave, south portal, Barga Cathedral, second half of twelfth century. Photo Alinari.

64 St. Nicholas Rescuing the Son of Getron from King Marmorinus. Chasuble of St.
Blasien, from Kloster St. Blasien. Österreichisches Museum für angewandte Kunst, acc.
no. 9125. Photo Hans Mayr.

The Son of Getron

Filius Getronis

TONE AND QUALITY

The Son of Getron has much to recommend it to a modern audience. It is as long as *The Image of St. Nicholas,* and it can have as much courtly pomp, splendor and military activity as the *Daniel* or the *Herod,* which follows in the "Fleury Playbook." The play is, moreover, blessed with seven distinct melodies, six of them the unique possession of persons who sing them and are thus characterized by them. Three of these characters are also individualized by their words and actions. About a third of the play is taken up with the extended laments and prayers of Getron's wife Euphrosina and the Consolers; while these are more lyric than dramatic, there is enough violent and miraculous action before and after that aria section to keep the play alive, and a goodly amount of travel between three *sedes.*

The only apparent objection to the play is its extravagant demand for eating and drinking. In successsive scenes the King is served a banquet and Euphrosina has a collation for the schoolboys and paupers of the town. The action shifts to another locality too soon for the food to be even partially consumed. But in the convention of the simultaneous *sedes,* the eating and drinking may continue after the shift, and so be entirely practical. In fact, because the eating scenes are adjacent, we have the double spectacle of Euphrosina's collation beginning, then the King ordering and eating his banquet, while the monastic collation continues. Neither location is required again in the play, so that the King and his officers may take their time, as may the Clerks and the Paupers, the latter groups needing only to be ready to move out to the *platea* for the celebration of the return of the kidnapped boy. What, therefore, seems at first glance extravagant and clumsy is actually an intentional part of the design of the play, and allows a direct contrast between the pagan excesses of the King and the pious works of Euphrosina.

Another objection levelled at the construction of the play is that, at one point, between one speech and the next, a full year must be assumed to have passed. No stage direction explains how this passage of time is to be made clear to the audience, because it could not be explained. Much later in the play the homesick Boy tells the King that it has been a full year since he was kidnapped. This is the only clue we have as to the break between the end of Euphrosina's prayer to St. Nicholas and Getron's suggestion that she pray to God now that the feast of St. Nicholas is imminent.[1] There would have been no problem if the Boy had not (at line 145) blurted out that the full year had passed, but since he does not mention this until long after the alleged break (between lines 84 and 85), I cannot see that anyone in the audience would have been confused. Literary analysts are bothered because they can turn back the pages, but in the continuous movement of the drama there is no turning back and little chance that a length of time will be missed if there is no break taken at line 85. Fortunately for dramatic art, the medieval producer had no curtain to lower to indicate the passage of time; he and the audience simply let it pass, as modern audiences have recently relearned to do. On two counts, then, the play has been arraigned for what turn out to be examples of sophisticated dramaturgy. As often with the plays of this repertory, imagined difficulties in the scripts disappear when the plays are produced.

DETERMINATION OF MAJOR EPISODES

In their own kind of simultaneous staging, some of the art works of the period give a summary of the high points of the play, including the same sense of simultaneous activity on the stage. So similar are the lintels on this subject from the Salvatore Church at Lucca and the cathedral at Barga (plates 62, 63) that one may surmise that either artist borrowed from the other or that both saw the play in some lost version similar to the Fleury. These sculptures seem to portray St. Nicholas rescuing the Boy from King Marmorinus, Euphrosina's welcome of the Boy and St. Nicholas at the gates of Excoranda, and a collation scene at the house of Getron. The Lucca version uniquely includes the schoolboys. The chasuble of St. Blasien (plate 64) simply shows the rescue from Marmorinus. Students of the play can no more afford to overlook these illustrations than can art historians afford to overlook the play. The legend as recorded by Mombritius is a much more sprawling narrative than either the illustrations or the play, both of which concentrate the story in their compositions and

[1] Young points out this difficulty as Sepet had done before him, but has no solution for it (II, 360).

reveal its significance. In like manner, the chasuble of St. Blasien (plate 64) emphasizes the climax of the narrative.

CHARACTERIZATION

No other play of the repertory gives as much attention to characterizing by melodic motif. The *Herod* does some of this, and so does the *Image,* but neither achieves such distinctions as have been remarked above: six of the seven melodies of *The Son of Getron* are the unique property of single characters. The Officers possess Melody A, King Marmorinus B, and the Boy, Adeodatus, C; Melody D is shared by Euphrosina, her Consolers, and Adeodatus; Getron has E; the Citizen(s) F; and Euphrosina another of her own, G. Adeodatus once borrows Euphrosina's Melody D,[2] and this use, only for lines 133–36, has a curiously umbilical effect. It may have been so planned by the playwright; had anyone else used it, one would have been suspicious of the playwright's intelligence.

Scholars have pointed out that the principal characters are reminiscent of leading characters in the *Herod* and *The Slaughter of the Innocents.* King Marmorinus is a blustering tyrant, out to destroy the Christians, while Euphrosina in her lament for her son is closely akin to Rachel, though her aria of lament, poignant enough, is less brilliant and more a set piece than the exquisite Rachel's. But perhaps this seems a valid comparison only because no one in modern times has actually heard Euphrosina's lament.

The Boy—Adeodatus, the son of Getron and Euphrosina—is the best juvenile role in any of the plays. He is much younger than the Three Clerks, as the visual portrayals testify (plates 62–64), and in fact he is the only real boy in any of the plays. He has the pivotal as well as title role in this play; no one else has scenes in all four locations of the play. He is, moreover, no poor little lost child in the Victorian tradition. He is homesick and admits it, is obviously miserable in the service of the King, but is not afraid to tell the King in hissing sibillants how deceitful and evil his majesty's pagan god Apollo is, how stupid, deaf, dumb, and blind ("mendax et malus est; stultus, caecus, surdus, et mutus est").

[2] This is like one playwright borrowing another's melody. Melody C appears also in *The Three Daughters* as the main melody, and in *The Image of St. Nicholas* (lines 112–35). On the premise that even a medieval artist is more likely to borrow from himself than from another, particularly when a series of plays on the same subject is involved, one could make something of a case that the three plays were composed by the same playwright. The other possibility is that Melody C is a folk tune and could thus be used by any artist without infringing another's right to it. This melody, however, seems rather consciously artistic in the medieval manner.

The Officers of the King are the same sort of people who surround Herod. If enough good voices were available there were three of them, according to the stage directions. While others have considered them courtiers in both plays, it was remarked in discussion of the *Herod* that a medieval military dictator would be more likely to surround himself with officers or knights than with courtiers. This point is underscored by the fact that one of the King's "Ministri" leads the attack of the common soldiers on the church of St. Nicholas, according to a stage direction for that pantomime scene. Incidentally, such a scene was close to the experience of a monastic audience: monasteries throughout the Middle Ages were frequently under threat of military attack.

The role of Getron is somewhat subservient to that of Euphrosina, mainly because he would lament less touchingly than she. He shows his strength, however, in his tender comfort and advice to her when she despairs of seeing their son again. In the legend both she and her husband built the church to the honor of St. Nicholas because he had granted their prayers for a son, but in the play itself, it is only she who is benefactress to the scholars and paupers.[3] One does not feel, however, that she dominates her husband like her lower-class counterpart, the Old Woman in *The Three Clerks.*

The Three Consolers were thought by Young, with no support from Mombritius' account or from the text of the play, to be Euphrosina's servants, "her women." [4] I prefer to think of them as her neighbors and friends, though the serving of the collation to the schoolboys and paupers would require some help from her servants. Since this action comes later in the play, the Consolers may then have doubled as servants, much as the Mothers and Consolers were doubled in the Greenberg production of *The Slaughter of the Innocents* and the *Herod.*

There is other doubling to be done. Some of the choir are presumably the Paupers at the collation, and they must also sing the epilogue, *Copiosae karitatis.*[5] The Schoolboys at the collation are no doubt choirboys of the church in which the play was performed, and they too in a sense double most appropriately at the collation, since, as we shall see later in considering the staging of the play, the Church of St. Nicholas was probably located in the choir and sanctuary area.

St. Nicholas has no lines in this play, but he is the man of the hour, in his usual efficient and modest way, when it comes to rescuing Adeodatus from the clutches of the King. The latter never knew what was happening

---

[3] Young, II, 492, reproduces the legend from Mombritius.   [4] Young, II, 357.

[5] See below, p. 345, for a modern transcription.

until the Boy had disappeared, whisked off by St. Nicholas. On the authority of the Barga architrave (plate 63), as I interpret it and plate 64, St. Nicholas stays with Adeodatus all the way back to Excoranda, watches from one side the general rejoicing, and perhaps bows when his name is extolled in the mensuralized choral antiphon at the end of the play.

MOVEMENT AND GESTURE

Under this heading may be considered a supposedly difficult piece of business, the transporting of Adeodatus by St. Nicholas from the King's court to the gates of Excoranda. The medieval producer was not above a mechanical engineering solution to such problems, as we have seen in connection with the star in the *Herod,* and shall see in the descent of the dove in *The Annunciation.* Young himself wondered if "the stage properties included some sort of mechanical aid to realism" in the present play.[6] To judge, however, from the gesture and movement with which St. Nicholas, in three illustrations (plates 62–64), snatches the Boy by the hair, no mechanical aid was needed, nor would it be appropriate to the style of staging this play. If the Boy was light enough to be so lifted—the younger he was the more appealing he would have been—and if his hair was long enough, St. Nicholas had only to lift him and the King's goblet inches above the ground and move across to the location of the gates to Excoranda. Since there is no intervening action, St. Nicholas could not have conveniently disappeared with the dangling Boy and appeared at the gates with him again suspended.

As a matter of fact, the stage direction for this movement is merely that St. Nicholas seize the Boy and place him, still held, before the gates ("apprehendat, apprehensumque ante fores componat"). Mombritius recounts the action thus: seizing the child by the top-knot, he carries him and returns him to his mother ("appraehendidit infantem per verticem capilli capitis sui, et reportavit et reddidit illum matri suae"). Neither Mombritius nor the visual artists nor the stage direction suggests anything more than lifting him slightly by the top-knot. Any audience that had accepted the convention of the King's court and the house of Getron being miles apart, instead of twenty feet, would have had no difficulty in understanding that St. Nicholas was performing another miracle, and a rather delightful one, in dangling the Boy across to Excoranda. The same action is, moreover, brought off satisfactorily, though more comically, when the Angel brings Habakkuk to the lions' den in the *Daniel.*

[6] Young, II, 360.

The attack of the King's soldiers on the Church of St. Nicholas begins as soon as the King gives the order, Herod-like, from his throne on the Court *sedes.* Since this attack comes after only two stanzas of singing, and the Church is then to be in the midst of a "sollempnitatem celebrandum" (a high service), with Getron, Euphrosina, the Consolers, Adeodatus, the choir, and the officiating clergy already present, the play probably opened with the mimed beginning of the service, which comes aloud after the King's order and remains alive until the Soldiers have marched to the Church and broken up the service. The extensive stage direction is clumsy about these matters, but clearly requires action to begin in the Church location at the opening of the play. The producer may have taken the matter one step further and had the choir begin to sing the antiphon, *Copiosae karitatis,* which later closes the play, as soon as the King gave his order. This familiar antiphon would have been broken up by the attack, but during the march of the Soldiers would have been heard long enough to be recognizable when repeated at the end of the play.

COSTUMES

For the King's costume, including his crown, the description above of Herod's outfit, in the play of that title, is apposite. The Officers' regalia is discussed in the same place. The Soldiers resemble those in the *Herod, The Visit to the Sepulcher,* and *The Conversion of St. Paul.*

Getron and Euphrosina are wealthy people, not of the nobility but roughly on a class level with the Father in *The Three Daughters* before he lost his fortune, or Simon in *Lazarus.* All that would distinguish their costumes from those of more common people, like the Marys and the Disciples, is the amount of trimming and ornamentation. Pictorial representations of Euphrosina (plates 62, 63) show her as hardly distinguishable from a Mary, even to the headdress. The Consolers are similar in appearance.

The Boy is bare-headed, of course, and barefoot, and wears a belted, sleeveless, but only knee-length tunic. The choir members doubling as Paupers would merely put ragged blankets over their vestments.

PROPERTIES AND FURNISHINGS

The most interesting property in the play is King Marmorinus's covered goblet, which the Boy clutches and carries back to Excoranda. This becomes a nice touch in the play, as it was in the legend and its depictions in art. Adeodatus has in effect kidnapped the goblet, which becomes a symbol of poetic justice. It is a large, regally ornamented goblet, as the illustrations show (plates 48, 62–64), and has a cover, perhaps to distinguish it from the ecclesiastical chalices. It has a knob on top like a pyx. See also plate 7.

The stage direction at the head of the play describes the throne of King Marmorinus as elevated. Such a level added vertically to the interest of the scene, and probably means that there were two steps up to the throne seat, in addition to whatever platforming was used for the court area. For the elevated throne see, for example, plates 36 and 67.

The remainder of the Court *sedes* was devoted to a covered table and an upstage bench for the banquet scene. The arrangements for the latter scene may be deduced from plates 24, 48, 64, and 66. Additional details of the table and its contents may be derived from the Hildesheim portrayal of a sumptuous repast at the Emmaus inn (plate 24). The illustrations of the table-setting for Marmorinus' banquet (plates 62 and 63, but not 64) show individual bowls for each participant.

The meal prepared by Euphrosina for the Schoolboys and Paupers is rather less sumptuous; the stage direction mentions no more than bread and wine for all, and no bowls. Young's translation of "mensa," in conjunction with the stage direction for bread and wine, as a "collation" is a happy intuition. Merely bread and wine, served buffet-style as collations are, would have been adequate for that occasion, and would have contrasted nicely with the King's banquet. There would, in any event, hardly have been time to put out more than bread and wine, the latter in small, plain chalices.

For the attack on the Church the four or five Soldiers would have needed swords, similar to the broadswords used by their kind in other plays of the repertory. Properties and furnishings for the Church were automatically present if the chancel area was used for these scenes. St. Nicholas would have had to forego his crosier in this play (as in plate 64) in order to be free to carry the Boy by the hair, unless the actor was strong enough to lift Adeodatus with one hand.

STAGING AND THE DEFINITION OF ACTING AREAS

There is a total of nine scenes in the play, including those with mimed action but without dialogue. These nine scenes are in four locations: the

Court, scenes 1, 3, and 6; the Church, 2 and 4; [7] the house of Getron, 5 and 8; before the gates, 7 and 9. The balance of scenes, both as to their alternation and as to their quantity and length, is artistically managed by the playwright.

For a variety of reasons, it seems likely that the court scenes were on the nave edge of the north (stage right) transept, the house scenes in a similar position in the south transept, and that the church scenes were played at and beyond the center opening of the choir. The advantage of this arrangement is that the real chancel can be used as if it were—the playscripts use the word "quasi"—the Church of St. Nicholas, with the choir and clergy placed as usual. There may be a witty connotation to the stage direction that places the Church of St. Nicholas "ab orientali parte civitatis Excorande" (in the eastern part of the town of Excoranda), the surmised location of the church in relation to the house and the town gates being thus easterly, as was the Fleury chancel. Another stage direction which may bear on the location of the chancel at Fleury is the otherwise curious entrance of the Consolers, who, at their entrance to the church scene, "exeant et dicant" (go out of [the cloister] and sing). How else but from the cloister door could the actors "exeant" and still be on stage? The door to the cloister in a typical monastic church is very far up the nave, at no great distance from the crossing.[8]

[7] This assumes no break in scene between lines 84 and 85.
[8] See Conant, pp. 20–21.

14. The Play of Daniel

65 Daniel in the Lions' Den, with Habakkuk and the Angel (top),
and Darius (bottom). *In Danielem,* from Santo Domingo de
Siles, 1109. London, British Museum, MS Add. 11695, fol. 239ʳ.
Courtesy of the Trustees of the British Museum.

66 The Feast of Belshazzar. The Gumpert Bible, before 1195. Erlangen, Universitätsbibliothek, MS 1, fol. 227ᵛ.

67 Darius. *In Danielem,* from Santo Domingo de Siles,
    1109. London, British Museum, MS Add. 11695,
    fol. 238ᵛ. Courtesy of the Trustees of the British
    Museum.

The Play of Daniel

Danielis Ludus

TONE AND QUALITY

During the twelfth century the cathedral school of Beauvais created two plays of extraordinary artistry, *The Pilgrim* and its companion piece, the *Daniel*. While the *Daniel* has the same astute sense of structure, the pattern and hence the spirit of this play are quite different from those of the intricate theme and variations of *The Pilgrim*. The form of the *Daniel* is processional, with eight choral processions implied in the script.[1] Five of these are labelled as choral; the word "conductus," which meant a musical procession, is the key word in five not otherwise very illuminating stage directions. The other three, including the first and last, are easily recognized. The eight processions were necessary as bridges between the many episodes.

The play is spectacular, full of pomp and circumstance. Like the *Herod,* it is a court play, no doubt lavishly produced at Beauvais at the Christmas season in the twelfth and thirteenth centuries, and probably attended by courtiers and prelates, schoolboys and clergy, in holiday mood. Of all medieval plays, the *Daniel* was naturally Noah Greenberg's first choice for revival with the New York Pro Musica in 1958.

A great debt is owed to Noah Greenberg for having courageously brought to the attention of the modern world a music-drama that had been neglected for 700 years, thus paving the way for the exploration and revival of the repertory of sixteen such produceable dramas. Nevertheless, one must observe that because Greenberg's production was a pioneer effort, it was hedged and protected by so many additions and modifications that the performance might be most accurately described as skillful adaptation of the original playscript. A description of these additions and modifications may serve to sort out what the original production was,

---

[1] E. Martin Browne, in his preface to Noah Greenberg, ed., *The Play of Daniel: A Thirteenth-Century Musical Drama* (New York, 1959), p. vi, counts a dozen processions, no doubt a reflection of the Pro Musica production.

and to provide a basis for judgment as to whether the adaptation is more or less satisfactory artistically than the twelfth-century original.

The largest single addition is the invented narrator's ten passages of English verse, composed by W. H. Auden in a contrived, archaic style of about the fifteenth century. These passages, which total 241 lines, are a substantial portion of the play, the original Latin and incidental French lines totalling 392 or only 62 percent of the total lines of the adaptation. One may reasonably object to this addition on two aesthetic grounds. While Auden's association with the production helped to attract the initial audiences, his additions gravely distort the proportions of the play, and too frequently disrupt the genuinely dramatic experience of the play with spoken intrusions by the Narrator, a breaking of the spell evoked by the Beauvais dialogue, as sung to its haunting melodies. On this latter point the stage director of the Pro Musica production, Nikos Psacharopoulos, at-temps a justification: "The problem posed for modern audiences by the Latin text is actually a minor one: Auden's narrative is sufficient to provide a clear exposition of the action. In addition, the Narrator has a further unifying function: his rendering of the narrative should create the world of the play, dramatize the incidents, and build the suspense." [2]

One wonders if the sense of insecurity which Greenberg and his produc-tion group admittedly felt about producing a twelfth-century play in Latin did not lead them into a kind of condescension to the play; Mr. Psacharop-oulos' claim for Auden's narratives leaves very little for the original play to do as a play. When Greenberg was preparing his production script for *The Play of Herod* several years later, he pondered the advisability of a Narrator for it, gathered critical opinions from those who had seen his *Daniel,* and cited his earlier fear that the modern audience would, un-assisted, reject these plays because it did not understand the Latin. His decision was to do the *Herod* without narrative explanations.[3]

The other large addition to the original playscript is the quantity of instrumental items, either alone or as an accompaniment. Unaccompanied singing of the roles of the play, as recorded in the Beauvais script, amounts to 383 bars in Rembert Weakland's modern transcription. This quantity is not much greater than the bars of the purely instrumental numbers added in the Pro Musica production, which for the overture are 249, and build to a total of 310. Greenberg, in commenting on the extent of such items in his production, cites the stage direction for the kithara players

[2] Greenberg, *Daniel,* pp. 112–13.
[3] The 1969 Pro Musica production, however, did add just such a narration, written by Archibald MacLeish.

and the dialogued commands for drums, harp players, and "the sonorous tones of strings," this last being in my opinion not necessarily other than another reference to harps. He argues that "on the basis of purely internal evidence—leaving aside our present knowledge of medieval performance practice—one can conclude that the Beauvais performances included the wide variety of instruments in use at the time." [4] The internal evidence positively supports only the use of drums, kitharas, and harps. That these instruments, and possibly others, were sounded in four-fifths of the score seems most unlikely, despite Greenberg's reference to "medieval performance practice." One would estimate that one-fifth would be nearer the maximum, even in as processional and courtly a play as the *Daniel*.

The Pro Musica adaptation also departs from the original script in the invention of Belshazzar's Prince, a role originally handled by the Satraps, and in another, rather damaging instance: the shifting of the Queen's *conductus* from the choir to the Queen and her (invented) attendants. This requires the Queen to brag of herself as "prudens, styrpe cluens, dives cum potentia; in vestitu deaurato" (prudent, of noble birth, rich and powerful, in golden dress). These lines come much more naturally to the choir of Satraps, and the Queen has appropriate opening lines shortly thereafter in her mannerly address to Belshazzar, beginning "Rex, in aeternum vive!" as the Beauvais manuscript has it. Furthermore, the last lines of the Queen's *conductus* are totally inappropriate for either the Queen or her attendants, for these lines prophesy that the Queen "will introduce a strange prophet through whose interpretation the King will have his ruin foretold." Neither the Queen nor her attendants would prophesy what she will indeed say as soon as she reaches Belshazzar. These lines are clearly more appropriate to the chorus of Satraps. Greenberg's invention of Belshazzar's Prince, and the transfer of the singing of the *conductus* to the Queen and her attendants, appear to have had the purposes of allowing responsorial singing and giving individual singers more opportunities.[5] The musical effect is heightened, but theatrical reality is diminished.

DETERMINATION OF MAJOR EPISODES

An analysis of the episodic pattern of the original play reveals several important theatrical matters. First of all, there are in my analysis some nine-

---

[4] Greenberg, *Daniel,* p. ix.   [5] Greenberg, *Daniel,* p. x.

teen episodes, of which thirteen take place in the palace, three at Daniel's house (one of these simultaneously with a palace episode), and four in the lions' den. This is of course an extraordinary number of episodes, though they require no more than the three locations or *sedes,* that are found in many plays of the repertory. Five of these scenes contain or are introduced by a choral *conductus,* as indicated by the Beauvais script, and the play itself opens with a choral *conductus,* which, although it is not so identified by the Beauvais scribe, seems obvious enough from the first stage direction, "Dum venerit Rex Balthasar, Principes sui cantabunt ante eum hanc prosam" (Now let King Belshazzar enter, his Princes preceding him and singing this song). There is likewise a choral *conductus,* of considerable length, on the first entrance of Darius and his attacking Persians: "venientque ante eum Cythariste et Principes sui psallentes haec" (And let there come before him the kithara players and his Princes singing this).[6] The play concludes with the *Te Deum,* which in many plays is an obligatory recessional, down the nave.

In addition to the eight choral processions, six or eight instrumental pieces were possibly used to bridge from one episode to another, to shift one location or action to another. These would have been considerably shorter than the choral *conductus,* and probably not in that musical form. They would have occurred, if at all, in the last fourth of the play, after the conducted entrances of the potentates and Daniel had been accomplished.

The processions have been discussed here because they serve to define the major episodes. Ten of these episodes are illustrated in the Greenberg edition from illuminated Bibles of the period, now in the Bibliothèque Nationale, and need not be repeated in the present study. Greenberg's illustration of the feast of Belshazzar is somewhat misleading, however; it is a circular composition which does not show the handwriting on the wall, as does plate 66 of the present study.[7] The "Mene, Tekel, Pheres" in plate 66 is between the cast and the audience, where theatrically it should be. Had Mr. Psacharopoulos seen this illustration of the episode he probably would not have placed the handwriting upstage in the first production, "making the cast turn toward it and away from the audience. In the second production we felt that if the writing was placed between the audience and the performers, the latter would then be able to wheel toward the audience and create a more compelling effect."[8]

[6] Greenberg, *Daniel,* pp. 14–19.   [7] Greenberg, *Daniel,* p. 103.
[8] Greenberg, *Daniel,* p. 113.

CHARACTERIZATION

The title role of Daniel is that of the young hero.[9] He is redeemed from
the romantic by his onerous necessity to win the favor of two glittering
kings, Belshazzar and Darius. His success with the former makes his near
failure with the latter all the more agonizing, and he is saved not only by
his own brilliant behavior but also by the miraculously friendly lions and
the God who controls them. While the play claims to show "the many
things faithful Daniel underwent and suffered," and Daniel repeatedly
refers to himself as "pauper et exulans" (a pauper and an exile), he has
really prospered until the Jealous Counselors throw the legal book at him
and Darius. At this point Daniel first goes to his house and prays, then returns to ask Darius to spare his anger, and finally prays again in the lions'
den. He is spared only by the interventions of an Angel with a sword and
later another with Habakkuk. His gratitude is expressed in a vision of the
coming of Christ, to end the kind of political opportunism that the play
portrays.

Daniel is certainly not a Greek or a Renaissance hero; he is heroic only
because God makes him a prophet and an example, and because in Daniel's tribulation he does not save himself but is saved. The medieval actor
of the role understood these conditions rather better than we can, though
divine destiny was also important for the Sophoclean hero, and Hamlet
spoke of the "divinity that shapes our ends." The play is not a tragedy, but
rather a celebration of the Christmas season, and Daniel is not a tragic
hero but a humble instrument of the Most High, as Belshazzar's father
had realized earlier.

The roles of Belshazzar and Darius could not have been doubled,
even with sufficient change of costume, because Darius's procession begins
as Belshazzar is murdered on stage. The differentiation is easier, anyway,
if two singer-actors take the roles, as in the Pro Musica production.
Belshazzar makes more fatal mistakes than Darius, who is reluctant to
throw Daniel to the lions and who has not desecrated the holy vessels.
Belshazzar is murdered, Darius is not. In fact, Darius by modern standards
faces a nearly tragic dilemma: by the laws of the Medes and the Persians
he cannot excuse Daniel, although he knows that Daniel's sentence is un-

---

[9] For his age see the discussion of *The Procession of the Prophets,* p. 317.

just. His brief solution has nevertheless some humility in it, as Pilate's did not: "Deus quem colis tam fideliter / Te liberabit mirabiliter" (The God you worship so faithfully / Will liberate you miraculously).

The Queen is just a loving and noble queen, and the Courtiers are also stock figures, though the latter were easy enough for the medieval actors to imitate from life. Some of these characters are shown in plate 66. One of the Magi, unable to interpret for Belshazzar, is pictured as an old graybeard, dejected by his failure and Daniel's success.

Habakkuk, as described above in *The Procession of the Prophets,* is a prophet and also a low comedy character. He is a lame old man, stooped and hunchbacked. While in the *Daniel* he does not eat radishes or beat people with his long palm branch, he is probably still to be regarded as a comic figure. When the Angel comes to him and tells him to take to Daniel the basket of bread he was trundling out to his reapers, he says he knows nothing about this Babylon place or any lions' den there—a comic reply, I believe. His retort is followed immediately by the Angel taking him by the hair of the head—surely not a serious action—and depositing the comic old man in the lions' den, where he offers the basket of bread to Daniel: "Surge, frater, ut cibum capias" (Rise up, brother, and help yourself). The Angel then returns him to his initial position, surely by the hair of the head, as the stage direction did not need to specify. I submit that Habakkuk entered and left the stage by that route, with more comedy than dignity, and that he was thus a welcome foil to the pomposities—and humilities—of the leading characters of the play.

MOVEMENT AND GESTURE

The play being processional, much of its movement is in this form: stately, elegant, and very little individualized. There is abundant and self-evident opportunity for gesture in the reactions to the handwriting on the wall and in the action of the den scene. For most gestures the medieval illustrations in the Greenberg edition are enlightening. The comedy of Habakkuk's movements and gestures, as he stumbles along with the bread basket, would have been emphasized if the Angel who had him "capillo capitis sui" (by the hair of his head) had led him as pompously as Daniel himself had twice been led to the two kings, the short Habakkuk processional representing a comic parody of Daniel's.

The Pro Musica production discovered a good deal about appropriate movement for this play. Because the direct experience of producing a medieval play is likely to be more informative than the most imaginative projections, I quote Mr. Psacharopoulos on this subject:

The Cloisters production made much use of emphatic movement and gesture to convey details of character and emotion: humility was expressed by Daniel's bowed head: arrogance by Belshazzar's bearing. The two lions assumed an heraldic pose after their entrance, giving an underlying sense of playfulness to their clawing and threatening. Dumb show can most effectively be used in certain scenes when the action is to continue without music or speech: immediately after the handwriting appears on the wall, when the entire court freezes and the Second Monk walks silently and sternly upstage through the court, giving a definite premonition of catastrophe: when Belshazzar, crushed by the prophecies, orders his attendants to adorn Daniel . . . the Court, drinking and reveling around its monarch: the bowed heads of the conspirators: the subdued lions being caressed by Daniel: the advance of the Persian army, with its warrior-king following, holding his sword before him like a banner.[10]

When the Jealous Counselors are thrown to the lions, the stage direction is: "statim consumentur a leonibus" (let them at once be eaten by the lions). The lions merely surrounded the Counselors so that the audience could not see that the lions were not really bolting them down. If there were two Counselors—the playscript does not specify the number—there would probably have been a minimum of three lions to mask their action, though Greenberg lists only two. The medieval illustration on the cover of the Greenberg-Auden edition shows seven lions, and plate 65 of the present study shows only two, but these reflect pictorial design requirements rather than theatrical practice.

COSTUMES

Regal costuming for the two kings has been described above in the sections on *Herod* and *The Son of Getron*. Darius's extreme pomp is illustrated in plate 67, and may indicate an interest in Persian style. Habakkuk's costume is suggested in *The Procession of the Prophets*. The Soldiers and courtiers are identical with those of the *Herod;* that is, they are Norman, particularly since the play is from Beauvais (see also, plate 66). In early lines of the play the Satraps praise Belshazzar for having clothed his subjects in "purpura et ostro" (purple), and Belshazzar promises to clothe the successful interpreter "insignitus purpura torque fruetur aurea" (in purple trappings and a gold collar).

[10] Greenberg, *Daniel,* p. 113.

Daniel is a prophet, and in spite of his poverty and exile would have been rather splendid, as in *The Procession of the Prophets* and in the several medieval portraits of Daniel reproduced in the Greenberg edition (see also plates 38, 65). He becomes regal when seated next to Belshazzar, "induto ornamentis regalibus" (vested in regal ornaments), a reference to the promised purple trappings and gold collar. This purple stole and gold collar are certainly used in the play; one does not promise this sort of thing in the theater, anymore than Belshazzar did, without delivering it. One doubts, however, the intention to clothe Belshazzar's entire court in purple.

The lions' costumes were of course designed for pairs of boys to wear. The image of the lions in plate 65 seems more in keeping with their "underlying playfulness" that those illustrated on the cover of the Greenberg edition. The Angels would have been costumed as elsewhere in the repertory; the wings of the Herald Angel at the finish would have been somewhat more elaborate than those of the other Angel or Angels.

PROPERTIES AND FURNISHINGS

The banquet table is clearly depicted in a twelfth-century Gumpert Bible illustration (plate 66). The artist had insufficient space to show all the food and drink that should be on the table, but plates 48 and 64 supply supplementary information. During the procession of Darius, Belshazzar is murdered and carried out. I believe his banquet table would also have been removed, and an elegant throne set up in its place for Darius, with a footstool for his feet, as in plate 67.

The distinction between Belshazzar's decadent court and Darius's military society is made in the illustrations not only by the contrasting costumes of the courtiers and the soldiers but also by the shields and spears carried by Darius' followers, as in plate 65. Another contrast between Belshazzar's culture and Darius's is in the style of scepter each holds; these are illustrated in plates 66–67).

There is an excellent illustration of Habakkuk's breadbasket, with four round loaves of bread in it for the reapers, on the cover of the Greenberg edition. The breadbasket in plate 65 is two-dimensional, and appears schematic rather than practical for the stage.

The sword of the Angel who protects Daniel from the lions is, one would suppose, modelled on the kind of sword used by the Cherub at the east gate of Eden, though not necessarily flaming.[11] The weapon carried by the Angel on his way to the den with Habakkuk, as in plate 65 and the cover of the Greenberg edition, is not a sword but rather a long-handled lion-tamer's instrument, on the order of a straight hoe. The Beauvais and the Hilarius stage directions call the weapon a "gladium," though Hilarius indicates that the sword should close the mouths of the lions, which sounds more like a task for a handler's instrument. One observes in the illustrations that the Angel does not leave his "gladium" at the den while he goes to get Habakkuk; he still has it when he returns with Habakkuk by the hair. The sketches by the costume designer for the Pro Musica production show no weapon, though sketches of the other characters do include authentic swords, spears, and scepters.[12]

The royal vessels from Jerusalem were probably whatever the keeper of the cathedral treasury would permit the producer to borrow for the occasion. I doubt if the communion vessels then in use at the cathedral would have been considered appropriate or proper for a play about heathen kings.

STAGING AND THE DEFINITION OF ACTING AREAS

In discussing the nineteen episodes of the play, I mentioned that all of them take place in no more than three stage areas, and that thirteen of them are set in the palace, three at Daniel's house (one of these simultaneously with a palace scene), and four in the lions' den. The locations are named in the manuscript stage directions: the "palatio," including a "solium" (throne) but inadvertently omitting the banquet table; "in domum suam" (Daniel's house); and "in lacum leonum" (lions' pit). The only other area is that in which the Angel finds Habakkuk and to which he is returned: "Angelus reducet Abacuc In locum suum." Habakkuk is not at his house when the Angel meets him; he is on his way to his fields with bread for the reapers. This, then, is no more a location, a *sedes,* than any other on-the-road *platea* scene in the repertory, and required no setting or platform. From its use in thirteen episodes, and by the large cast which had to be accommodated, one may reasonably assume

[11] Genesis 3:24.   [12] Greenberg, *Daniel,* pp. 116–17.

that the palace *sedes* was of considerable size and that it was centered in the total playing space, with the smaller structures flanking the central platform at some distance from it. The Romanesque church of Beauvais could at the crossing have comfortably accommodated the three structures with ample space between them.[13] There may be some interest in determining which of the subordinate structures was at which side of the main platform. One medieval illustration, reproduced in the Greenberg's edition, places Daniel's house stage right of the Legates who have come to get him. Since forward action is in all Western arts represented as from left to right, Daniel's forward action would therefore begin at the audience's left and conclude in the lions' den at its right.

The palace platform was probably more elevated than the two side platforms, as well as much larger than they. Its superior elevation would have helped to give the feeling of a pit to the lions' den, and of humility to Daniel's house, and would have made unnecessary any other indication of the den's being below ground level. Some ornamented framework at the top of the palace platform would have been necessary to provide a space for the handwriting in the position required for it, as described above and pictured in plate 66.

I have found no medieval illustrations that show the nature of the walls of the den. Some low-lying partial wall or fence would have been desirable to give the sense of an enclosure so that neither the lions nor Daniel could escape. It is conceivable that this kind of wall was placed on the floor level, without a platform under it; the only disadvantage of this level would be the impairment of vertical sight lines, and the lions were surely to be shown off in these exciting scenes.

At the end of the play the Herald Angel "ex improviso" (without warning) appears at presumably a high level, possibly even in a gallery,[14] for the Christmas hymn. This same hymn is sung in the brief Magi play from Limoges; "unus puer psallit retro majus altare, ad instar Angeli" (a choirboy, in the likeness of an angel, sings from behind the high altar).[15] This stage direction suggests another practical location for the Herald Angel, the high altar and sanctuary being usually several steps above the level of the nave. This position for a triumphant announcement I have likewise found effective for Mary Magdalene's "Resurrexit hodie" in the Fleury *Visit to the Sepulcher*.[16]

---

[13] For data on the building of the present cathedral, apparently a half-century later than the composition of the *Daniel,* see Paul Frankl, *Gothic Architecture* (Baltimore, 1962), pp. 24–25. For the date of the play see Young, II, 486.

[14] Sepet places it there; see Young, II, 303, note 1.   [15] Young, II, 35.

[16] See above, p. 60.

MAKEUP: BEARDS AND HAIRSTYLES

Most illustrations of the Daniel story from the first half of the twelfth century, such as plates 65 through 67, show a well-trimmed beard for Belshazzar and none for either Darius or Daniel. Daniel's lack of a beard reinforces the idea of his youthfulness. The Magi have long white beards as becomes their station. Habakkuk is presumably bearded, as he was in *The Procession of the Prophets,* although illustrations of the Daniel story show Habakkuk clean-shaven. In the role of an old man in the comic tradition, as I have proposed above, he would have had to be bearded—but not well trimmed. Belshazzar's courtiers may or may not have been bearded, but neither Darius's soldiers, with their Norman cowls, nor Belshazzar's Satraps would wear beards if they were played by the choirboys of the cathedral school at Beauvais.

LIGHTING

A single crown light, suspended from the ornamented frame over the front of the main stage platform, would have been in the way of the handwriting. If there were any—and no illustration within my knowledge shows such a light for the *Daniel* palace scenes—they would have been suspended near the ends of the overhead frame.

SOUND EFFECTS

The Greenberg edition lists the instruments used in the Pro Musica production, and this list represents a maximum of winds, bells, plucked strings, and percussion. The sleigh bells surpass the maximum, but otherwise, Noah Greenberg's flair for medieval instrumentation seems within the bounds of possibility.[17]

[17] But see above, p. 246–47, for the proportions of instrumental pieces.

15. The Play of the Annunciation

68   The Annunciation to the Virgin. Florentine relief,
ca. 1200. Courtesy of the Metropolitan Museum of
Art, Cloisters Fund, 1960.

69 The Annunciation to the Virgin (left), and the Meeting of the Virgin and Elizabeth. "Echternach Gospel Book," 962–1056. Nuremberg, Germanisches Nationalmuseum, MS 156142, fol. 18ᵛ. Courtesy of Germanisches Nationalmuseum.

The Play of the Annunciation

In Annunciatione Beatae Mariae Virginis Representatio

TONE AND QUALITY

PRESERVED in fourteenth-century manuscripts, *The Lament of Mary* from Cividale, *The Annunciation* from Cividale and Padua, and *The Purification* from Padua share the distinction of being the only music-dramas in the repertory of which there are no extant versions from the twelfth or even the thirteenth century.[1] In the prime period of play composition the annunciation subject probably did not appear in play form; when it did, it was in as primitive a condition artistically as the playlets of the tenth and eleventh centuries. The visual artists of the prime period are profuse in their portrayals of the annunciation, the narrative in Luke is full of available dramatic dialogue, and the liturgical antiphons provide musical settings for that dialogue. Yet the material from Luke, assisted by the antiphons, is in *The Annunciation* very little shaped. With the exception of only twelve measures (Elizabeth's *Salve cara* in the Cividale version[2]), the play is a medley of lovely antiphons, interspersed with plainchant readings of the narrative portions of Luke 1:26–56.

For some reason that Young does not explore, the playwrights shied away from the subject of the Annunciation. Perhaps the fact that the *Magnificat,* the last third of the annunciation story in Luke, is a fixture of Vespers and also appears as the epilogue of some versions of *The Pilgrim* disqualified it for general use in Annunciation dramatizations, and so inhibited the growth of Annunciation plays.[3] On the other hand, the use of the *Te Deum* as the epilogue of many of the plays, perhaps because it is nonnarrative and less personal, does not seem to have been discouraged by its daily use in the Matins service. The trouble may have been that

---

[1] Young, II, 484, notes two reports of "dramatic commemorations" from the thirteenth century, but no dramatic texts.

[2] The literary texts of both versions are printed by Young, II, 247–50. The stage directions of the Paduan version are contained in embryo in two Cividale ordinaries.

[3] See the text of *The Pilgrim* in Young, I, 453–54, and his comments, I, 456–58.

while there is much ready-made dialogue, only two actions are possible in the Annunciation story: Gabriel's appearance at the beginning, and Mary's visit to Elizabeth. *The Lament of Mary,* with no more action in its sources, may have been late appearing for the same reason.

In spite of these handicaps, when the more complete text and score of the Cividale version of *The Annunciation* are combined with the unusually detailed stage directions of the very similar fourteenth-century Paduan version, a consistent and dramatic structure emerges, primitive but eminently stageable.

Of the plays of the repertory, the nearest approach to the structure of *The Annunciation* is in *The Procession of the Prophets,* where an interlocutor introduces each member of the cast. The situation in *The Annunciation* is even less illusory, since the medieval audience was quite aware that the Deacon and Subdeacon were singing the Lesson and the Gospel as they would in any Annunciation service. As Young comments, "this arrangement is accurately described in the sentence (from one of the Cividale *ordines*) 'Cantatur evangelium cum ludo.' " [4] This is a singing of the gospel with a play, not the reverse, yet the Cividale playscript calls the bare dialogue a "representatio," inviting comparison with the full title of the Fleury *Herod,* "Ordo Ad Representandum Herodem."

DETERMINATION OF MAJOR EPISODES

The artists of the period naturally chose the two major episodes of the Annunciation: Gabriel's announcement to Mary and her response, and the visit of Mary to Elizabeth (plates 61, 68). Often the two episodes are portrayed in twin panels, as in plate 61, even though the second episode is only a sequel to the annunciation. The presence of both episodes in the play is therefore not a dramatic invention but is in line with a visual artistic tradition which long preceded the performance of the play. The narrative in Luke was an even older precedent, and conditioned the artists.

CHARACTERIZATION

Mary's directness in questioning how she could possibly be pregnant, and her wholehearted acceptance of her destiny, are of course well known

[4] Young, II, 248.

to readers of Luke, and are not modified in the play. The stage directions do emphasize this direct quality in describing the appropriate voice for Mary's question as "plana voce," which means softly, simply, without challenging Gabriel's "alta voce" of authority.[5]

Elizabeth is a much older woman, yet she has full respect for the young cousin who is to be "the mother of my Lord." Elizabeth contrasts with Mary, not only in age but also in the miraculous events of her life: Gabriel's annunciation to her husband Zacharias and his consequent dumbness. He is still unable to speak when Mary comes to visit, Elizabeth being then six months pregnant.

Joseph, another elderly person, more of the generation of Elizabeth and Zacharias than of Mary, is only a figurehead in the play. In a version of the English medieval ballad, *The Cherry Tree,* Mary picked cherries "while Joseph stood around." This is also the extent of his action in the play, which may have been sufficient to conform to medieval expectations; it is consonant with many illustrations of the Nativity—yet oddly not with illustrations of the Annunciation scene.

Joachim (apparently a scribal error for Zacharias, since Mary's father can hardly be intended) is a retired priest of the temple, "well-stricken in years." Since Joseph apparently does not move from his original location in the play, Joachim-Zacharias will also be alone and literally speechless during Mary's visit, except for his formal mute welcome when she arrives.

Gabriel has been encountered in *The Visit to the Sepulcher, The Shepherds, The Wise and Foolish Maidens,* and the *Herod;* he is the same Archangel in this play. In Luke's account he so identifies himself to Zacharias: "I am Gabriel, that stand in the presence of God." Except in *The Visit to the Sepulcher* this role was always played by a "puer," a choirboy. The Paduan version so specifies, in conformity with the dramatic tradition.

MOVEMENT AND GESTURE

The business of the dove's descending and Mary's putting it under her cloak is another instance of the medieval love of gadgets. To judge from fifteenth- and sixteenth-century stage directions, the dove (usually alive) was let down on a string from a roof or gallery over or adjoining the

---

[5] "Plane voce" is defined in a thirteenth-century version of the *Visitatio* from the same Paduan Duomo as "ita tantum quod audiri possint" (only loud enough to be heard). This version is in Young, I, 294.

playing area.[6] In the Paduan stage directions the method is not specified, but Gabriel points up to the descending dove, Mary soon opens her arms, and shortly thereafter the dove is in her grasp. A short line later she puts it under her cloak, a practical as well as a symbolic gesture, for the live dove or pigeon will not struggle and flap its wings once it is covered by her cloak.

Gabriel's first gesture is carefully described in the Paduan directions: "duobus digitis manus dextrae elevatis" (holding up two fingers of his right hand). A twelfth-century Tuscan relief (plate 68) illustrates the gesture exactly. Mary's responsive gesture is indicated in the same relief. Artists were divided as to whether Gabriel should kneel to Mary. He does not kneel in plates 61 or 68, although he does in many others, with which the Paduan stage direction agrees. This may reflect a difference between customs of the eleventh and twelfth centuries, the period of the cited illustrations, and those of the fourteenth century and the Renaissance.

The gestures involved in the beginning of the second action, the reception of Mary by Elizabeth at Zacharias's house, are a good example of the expansive needs of the playwright as compared with the account in Luke and the pictorial artists' similar portrayals of the reception. The Gospel reads, and in the play was sung: "Exsurgens, autem Maria in diebus illis abiit. . . . Et intravit in domum Zachariae, et salutavit Elisabeth." (And Mary arose in those days and went . . . and entered into the house of Zacharias, and saluted Elizabeth). The eleventh-century Echternach illustration, along with others of the twelfth and thirteenth centuries, shows Elizabeth and Mary standing in a mutual embrace (plate 61).

The Paduan stage direction, while showing awareness of what the Deacon had just sung, is more dramatic: "Interim Maria descendat de loco suo et vadat ad locum Helisabeth et Ioachim, et ambo suscipiant Mariam sicut scriptum est in evangelio. Hoc facto, Helisabeth genibus flexis tangendo corpus Mariae cum ambabus manibus . . ." (Meanwhile [during the singing of the Gospel verse] let Mary descend from her platform and go to the platform of Elizabeth and Joachim [Zacharias] and let both of the latter help Mary up, as it is written in the Gospel. This being done, let Elizabeth, kneeling, clasping the body of Mary with both hands . . .). Despite the playwright's assurance, the action of hospitably assisting Mary up the steps to Elizabeth's house is not to be found

---

[6] Young, II, 246–47.

in the Gospel; it is a theatrical trope of the Gospel account, as are Elizabeth's kneeling and clasping Mary's body while she sings to her the antiphon, *Benedicta tu in mulieribus.* In addition to getting Mary up the steps, this stage direction gives Zacharias something to do. It is the only time in the play that he has any direction for movement. More importantly, this Paduan invention of movement and gesture for Elizabeth permits her to deliver the first antiphon to Mary in a kneeling position, to rise from it, and standing ("erigit se, et stando"), to sing her second antiphon, *Et unde hoc michi.*

In fact, the attention to movement, gesture, and voice in the Paduan script is comparable to that in the Cividale *Lament of Mary,* and suggests that in the Venetian area at that period a playwright-director was extremely precise with his actors. This precision may be explained by the fact that in both plays the leading actors were boys, whose changeable voices caused them to be replaced often. The last direction in the Paduan *Annunciation* for Mary is "Et Maria vertat se versus populum," while Cividale's last for Mary in *The Lament* is "Hic se vertat ad populum," similar and effective in both plays. Not only are the movements and gestures almost as detailed and frequent in *The Annunciation* as in *The Lament of Mary,* but also the quality of voice to be used by the singer-actors is prescribed for five of the seven items. Gabriel is to sing "alta voce"; Mary first "plana voce"[7] and later "alta voce" (twice); and Elizabeth is to begin "humili voce," in contradiction to the Gospel's "And she spake out with a loud voice." All of these vocal directions are dramatically appropriate and interpretive of character and emotion.

PROPERTIES AND FURNISHINGS

As mentioned above, a live dove or pigeon was probably used to represent the Holy Ghost. A similar though less difficult problem was encountered in relation to the Suitor's falcon in *The Three Daughters.* Whether suspended by his legs or by wired wings, the pigeon's descent upon Mary required some ingenuity on the part of the producer; the effect, in any case, was neither grotesque nor comic. Precisely how Mary puts the dove under her cloak was not specified, but the sexual implication in Luke can hardly be overlooked. In the ceiling of the south transept of the Paduan Duomo, where I infer the play was performed, there were still in 1968 a series of plugged holes, of which the largest and most eccentrically

[7] See the Paduan definition of "plane voce," above, p. 262n.

plugged is at the peak of the half-dome, in an excellent location for the play down below, and of sufficient size to accommodate a pigeon—or the shower of wafers called for in the Paduan version of *The Pilgrim*. Such holes were common for this purpose.[8]

Gabriel bore some kind of ornamented staff, perhaps as elaborate as the candelabra staff he carried in *The Visit to the Sepulcher* or as comparatively simple as the staff in the Tuscan relief (plate 68). His staff in the Echternach illustration (plate 61) is between these two in terms of size and complexity of design.

The Deacons are directed to read from "libros argenteos," which refers to the silver covers of the Evangelarium or Gospel Books from which they sing. The covers were not only of silver but were certainly highly ornamented with semiprecious stones, as books of this sort were in the Middle Ages; the Echternach Gospel Book is a rich example. The dimensions of such a book varied, but nine inches by twelve is typical. In the Paduan production it is probable that the Deacon and Subdeacon sang their roles from these books, and that the purpose of the direction concerning them was to assure that the most spectacular Paduan copies, those bound or embossed in silver, were used in the play.

In many illustrations of the period, Mary has a book in her left hand when Gabriel appears (as in plate 68). This book is probably an Old Testament, in size similar to the Gospel book John sometimes carries in postcrucifixion scenes like those of *The Lament of Mary*. As in that play, a Testament may have been of assistance to the boy actor in the role of Mary, or may have been a real handicap to thim. If he carried one at the beginning of the play, he would have had to dispose of it before the dove descended for him to grasp, for he could not have managed that business with one hand. If Mary were seated at the beginning of the play, she could have risen at the entrance of Gabriel and simultaneously left the book on the bench or stool. This is the only article of furniture in either set, and would have been plain, in order to indicate "the low estate of his handmaiden." No furnishings seem to have been required for the scene at the house of Elizabeth and Zacharias.

The chair on which the choirboy-player of the role of Gabriel is mounted has special interest because its use seems to have been unique to the Paduan *Annunciation* and *Purification*. In a survey of eighty dramatic texts in which one or more angels appear, I find no other mention of a "cathedra" chair, and we may infer that its theatrical use was the in-

---

[8] See Chambers, II, 66, note 1; and Young, I, 484, 488, 490–91; II, 245, 257.

vention of the producers at Padua. They were apparently fond of spectacular devices, as we have seen in their handling of the dove in this play and of the wafers in *The Pilgrim.* The chair serves the practical purpose of suggesting that the messenger has come from on high, not down the street.

The "cathedra" chair is, and was, a heavy, carved, wooden chair with substantial back. It is customarily used in the sanctuary by a bishop, and occasionally in a procession to carry a high prelate. Gabriel was of course of a rank comparable to that of the highest prelates. The directions specify that the choirboy playing Gabriel is to be carried on the "cathedra" from the Baptistry, presumably on the shoulders of four sturdy clerics, to his position on stage in the cathedral. The practical nature of other stage directions for the Paduan plays is a strong indication that the producers actually went through with this ponderous display. The back of the "cathedra" must have helped prevent Gabriel, standing on the seat, from toppling over backwards as the chair was carried a distance of some eighty feet to its position in the south transept.

STAGING AND THE DEFINITION OF ACTING AREAS

By checking the copious stage directions for the beginning of the Paduan *Annunciation,* and a parallel set for its *Purification,* against present architectural conditions in the Paduan Duomo and Baptistry, one may with some confidence derive the exact location of both plays in the cathedral. The scarcity of this kind of information for other medieval music-dramas will, I trust, justify its inclusion here. The initial stage direction reads:

In die Annuntiationis post prandium hora consueta pulsetur campana magna, et interim clerici conveniant ad ecclesiam, et in sacristia maiori preparent se aliqui de clerici cum pluvialibus et aliis necessariis. Et in dicta sacristia stent Maria, Elisabeth, Ioseph et Ioachin preparati cum diacono et subdiacono portantes in manibus libros argenteos. Et hora debita exeant processionaliter de sacristia, et pergant ad loca eis preparata. Hiis dimissis, processionaliter pergant ad baptisterium, et ibi stet puer preparatus in modum Gabrielis super cathedram; et de baptisterio elevetur et feratur in ecclesiam a latere plateae, et portetur super scalam versus chorum. Et clerici stent per medium ecclesiae in modum cori; et interim subdiaconus incipiat prophetiam. . . .[9]

[9] Young, II, 248.

The Play of the Annunciation

(On Annunciation Day after the meal, at the usual hour, let the tower bell be rung, and while it is ringing let the scholars convene at the church, and in the sacristy let some other scholars prepare themselves with copes and other properties needed for the procession.[10] And so in the sacristy also let there stand Mary, Elizabeth, Joseph, and Joachim [Zacharias], ready in their costumes, with a deacon and a subdeacon carrying in their hands the silver-bound Gospel and Epistle books. At the proper time let these persons leave the sacristy in procession [in the order listed above], and let them proceed to the stage area prepared for them. When they have gone, let the priests and the other scholars go in procession to the Baptistry, and there let a choirboy be already costumed as Gabriel and be standing on the "cathedra" chair. Let them pick up him and the chair, and let them carry him from the Baptistry into the Cathedral by the side alley, and carry him beside the platform that is nearest the chancel. And let the scholars stand at the crossing as a choir, and meanwhile let the Subdeacon have begun to sing the epistle. . . .)

The interior of the Paduan cathedral, while considerably remodeled since the fourteenth century, has retained its basilican arrangement of nave, transepts, and chancel.[11] The Baptistry at Padua is an adjoining building, not as much remodeled, standing alongside the west end of the Cathedral's south wall, and extending along that wall to within about eighty feet of the south transept. A back door of the Baptistry faces the side of that transept. Forty feet from the Baptistry door is a wider door which opens on the first bay of the nave. The outline of the original Romanesque brick arch over the outside of the cathedral door is still visible, and the remodeled doorway is even now the only side entrance to the Cathedral. There is, of course, no door at the end of the transept.

The problem for the producers was that Gabriel could not be effectively costumed, with wings strapped on, in the sacristy because he would give away his spectacular costume and lofty entrance to the set if he went with the other four actors and the Deacon and Subdeacon to the location of the play. Furthermore, he has to make an entrance during the play, while the other four actors come on stage to take their places and so begin the play. No area adjoining the set could have been sufficiently screened to hide Gabriel when he stood on the elevated chair. The only solution was to costume him in the Baptistry, a separate and concealed area. After all, the distance from the back door of the Baptistry to the

[10] The similar stage directions for the preliminaries to *The Purification* (Young, II, 253) identify a staff cross and tapers as some of the properties necessary for the procession of the actors.

[11] This cathedral is known locally as the Duomo, and is not to be confused with the more beautiful Basilica di Sant' Antonio in the same city.

side door of the cathedral is only about fifteen paces, and once inside the cathedral door he could almost immediately be turned to the right and make his surprise entrance to the adjoining transept. As the stage directions indicate, the play would already have started with the Deacon's singing of the Gospel, which would be interrupted at Gabriel's cue, "Et ingressus angelus ad eam dixit" (and the Angel, entering, says to her).

A transept generally made a better stage than did a bay of the nave; although both were enclosed on three sides, the transept had greater depth. At Padua the south transept has a floor area of forty feet in width by about sixty feet between the transept altar and the south aisle, adequate space to accommodate the two stage platforms and the audience, which probably extended from the platforms out as far as the crossing. The priests and scholars were instructed to stop at the crossing and to become the choir for the play ("Et clerici stent per mediam ecclesiae in modum cori"). From the markedly similar stage directions for the preliminaries to *The Purification* in the same cathedral we learn that the plays in the south transept were near the altar of Saints Fabian and Sebastian.[12] I surmise that this altar stood along the west wall of the transept, near the crossing, and that the platforms for the play were set deep in the transept.

These two platforms, with steps at side or front, left sufficient floor space between them to allow Mary to simulate a journey from Nazareth to Juda, along the usual *platea*. The steps, and therefore the raised platforms, are definitely stipulated. Mary, the stage directions tell us, descends from her house, goes to the house of Elizabeth and Joachim [Zacharias], and both help Mary up the steps.

An important feature of the staging of this play is the handling of the platform, the portable "cathedra" on which Gabriel is transported from the Baptistry to the cathedral door and then to Mary's platform, and on which he is finally carried out of view at the end of his scene. There would be less awkwardness in his remaining perched throughout on the "cathedra" than in attempting to land on Mary's platform. He could, once landed, stay on the platform to the end of the play, along with Joseph, except for the fact that the play ends in a procession, and that this event would require him to embark again on the elevated "cathedra." One doubts that such a precarious and ungraceful movement would have been performed in view of the audience. The first mounting of the "cathedra," indeed, was hidden away in the Baptistry, partly because of its

---

[12] Young, II, 253. This altar is no longer in existence at the Duomo.

inevitable awkwardness, no matter how carefully rehearsed. In addition to the difficulty the carriers of the chair would have in bracing rigidly against the step and thrust of Gabriel's standing and top-heavy figure, Gabriel's own equilibrium is somewhat disturbed by the weight of the wings behind his shoulders, to judge from modern productions involving winged Gabriels in the medieval repertory. Quite apart from these technical considerations, which can nevertheless make or break a play, the first scene is Gabriel's but the second entirely Mary's. No playwright would plan to leave Gabriel on stage, even if on a different side, for Mary's second scene and its climactic *Magnificat*.

16. The Purification

70   The Purification. Detail of plate 27.

71 The Purification. "Echternach Gospel Book," 962–1056. Nuremberg, Germanisches Nationalmuseum MS 156142, fol. 19ʳ. Courtesy of Germanisches Nationalmuseum.

The Purification

Purificatio

TONE AND QUALITY

MUCH that I have said about *The Annunciation* applies also to *The Purification*, which was a companion piece to that play, performed in the same cathedral. Indeed, many of the explicit stage directions, particularly those having to do with the preliminary procession and the arrangements for Gabriel to be borne in from the Baptistry, are nearly identical with those of *The Annunciation*. *The Purification*, however, resembles an "evangelium cum ludo"[1] only in the penultimate item which introduces Simeon's *Nunc Dimittis*, and then in the form of an antiphon, not as a direct, intoned quotation from the Gospel (Luke 2:28). Simeon and the three Angels have all the dialogue, while Mary (with an image of the Christ Child in her arms), Joseph, Anna, and four other prophets have much of the action during the singing of the antiphons by the angels. Young characterizes the play as "an elaborate dumb-show," which rather exaggerates the proportions of the action by the nonsingers.[2] For example, the initial item, *Ave, gratia plena*, is not narrative but a piece of dialogue sung by the Angels directly to Mary as she and the others approach the platform-set of the Temple. The other items, with the exception of the second and the fifth, are also dialogue rather than narrative.

The play builds to the final *Nunc Dimittis* just as *The Annunciation* builds to the final *Magnificat*. The dramatic sequence of *The Annunciation* is identical with that of the Luke's account—of necessity if it were to be an "evangelium cum ludo"—while *The Purification* considerably alters the narrative sequence of the Gospel in order to conclude with the *Nunc Dimittis*. This comparison suggests that *The Purification* may have been composed after *The Annunciation* and been influenced by it structurally as well as in its staging arrangements.

[1] See above, p. 261.   [2] Young, II, 255.

DETERMINATION OF MAJOR EPISODES

There is only one major episode in *The Purification,* though the play is introduced and concluded by processions of the characters, the choir, and the clergy. This episode is illustrated in the Gospel Book of Henry the Lion (plate 27), and in the Echternach illumination (plate 71).

CHARACTERIZATION

Mary is hailed in the first item, but the play becomes Simeon's as he takes stage in the Temple, and remains his in the final *Nunc Dimittis* as *The Annunciation* had been Mary's in the final *Magnificat.* Simeon is described by Luke as "just and devout, waiting for the consolation of Israel." He had been told by the Holy Ghost that "he should not see death before he had seen the Lord's Christ." [3] Most medieval illustrations (like plate 27), show Simeon as an old man, though his age is only suggested by Luke and is not specified in the stage directions of the Paduan version of the play. The Echternach illustration (plate 71) shows him as middle-aged, but another twelfth-century dramatic ceremony from Augsburg cathedral [4] assigns the role of Simeon to "unus senior ex presbyteris" (one of the senior priests), which suggests that the tradition of Simeon's age was liturgical as well as pictorial, and therefore may be accepted as a part of his character in the play. In the Laon version of *The Procession of the Prophets,* he is described as an old man in a silk cope, and in the Rouen version simply as an old man ("senex"). [5]

Two individual touches characterize Simeon in this play. One is the stage direction, "Symeone cum Puero garulante" (Simeon chatting with the Christ Child), which apparently represents an attempt to entertain the Child, somewhat as a priest rocks in his arms a baby who is being christened. The other is Simeon's action on taking the offering of doves. He turns to the audience, and "respiciat sub allas, si boni sunt" (let him look under the wings of the doves to see if they are plump).

Anna the prophetess "was of a great age, and had lived with an husband seven years from her virginity; and she was a widow of about fourscore and four years, which departed not from the temple, but

[3] Luke 2:26.   [4] Young, II, 251.   [5] Young, II, 145, 163.

served God with fastings and prayers night and day." Like Simeon, she "looked for redemption in Jerusalem." [6]

The four Prophets are straight out of *The Procession of the Prophets,* and one can only guess which prophets they are. Isaiah is surely one. Among others eligible are David, Jeremiah, Moses, and Daniel.

Joseph, who carries the doves in a wicker basket on his shoulders, is unobtrusive as usual. He always gives quiet direction to Mary, whether at the inn, on the flight to Egypt, or in the Temple. He is elderly, as he was in *The Annunciation.* The two guardian Angels are cathedral scholars, the winged Angel on the "cathedra"' is a choirboy.

MOVEMENT AND GESTURE

As in *The Annunciation,* Joseph is given something to do. Initially, he carries on his back the basket with the doves. After Mary has been hailed in the first item, and just before the group ascends the steps to the Temple set, we find "Anna et Joseph Puerum in ulnis portante" (Anna and Joseph with the Boy in arms), Mary having gone ahead up the steps with the two guardian Angels. There may be some question as to whether Joseph or Anna has taken the Child from Mary; the stage direction is ambiguous. In the twelfth-century illustration from Gmunden (plate 27), Mary herself presents the Child, another instance in which the graphic artist's compositional problem is different from that of the playwright, who requires more complication in the movement of the characters and the event. There seems to be no pictorial evidence that Joseph should hold the Child. Nevertheless, one is disposed to have Joseph present the Child to Simeon, because Anna has already been described as "cum carta magna in manu" (with a large sheet of parchment in her hand). Since both Joseph and Anna are somewhat encumbered, the fact that Joseph's burden is on his back makes it more convenient for him to carry the Child in his arms than it would be for Anna to carry him in one hand. In fact the intention behind the stage direction that Joseph's wicker basket should be "super humerum" (on his shoulders) may well have been to leave the actor free to hold and to present the Child.

We have already noted the effective gesture of Simeon's chatting with the Child, and the more spectacular matter of the introduction of the Angel on the "cathedra" (exactly as in *The Annunciation*). What has not been remarked in the pattern of movement is the positioning of the

[6] Luke 2:36–37.

three Angels in relation to the central action of the presentation. When the procession enters the cathedral from the Baptistry, the order of entrance is "Angelis cum Maria et Anna praecedentibus, post sequente Angelo qui est super cathedram" (The Angels with Mary and Anna leading, followed by the Angel who is up on the "cathedra"). The single Angel and his chair are placed, as in *The Anunciation,* to the choir side of the Temple platform. The two guardian Angels, as a kind of bodyguard, follow Mary and Anna up onto the the Temple platform, and presumably take their positions left and right of the principals.[7] There are also two choirboys is dalmatics "qui cantare debent *Ave, gratia plena"* (who are to sing the *Ave, gratia plena*), the first item. These choirboys, earlier called "clerici" and never really identified as angels, have already taken their places on the platform before the arrival of the procession from the Baptistry. Presumably the position for these singers would be up-center, and possibly somewhat elevated above the platform level so as to be seen as they sing the first two items.

The third item is sung by the winged Angel on his "cathedra," the fourth by the two guardian Angels, who flank the other actors on the platform. The fifth item is also the two Angels', after which Simeon sings the *Nunc Dimittis,* and the cast joins in the *Gloria Patri* with organum harmony. The choir, which has stood with the audience at the crossing, answers with "Sicut erat," the conclusion of the *Gloria,* after which the entire cast leaves in procession. This is an interesting pattern, with a conscious effort to achieve variety and composition in what could have been a huddled group of soloists and choir, since all the items are antiphons.

In this play, in contrast to the situation in *The Annunciation,* there is no indication of the exit of the single Angel on the "cathedra." He could not leave during the play, nor does it seem certain that he would join the specified procession back to the sacristy. One might speculate that in this instance the Angel remained on the "cathedra" until the procession and the audience had left that area of the cathedral, and then unceremoniously dismounted and walked back to the Baptistry.

COSTUMES

The single Angel on the "cathedra" is presumably Gabriel, dressed elaborately as in other plays in which he appears. He was undoubtedly winged,

[7] The two figures flanking the central group in plate 27 are not angels, since they are in women's dress.

and the Paduan direction in this play equips him also with two candles and a cross. The stage directions twice mention that the two choristers who sing the first two items wear dalmatics, elegant ecclesiastical vestments. The intention here is probably to have them represent the churchly audience and to greet Mary on her entrance.

The costumes of the other characters are not specified but can be derived from the specifications of other plays in which they appear: the four prophets and Simeon from *The Procession of the Prophets,* and Mary and Joseph from innumerable plays and depictions. Anna the Prophetess is more difficult; I have not found an illustration in which she can be certainly identified in costume. Philippe de Mézières's famous but late account of *The Feast of the Presentation of the Blessed Virgin Mary* (1372–1385) describes Anna's costume as follows: "Anna vero induetur de lino albo, tam in corpore quam in capite ad modum antiquae honestae matronae. . . ." [8] (Let Anna, indeed, be dressed in white linen, both on her body and on her head, in the style of an old and worthy matron).

PROPERTIES AND FURNISHINGS

Hand properties are numerous and characterizing in this play. Joseph has the covered wicker basket with the doves inside, Anna holds a large sheet of parchment, Mary carries the image or effigy of the Christ Child, and the single Angel on the "cathedra" has two candles and a staff cross. [9] The doves are presumably alive, as in *The Annunciation,* and must have been bound only by their legs, so that Simeon could lift their fluttering wings to show the audience that their breasts were well fleshed out.

There is no indication in the stage directions as to the furnishings of the Temple on the platform. Plate 27 shows a rather small altar with a floor-length ornamented cloth or pall over it. With eight of the cast on the Temple platform, the space available for the stage altar could not have been large.

STAGING AND THE DEFINITION OF ACTING AREAS

Except that there is only one platform in this play, while two are required for *The Annunciation,* the staging conditions were presumably the

[8] Young, II, 229.
[9] For details concerning the "cathedra" chair and its use, see above, pp. 265–66.

same. The stage area was in the south transept of the Paduan Duomo, and "post altare sanctorum Fabiani et Sebastiani," which gives little indication of its exact location. Surely the platform was not hidden behind the altar and reredos. The altar may have been near the northwest corner of the transept, near the crossing, and thus the platform would have been located deeper, beyond the saints' altar.

The positioning of the single Angel is directed to be the same as in the companion play.

MAKEUP: BEARDS AND HAIRSTYLES

Mary and Anna, the two women in the play, would have had veils covering their heads, since they are to enter the Temple. Hence their hairstyles, fortunately for the boys who were to play these roles, were hidden, and no wigs were required. Joseph is usually bearded, as is Simeon, whose beard in plate 27 is long and white, his head bald to the crown. He is also bearded in the Laon version of *The Procession of the Prophets*.[10] The three Angels would not be bearded, nor would be the two boys in dalmatics who sing the opening items.

LIGHTING

Young calls attention to the fact that the feast of the Purification of the Blessed Virgin Mary was initiated in Western Europe in the fifth century, and that "as early as the seventh century the liturgy of the day at Rome included a procession, and throughout the Middle Ages this ceremony gave prominence to the carrying into church of lighted candles, symbolizing the entering there of Christ, the 'lumen ad revelationem gentium.' "[11] Inasmuch as the Paduan directions emphasize the processional nature of the play, we may assume that the processions included an unusual quantity of lighted tapers, "to lighten the Gentiles."

SOUND

One of the "aliis necessariis processionaliter" was certainly bells, as Hardison makes clear in his description of the "bells-illumination-procession sequence."[12]

[10] Young, II, 145.   [11] Young, II, 250–51.   [12] Hardison, p. 213.

Notes on Production

Notes on Production

The following pages present additional specific information about certain aspects of the production of most of the individual plays, and are therefore organized in terms of the production categories of each play (with the exception of *The Conversion of St. Paul,* the *Daniel,* and the *Purification,* which have been fully treated in the preceding section of this work). Cross reference is made to pages of that section under the play-headings of this one, to remind the reader that the present section does not contain a complete account of production matters.

What is set forth here is of special interest to those who are concerned with an accurate production of a play, and is intended to supplement the discussion of general considerations and the interpretations of individual plays presented above. All readers may not wish to go so deeply into the subject, but I hope that many will, for it is a truism in the theater that those who are totally involved in the production of a play—even unto consideration of its furnishings, hairstyles, lighting, and sound effects—usually move closer to an understanding of the nature of that play.

The Visit to the Sepulcher

(See above, pp. 46–84)

MOVEMENT AND GESTURE

THE Dublin version of *The Visit to the Sepulcher*,[1] uniquely related to the Fleury version by the full correspondence of six of their first ten stanzas of verse, offers alternate possibilities for movement in the first scene, that of the entrance and approach of the Marys to the tomb. Dublin not only has the Marys sing the opening stanzas alternately, as in the Fleury version, but also introduces them to the "stage" singly rather than as a group, so that they meet only after the sixth stanza. The entry of each Mary is to the choir level opposite the apparently anastasis type of sepulcher ("ad ingressum chori versus Sepulcrum"), which I suppose means that they enter from the sacristy. Having met, they move together to the steps from choir to sanctuary and sing together for the first time ("Tunc se coniungant et procedant ad gradam chori ante altare simul dicentes").

What they sing is a stanza beginning "Iam, iam, ecce! Iam properemus ad tumulum" (Now, behold! Now let us hasten to the tomb), at which point they move near the sepulcher ("Deinde procedant simul prope Sepulcrum"). They then alternate in singing three stanzas, after which the Archangel appears and asks the usual question, "Quem quaeritis?" The separate entrances of the Marys, whether from the sacristy, from some other point or points alongside the choir area, or from three locations at the rear of the church, constitute an attractive suggestion for movement, Fleury being silent about these logistics.

COSTUMES

Plates 2–5 and 9–15 show a dozen detailed illustrations of Marian costumes, and demonstrate conclusively the style of their costumes. Eight of the illustrations are of the twelfth century, four of the first half of the

[1] Text in Young, I, 347–50.

thirteenth, so that an historical consensus can be had. The veil, with its ends hanging in folds to breast level, so that it often resembles a cowl, is in most of the illustrations caught back of the ears so that the facial profile is never covered even when the wearer leans over. In many of the illustrations, most clearly in plates 4 and 10 (one of which is Italian, the other German), there is an indication of the method of draping the hood or veil. It appears to be a long piece of cloth wrapped around the head and lapped over, turban-style, the two ends falling over the shoulders and caught either in front or at the side, or left hanging as in plate 3. For actors of women's roles in the plays the exposure of the ears is crucial to hearing the musical cues, which cannot be lip-read as spoken dialogue can. The method is described as "vinctus in modum mulieris caput circumligatus" (the headdress wrapped around and lapped under in the manner of a woman).

The underdress is a loose, full, floor-length tunic, girdled, over which is draped a shorter mantle or cape, full enough to enclose the arms and even the hands in its folds. In effect, the mantle is somewhat like a very long shawl. One should note that none of these three staples of Marian dress is fitted; all are draped very fully, in a tradition of dress that reaches back to the tunic and chiton of the Romans and Greeks.[2]

In visual representations from the period no stylistic distinction is made among the costumes of the Marys, except in color, where the tradition of red for Mary Magdalene is generally observed, and even the plays have some stage directions to this effect.[3] The Mary blue is reserved for the Virgin and is not used for Mary Jacobi or Mary Salome. The palette for *The Visit to the Sepulcher* therefore is controlled by Mary Magdalene's shade of red, especially since she is the central character and remains onstage throughout the play. For the texture of materials for the Marys' costumes, we have an occasional stage direction, such as that from the Dublin version of this play, which notes that the Marys are to be clothed in "superpelliceis" (literally, surplices) and capes of silk.[4] In the Cologne plaque (plate 10) the Marys are dressed in what Thomas P. F. Hoving describes as "wet, clinging drapery which reveals the parts of the body."[5] One may wonder whether the use of silk in the Marys' capes may not have inspired the Cologne workshop to use this, its typical but not unique style. The dress of the Archangel in the same plaque is also

[2] For further details of the costume, see above, p. 21.

[3] The Fécamp version (Young, I, 264) dresses Mary Magdalene "in capa rubea."

[4] Young, I, 347. For the directions for silk, see also the versions from Fritzlar and Le Mans, Young, I, 257 and 289.

[5] Hoving in Rorimer, *A Medieval Treasury,* note to plate 23.

rather clinging, as it would not be in dramatic costuming because the Archangel is dressed as a male ecclesiastic. The Cologne artist, however, had to make it clinging in order to harmonize his composition. There is, incidentally, nothing to prevent the opposite conclusion that the Dublin stage direction was inspired by the Cologne plaque, the playscript being later. The textual relationship between the Dublin and Fleury versions of the play is close, and we know that the Cologne center was in even closer communication with the latter in the twelfth century.

A comparison of costume style for the Marys with that of other women in other twelfth-century plays of the repertory, as for example in plates 24, 27, and 58, confirms what one would expect, that all women's costumes were contemporary and alike. The same situation exists in respect to the usual men's costumes, such as those of Peter, John, and the Spice Merchants. With the omission of the veil for men, there is very little difference between ordinary men's and women's garments in this period. This fact is made vivid by comparison of the Spice Merchants' dresses with those of the Marys in the Saint-Gilles lintel (plates 2, 3) and in the Italian companion statues of the Virgin Mary and John (plates 15, 16). One significant difference is in the fastening of the men's cloaks, either center front or at the front of one or both shoulders (plates 25, 32, 33, 39, 40, 60). A band of trim on the cloaks is common, either in a solid, contrasting color or in a formal pattern.

Another important difference is that the women invariably wear dark, soft-soled shoes; a medieval woman would no more think of being seen barefoot outdoors than bareheaded in a church. The men, on the other hand, are consistently barefoot in the illustrations and in occasional stage directions, as for example in the Dublin version, in which the two apostles are reminded to be "nude pedes." The only apparent exceptions are soldiers and Magi. The Christus—as well as the angels, who are considered male—are always barefoot in the visual arts of the period. Even the pilgrims in *The Pilgrim* wear no footgear.

PROPERTIES AND FURNISHINGS

Some of the hand properties required for the production of *The Visit to the Sepulcher* have already been described, and the present account of them is merely supplementary.[6]

The pyx is so common in illustrations of the Marys at the sepulcher

[6] See above, pp. 22–23.

(e.g. plates 2–11) and is so frequently specified in dramatic or semi-dramatic texts of *The Visit to the Sepulcher,* that one need hardly do more than accept the pyx as the usual hand-prop for all three of the Marys.[7] In the Fleury version of the play the use of the pyx may be inferred from the dialogue of Mary Jacobi and Mary Salome in the last two verses of the nine-stanza procession, and no doubt made unnecessary an explicit stage direction for so customary a property.

While there was some variation in the shape of the pyx, as in all traditional objects, its general contours were invariable: the metal or alabaster body was round, with or without a flared base; the lid surmounted with a round button knob, and the entire outer surface lavishly ornamented, either in enamel or etching.[8] The pyxes of the period shown in plates 7 and 8 exhibit the extremes of their contour variation.[9] The Malmesbury pyx or ciborium, ornamented in blue enamel, is about five inches in diameter at its widest point. To judge from pictorial evidence, this is a maximum diameter; most of the pyxes can be estimated in relation to a pictured woman's palm as being closer to four inches for convenient carrying in the traditional fashion, supported underneath by the left hand. The two surviving specimens show the hinged lid, which again made for safe holding in one hand. Hinged lids were necessary for two of the pyxes used in the St. Quentin version, in order that the business of opening and receiving their loads from the Spice Merchant might be performed with some degree of realism. The weight of the Malmesbury pyx, made of thin copper-gilt, is less than three pounds, and actors would therefore be able to hold a pyx in a fixed position throughout the long procession to the sepulcher. The medieval producer had to determine the moment and place at which the Marys disposed of their pyxes. If the anastasis type of tomb was used, the Marys could easily enough have deposited their pyxes inside it, out of the actors' way and the audience's sight.

The contents of the pyx, as described by the two Marys in the Fleury version of *The Visit to the Sepulcher,* are an oil base ("Nardi"—hard oil) into which have been mixed ("commixcio") the ground and aromatic spices ("condimentis aromatum") purchased from the Spice Merchant. These strong embalming spices were used so that the body "ne putrescat in tumulo" (will not rot and smell bad in the tomb).[10]

[7] See, for example, Young, I, 264, 347, 413, 639.

[8] I do not understand Young's description of the pyx as an "incense-boat," I, 404.

[9] The type represented by plate 8 is used in the tenth-century Hartker *Antiphonary.*

[10] The force of the verb "putrescare" seems clearly to include the olfactory results of putrefaction, as in the Biblical narrative and medieval play about Lazarus, upon whom apparently the embalming ointment was presumed to be ineffectual, as it doubtless was.

As for the thuribles carried by one or more of the Marys, there seems to have been no visible change in their design between the tenth-century Hartker miniature and examples from the art of the twelfth- and thirteenth-centuries (plates 9, 10) or the censers found in Catholic churches today. There is thus no need to describe them in detail. Some practice is required to accomplish the fueling and ignition of the thurible, and to control the chains by which it is swung. When carried, as by the Marys, the joined chains are held in the fingers of the right hand, and extended in front of the mantle. The hand is kept waist high, most of the swinging being accomplished by the wrist, as indicated in plate 10. The best quality of incense had a sensuous combination of spices, and added another exotic dimension to *The Visit to the Sepulcher*. After one or more Marys had in effect censed the audience on the Marys' way to the sepulcher, the fragrance would linger throughout the play.

Disposition of the thuribles after the Marys reached the choir was the same as that suggested for the pyxes: somewhere inside the anastasis. In the tenth-century *Regularis Concordia* from Winchester there is a rather full rubric for their disposition. The Angel shall sing to the Marys the "Venite et videte" and shall show them the graveclothes; upon seeing this, "the three shall lay down their thuribles in that same 'sepulchre' and, taking the linen, shall hold it up before the clergy. . . ." [11] It has often been remarked that the *Regularis Concordia* itself explicitly acknowledges indebtedness to Fleury practices, and we have called attention above to the likeness of the "pedetemtim" stage direction to a Winchester rubric and two others. The twelfth-century play of *The Visit to the Sepulcher* probably followed a Fleury ritual of several centuries in fixing the time and place of disposing of the thuribles. The position of the "Venite et videte" antiphon, however, is so late in the matured play that one doubts the Marys would have been burdened with the thuribles for so long a time. At least the *Regularis* seems to indicate an awareness of the problem even in a much shorter dramatic ceremony, and we can imagine that the producer of the Fleury play also took steps to get the thuribles out of the hands of the Marys and into a fireproof place at the earliest feasible moment. The St. Quentin version, in which the Marys were played by nuns, dodged the problem by introducing into the cast a Priest whose chief function was to lead the procession and swing the thurible.

Another traditional prop is the staff-cross, which some illustrations (plate 12) show as Christ's gardening tool in the "Noli me tangere"

[11] Thomas Symons, ed., *The Monastic Agreement of the Monks and Nuns of the English Nation: Regularis Concordia* (New York, 1953), p. 50.

scene. In many versions of the resurrection story in art and in drama, the episode of the harrowing of Hell immediately follows the "Noli me tangere" scene, and for its symbolism the Christus must have had a cross for the harrowing.

The graveclothes, identified in some stage directions collectively as the "sindon" and singly as the large "linteamina" for wrapping the body, and the small "sudarium" for the head, were simple enough to cut, prepare, and use.[12] Their material was unbleached linen. Hartker's *Antiphonary* illustration (tenth century) is as good as any. No attempt was made to show a "veronica" imprint on the "sudarium" or bloodstains on the "linteamina." These cloths were placed in advance on the sarcophagus, draped over the front edge for all, including the Marys, to see. This is one of those happy theatrical moments when the audience knows something before the actors (the Marys) do.

Properties for the Archangel and for succeeding Angels are of some importance. The palm frond is repeatedly depicted in art (see plates 6, and 9–11), and called for in rubrics and stage directions, which specify "palmas in manibus" in the several forms of *The Visit to the Sepulcher.* What is unexpected in the visual representation is the width of the traditional palm frond. Unlike what is provided for Palm Sunday in modern churches, the medieval palm frond was not real. It was an image of a palm frond, more substantial and narrower, but colored to look like the real thing, which only the pilgrims in the audience had ever seen.

The two hand-props for the Christus on his final glorious appearance in the Fleury version are specified thus: "crucem cum labaro in dextra, textum auro paratum in sinistra habens" (having in his right hand a cross with a banner, in his left a pall of woven gold). The banner on the cross was as short as a flag so that it did not drag behind the actor. The gold pall could be considered part of his costume, but if it was used to gesture with, it became a shining, swirling prop.

Properties for the spice-merchant scene are clearly visible in the Saint-Gilles lintel (plate 3), and since only the spices, the coins, and the scales are hand props, they may be considered part of the counter, briefly treated in the next section. If one desired to make much of this scene in presenting the St. Quentin version of the play, one might introduce the mortar and pestle of the sculpture showing one of the Marys grinding spices (plate 5). The business would then be that one Merchant weighed out the spices and the other ground them and poured them into the two

[12] See Young, I, 134–35, for medieval confusions in use of these terms. Mine are consequently no better.

Marys' pyxes; or the Marys could do their own grinding with the mortar and pestle on the counter.

STAGING AND THE DEFINITION OF ACTING AREAS

If the action within the monument was to be clearly visible to the audience, this structure, much more than head high, must have consisted of some widely spaced columns joined by Romanesque arches and pediments, and topped by a tiled or gilded dome. To accommodate this structure, depth in the choir area was essential, for the sarcophagus within the anastasis could not have been foreshortened to less than the imagined length of the corpse—although Christ's was not actually inside, Lazarus's was eventually present. Modern productions using this anastasis structure have found that with an audience at normal distance from the chancel the sarcophagus must be about six feet in length, the width of the base of the anastasis seven or eight feet, and the overall height to the top of the dome at least ten feet.

Visual representations of the period do not have such spatial problems, and sometimes are misleading in omitting the anastasis in which the sarcophagus is placed (plates 2, 9, 11). These views of the scene are close-ups, and intentionally focus on the tight grouping of the Archangel and the Marys around and on the sarcophagus. The shape and style of the sarcophagus may be deduced from these same plates. Notable is the raked lid of the sarcophagus, as seen in plates 9 and 10 and in most pictorial closeups. The purpose of the raked lid is to show that the sarcophagus has been opened and is empty.

The principal acting area was located in reference to the anastasis structure and the sarcophagus within. Since these were usually placed at the extreme right of the choir area, sufficient space remained for the "Noli me tangere" scene and for sight lines to the altar upstage. Specific problems of movement in these areas are considered in the section on movement and gesture (pp. 75–77).

In no version of the play is mention made of a change of location, a *sedes,* for the "Noli me tangere" scene, though one notices in the art of the period a fairly consistent use of a tree or shrub to indicate a garden setting for this scene. There is no reason to rule out such a scenic structure for the play. If styled in the manner of the art of the time (plates 12–14) and of the architecture of the anastasis, and placed well to stage left in the choir, such a handsome set-piece would have enhanced the staging and served as a counterbalance to the eccentric location, stage right, of the large monument structure.

The spice-merchant setting for the St. Quentin version can be derived from the Saint-Gilles scene (plate 3). Attention is called to some realistic details in it: the hand scales, the pyxes (open and shut), the pile of coins on the counter.

MAKEUP: BEARDS AND HAIRSTYLES

The generalizations made about hairstyles and beards in the Introduction apply to the male characters in *The Visit to the Sepulcher*. John, young and tender, has short curly hair (perhaps a wig), and rarely has a beard in illustrations, of which plate 16 is typical. These matters are never mentioned in any version of this play. Peter, on the other hand, usually has a beard, of the same type as Paul's (plates 43 and 45), but shorter and broader, as in the Byzantine portrait of Peter in the Lazarus resurrection scene (plate 41). None of the Angels is ever bearded in the art of the period (plates 9–11, and 17), and their hair is either long and wavy or short and tightly curled.

Most of the illustrations of the Christus in the "Noli me tangere" scene (plates 12–14) show him with shoulder-length hair and a beard not much longer than a chin-beard. In the Pembroke Gospel Book illustration (plate 14), the beard of the Christus is the same in the "Noli me tangere" scene as it is in scenes of the Harrowing of Hell. It is perhaps significant that the Christus's beard in this vivid group of illustrations is noticeably shorter than those of the disciples. Sculptured crucifixes usually show this same kind of beard, but shorter hair. Other examples of the Christus's beard may be studied in scenes from the *Lazarus* resurrection (plates 39 and 41) and from the *Peregrinus* (plates 19–25). The exception is the miniature, plate 40, which shows him beardless.

The styling of hair and beard for the Spice Merchants is so clearly carved in the Saint-Gilles and Modena scenes (plates 2–4) as to require no comment here, except to question whether in the Antelami portrayal (plate 4) the Merchants have headdresses somewhat like those of the Marys. If there is no headdress, there must be a headband or fillet, similar to what appears to be on the center Merchant in the badly disfigured Saint-Gilles portrayal of this feature (plate 3).

There is no problem with the length or style of hair for the Marys.

Each has a long hood or veil which would cover even the long hair of medieval women. This type of veil, wrapped so that it does not cover the ears or profile of face, would make unnecessary any concern with the actor's hair, including the alleged red hair of Mary Magdalene. The audience could not have known the color of her hair from her appearance in this play, unless her veil was farther back on her head than it should have been. Her role and hairdo in the *Lazarus* are something else again.

LIGHTING

The use of the crown light in *The Visit to the Sepulcher* was outlined above in the general description of that medieval stage-light.[13] It was lighted by the Archangel as a cue to the Marys to begin their procession or individual entrances. The stunning of the Soldiers was accomplished by the Archangel with his flaming staff-candelabrum as described above.[14]

The disposal of the Soldiers, who took their places before the procession, and the lighting of the crown light, which must have hung above head height and slightly in front of the monument, were the first two unofficial actions of the play. The Archangel probably appeared from within the anastasis as soon as the Soldiers set their watch, brandished his lighted candelabrum over them and stunned them, and then turned and briskly lighted the crown light with his candelabrum. He would then have gone inside the anastasis and remained in plain view, still bearing his candelabrum (as in plate 2), lighted or snuffed. There he awaited the Marys, who at this moment (or after the choir had concluded and had sat down) began their "Heu's" at some distance from the monument.

The Archangel would have led the processional and would have gone directly into the anastasis. The Soldiers, bringing up the rear of the procession, would have gone to their stations below the monument. I have suggested above that the choir may have proceeded, each member with a candle, in accordance with the St. Quentin stage direction.[15] At their entrance to the choir area they would perhaps have inserted these candles into standing candelabra, to augment the lighting of the scene.

The lighting of the spice-merchant setting was another matter, and perhaps could have been handled by having the Merchants bring out floor-based candelabra while covered by the choir, before the Merchants took their seats at the already placed counter.

[13] See above, pp. 38–41.   [14] See above, p. 70.   [15] See above, p. 73.

At the conclusion of the play the Archangel would have led out with his candelabrum (still lighted?), followed by the entire company of actors singing the *Te Deum laudamus.* The choir brought up the rear, pausing en route to retrieve their candles. The crown light would have held the audience's attention upon the sepulcher until, at the conclusion of the *Te Deum,* the great tower bells tolled the end of the drama.

SOUND EFFECTS

The musical score of Smoldon's edition of the Fleury version is so skillfully managed, and by now has been seasoned by so many performances, that fools should not rush in where angels have trod. The use of harp, chime bells, and organ is musically and dramatically quite satisfactory, such instrumental interludes being of value as punctuation, a concept which the Fleury composer certainly understood. An example of its dramatic use (in this case the harp alone) is upon the rising of the Archangel to ask the Marys "Quem quaeritis," then again before the two Angels ask Mary Magdalene "Mulier, quid ploras," and upon the entrance of Christ as the gardener. The harp does not repeat its theme for the entrance of Christ in his glory. The edited score at this point calls for a sustained organ tone (partly to give the Christus his pitch) with "if possible, the stroke of a heavy bell." Lacking the proper weight and pitch of bell, I have the temerity to suggest a single clash of medium-sized cymbals, since their pitch is less definite and thus less competitive with the sustained note of the organ, yet still gives a startling emphasis to the entrance of the Christus. A further use of cymbals may have been as an accompaniment to the Archangel's brandishing of the candelabrum over the Soldiers, at the beginning of the play.

The Lament of Mary

(See above, pp. 85–98)

MOVEMENT AND GESTURE

FREQUENTLY, as with the seventeen breast-beatings in *The Lament of Mary*, some interpretation is needed. In the first modern performances of this play, the original stage directions were taken as the basis of production with two different casts, and the directions were followed literally in early rehearsals. After the performances, the original directions were studied again in the light of our production script, in which gesture and movement were recorded rather fully. The results of this study are here presented for whatever value they may have in the interpretation of stage directions which are at once specific and ambiguous. The references to items follow the numbering in the Smoldon edition.[1]

ITEM 1. The four principals enter in turn during the interpolated prelude and the singing of the *Serena virginum,* and assume positions in relation to the cross. All portrayals of the Passion scene show the Virgin Mary to the left of the cross, John to the right, and the other two Marys left of Mary Major. See plates 2 and 17 as examples of this traditional blocking.

ITEM 2. Mary Magdalene, with arms outstretched, moves center and gestures out and to her right for "O fratres" and to her left for "et sorores." She then holds this gesture, both arms extended, through "Ubi est spes mea?" On "Ubi consolatio mea?" she beats her breast with her left hand.

In practice the business of breast-beating is not as melodramatic or monotonous as the repeated "Hic se percutiat" and its variants may suggest. "Beating" is rather too strong a word for the action. Variety is easily achieved by alternately striking with the open left or right hand slightly above the breast, by striking both clenched hands below the throat, by alternately striking the open left and right hand on opposite collarbones, and by crossing the open left and right hands above the breast. Some

---

[1] Smoldon, *Planctus Mariae.*

of these varieties of breast-beating are illustrated in the art of the period, as in plates 15 and 17.[2]

Mary Magdalene raises her right hand to the cross on "Ubi tota salus," and bows her head on "magister mi." This is almost exactly the sequence of gestures represented simultaneously in the Byzantine plaque (plate 17), with left hand still clenched against upper breast, right hand extended to the cross, head bowed. After she has finished singing, she prostrates herself at the foot and to stage left of the cross. Whether the prostration is complete, as the Latin "sternat" requires and plates 40 and 41 illustrate, or is a kneeling with torso and head deeply bowed, would have depended on vertical sight lines, which would have had to be exceptionally good to permit total prostration, better than in the north transept of Cividale.[3] After the prostration or kneeling she may slowly raise her head to contemplate the cross, though the playscript does not specify this. She holds this posture during the next item.

ITEM 3. Mary Major turns from focus on the cross and faces the audience with hands clenched together during the "O dolor! Proh dolor!" With hands open and arms stretched out and up, she turns to the cross on "Ergo quare," the first statement of the leading melody, and holds this gesture, grief heavy on her face. The stage direction, "Hic percutiat manus," is interpreted as a clenching of the hands, not a striking. Here again, as in the case of "prostrates" for "sternat," the Latin verb of action cannot be interpreted literally without farcical excess.

ITEM 4. John has been standing in a position illustrated by plate 16 or 17. After Mary Major finishes Item 3, he imitates her gesture to the cross, and sings "Rex celestis, pro scelestis." On "Alienas" he takes one or two steps forward ("proiiciendo se," as emended by Young from the manuscript's apparent "percuciendo se" which would be an additional breast-beating!). He gestures outward to the audience as Mary Magdalene did in Item 2, lowers his arms on "Agnus sine macula," and holds.

ITEM 5. Mary Jacobi's first gesture, to the cross, imitates those of Mary Major's second in Item 2 and John's first in Item 4. She beats her breast on "Pro peccatis hostia?" One should observe that all shifts of gesture oc-

[2] Other interesting illustrations of this gesture may be consulted in the following: L. M. J. Délaissé, ed., *Miniatures médiévales de la librarie de Bourgoyne au cabinet des manuscrits de la Bibliothèque Royale de Belgique* (Geneva, 1959), p. 67; C. Gaspar and F. Lynn, eds., *Les Principaux Manuscrits à Peintures de la Bibliothèque Royale de Belgique* (Paris, 1937), I, plates 51 and 67; Porcher, *L'Enluminure Française,* p. 67; and Santangelo, *Cividale,* pp. 137, 139, 141, 158. It is regretted that these excellent illustrations, many of them in color, could not be included in the present publication.

[3] See above, pp. 96–98, for discussion of the probable staging of the play in its original production at Cividale.

cur at breathing points. The location of the original stage directions, above the dialogue, usually suggests the correct timing of the gestures.

ITEM 6. By the process of elimination, beginning with the absurd assignment of this item to John, and not wishing to run two items for one singer together, one concludes that Mary Magdalene is the only possible singer of Item 6. She rises from her position at the foot of the cross, moves to Mary Major, and brushing away her own tears with one hand (an interpretation of "suas lacrimas ostendendo" which saves her from "pointing to her own tears").[4] The next direction, for breast-beating, is optional, and would be desirable only if there were space enough for her to cross to Mary Major by the end of the item, "Felix puerpera." Whatever the spacing, since Mary Magdalene would not have kissed Mary Major on the cheek ("Hic salutet Mariam") until the item had been sung, this stage direction seems obviously misplaced.

ITEM 7. Mary Major responds to Mary Magdalene's kiss by embracing her "ad collum," with both arms around her neck; this is done, I think, at a slight distance, without torso contact. She pauses in her singing after "fideles animae," where the end of the musical phrase is a full measure in length. In the pause she goes to Mary Jacobi, ("aliam," the other one) who would be nearby so that the interruption of the singing is just long enough to be dramatic, and embraces her in the same fashion. She breaks from the embrace, and resumes her singing with "Flete, sorores optimae." She beats her breast on the word "doloris," holding the gesture to the end of the item.

ITEM 8. Mary Major, still holding her gesture, now moves nearer the cross, so that Mary Magdalene and Mary Jacobi may with outstretched hands encompass Mary Major and the cross, as the stage direction says, "cum manibus extensis ad Mariam et ad Christum." This gesture is important in tying together Mary Major and the crucifix which is referred to in this item. Near the end of the item, on "ut praedixit psalmista" the women curtsey low to Mary Major as a salutation ("se inclinant cum salute"). This was a court curtsey, not a bob.

ITEM 9. Mary Major's gesturing twice to the cross seems excessive; and the manuscript may have been offering alternatives. One gesture would have been enough, after "crucis et lanceae." The gesture to the angel ("angelum") has occasioned some editorial speculation.[5] If, as explained below, the play were staged in the north transept, the figure of the angel

[4] Smoldon, *Planctus Mariae,* p. 4, translates this direction as "pointing to her tears," because he retains John as the speaker.

[5] See Young, I, 513, and Smoldon, *Planctus Mariae,* p. 6n.

would have had to be adjacent to that area. No such figure of the period remains at Cividale, either in the refurbished church or in the local museum. In the opposite, south transept there has been since the early sixteenth century a large painting of the Annunciation scene by Giovanni da Udine (1487–1564). If this location for the Annunciation chapel or altar was traditional, the gesture to Gabriel would have been over the audience, by whom it would likely have been accepted without the distraction of turning to see the well-known object.

ITEM 10. This also is Mary Major's item. After she finishes the preceding item, she moves to John and embraces him closely. Meanwhile, Mary Magdalene and Mary Jacobi may have varied their positions and gestures with a similar embrace. Mary Major would hold her embrace with John until "Tempus est lamenti," only gesturing to the cross with her head on "Fili novo," two lines earlier. She then beats her breast with both hands, on "immolemus intimas," and lowers her hands on "Christo morienti." She has moved away from John before the breast-beating.

ITEM 11. Before he sings, John moves to Mary Major with arms outstretched. His only other gesture, to the cross, should come after the item, rather than before the last line as specified by the scribe and repeated in the modern edition. If delivered during the singing, the gesture to the cross is at odds with the meaning of the words.

ITEM 12. Mary Magdalene breaks her embrace with Mary Jacobi, and kneels before the cross, her torso erect so that she can then sing "O Pater benigne." On "Noli me" she may risk an over-literal, John-Brown's-baby gesture if she beats her breast with one hand. The next breast-beating is with the other hand, and both are held to her breasts until she is called by Mary Major in the next item.

ITEM 13. Mary Major's longest solo is in contact with Mary Magdalene throughout, the entire item being addressed to her. The sequence of gestures, for the most part properly located by the scribe, is:

She reaches out a hand to the kneeling Mary Magdalene and helps her to rise.

She gestures to the cross, Mary Magdalene's eyes following.

She embraces Mary Magdalene with both arms around the neck, a little more closely than as described above in Item 7.

Relaxing with one arm her embrace, she half turns to John ("ad aliam partem").

She breaks the embrace entirely when she turns to look at the cross.

She turns back to Mary Magdalene.

She turns again to the cross and moves toward it slightly.

She turns again to Mary Magdalene and then moves away.

At sufficient distance she gestures to Mary Magdalene.

She drops her gesturing arm. (I understand the "deorsum" [behind] of this direction only as indicating that the swing of her gesture has been somewhat behind her, and that she now brings her arm forward to her side when she drops the gesture.) [6]

She returns to embrace Mary Magdalene as she had at the beginning, and holds this embrace to the end of the item.

The pattern of movement and gesture in this item is formal and dance-like, even to the framing repetition of the embrace. In this long melodic flight there must have been more movement and gesture than the directions specify. The strong patterning of the movement suggests how formal a style, similar to that of the secular *rondeau, virelai,* and *ballade,* and perhaps influenced by them, is demanded by such a play. If a fourteenth-century play in the repertory required this degree of formality in its acting, we may suppose that the earlier acting style was not different in kind but only in degree.

ITEM 14. This is Mary Magdalene's response to Mary Major's preceding eloquent expression, which ends in an embrace and Mary Major's affectionate "Dulcissima Magdalena!" The stage direction thereafter is "Hic salutet Mariam cum manibus tantum" (Here she salutes Mary Major with her hands only). Obviously the women must break from the embrace, after which, lingeringly, Mary Magdalene and Mary Major hold hands ("cum manibus tantum"). In this position Mary Magdalene sings "Mater Jesu crucifixi," and then with one hand brushes away her tears, as she had in Item 6. The next two stage directions may also be alternatives, as in Item 9. The first of these, "Hic se ipsam ostendat," is by itself another woodenly demonstrative gesture, but when combined with the second, "Hic se percutiat ad pectus," it merges into a one-handed breast-beating on "ex dolore cruciata," and is followed with the other hand (or both together, the first hand having dropped) in a two-handed breast-beating on "Sum in corde vulnerata." Mary Magdalene, looking at the cross, holds this agonized gesture in tableau until her Item 18.

ITEM 15. Mary Major, who throughout the preceding item was playing to Mary Magdalene, dropped her hands when Mary Magdalene began her breast-beating, and now turns full front and stage right as she ad-

---

[6] Smoldon, *Planctus Mariae,* p. 8, translates, as cryptically as the scribe, "Here she releases her hand from behind." See Santangelo, *Cividale,* p. 142, for a probable illustration of this gesture.

dresses the "homines" of the audience (the "fratres" of Item 2), and reaches out to them with open hands as she sings "Ubi sunt discipuli." She turns to stage left and gestures (as Mary Magdalene had in Item 2), to the "mulieribus" on "Ubi sunt apostoli," with a turn of gesture to the cross on "quos tantum amasti?" Then she whips back, with both hands, to the audience on "Qui timore territi," and swings to gesture at the cross on "in cruce dimiserunt." On the last anguished line, "Heu me," she beats her breast, once for each "Heu," and then holds, looking at the cross.

ITEM 16. The first stage direction contains another wooden gesture, upon which I have already commented. Of the two gestures prescribed here, the first calls for Mary Jacobi to look at those around her ("ostendendo circumcircha"). Smoldon translates this phrase as "indicating the bystanders," with the implication that the bystanders are imaginary, like the "fratres et sorores" of Item 2, and the "populum" of Items 4 and 17. In those items I have suggested that the audience is intended, that it is deliberately being involved with the action of the play. Because in the next item, the "O vos omnes," Mary Major must speak directly to the audience with open hands, I do not think Mary Jacobi would be directed to anticipate her by speaking to the audience, openhanded or otherwise. I would prefer that she ask her question, "Quis est hic qui non fleret?" of Mary Magdalene and John, with a simple gesture toward Mary Major, whose "tanta tristitia" is being observed by all three characters.

The gesture of hands to eyes, followed by a breast-beating, seems wrong not only in point of acting style but also in dramatic terms, for Mary Jacobi calls attention to herself when her whole item is designed as a comment on Mary Major's sorrow. The sense of Mary Jacobi's item is that any one would weep to see the mother of Christ in such sorrow, not that this sorrow makes Mary Jacobi weep. The source of these lines is the famous sequence, *Stabat Mater,* the subject of which is entirely the "Mater," and the medieval audience was certain to recognize this allusion. The force of the reference, therefore, is weakened by the self-display this stage direction requires of Mary Jacobi, and causes one to wonder whether this direction was confused by the scribe with the rather similar directions for Mary Major's following item. Remote from the performance of the play, as I suggested above, he could easily misplace such directions and assign them, as he did Items 6 and 18, to the wrong character. In any event, Mary Jacobi does not need them. Her item is short, and the "ostendendo circumcircha" gesture is enough: she turns to Mary Magdalene, then to John, and finally to the sorrowing Mary Major.

ITEM 17. Mary Major turns away from the cross to the audience, begins the "O vos omnes," and gestures to them with open hands. Omitting the putting of these hands to her eyes, she gestures to the cross on "et meum dulcem filium," and punctuates each of the last three lines of the item with a variety of breast-beatings. The final cadence is on the same notes and syllables as ended her previous item (15), indicating that she should hold, looking at the cross, at the end of the present item.

ITEM 18. Coussemaker's emendation of the manuscript's "Maria sola" to "Mary Salome" was picked up by Young, who commented, "Particularly noteworthy is the increase in the number of the speakers to five." [7] Smoldon's edition translates "sola" as meaning "alone," which is a better solution, since Mary Salome is nowhere else referred to in this play, can have no other lines, and would be superfluous and in the way of the other four characters. What remains unclear is whether the "Mary alone" is Mary Jacobi or Mary Magdalene. The substance of the item is perhaps more appropriate for the latter, since Mary Jacobi in her last item (16) understood very well why Mary Major was in deep sorrow, and would hardly now reverse herself to ask Mary Major "Cur merore deficis?" (Why exhaust yourself with grieving?). The item therefore is more appropriately Mary Magdalene's, and this assignment works well in performance. She has been in tableau looking at the cross since the end of her Item 14. After Mary Major's Item 17, Mary Magdalene moves to her to console her ("Consolare, Domina"). This is evidently what was intended by the stage direction "Hic versus Mariam maiorem." As she moves to comfort her, Mary Magdalene would naturally extend her hands to her, and the "ostendat" should probably be emended to "cum manibus extensis." I conjecture that Mary Magdalene then touches Mary Major on the shoulder with one hand, comfortingly, and raises that hand on "levat." She lets it fall ("Hic relaxet manus") on "ruina." Mary Major gives some indication that she has heard and appreciated Mary Magdalene's comforting words, and may even place her hand over Mary Magdalene's before moving a step away.

ITEM 19. Mary Major is still not enough comforted or resigned to cease her questioning. This item is built around the bitter question, "Cur te modo video in cruce pendentem" (Why do I see you this way, hanging

[7] Young, I, 513.

on the cross?), and the thrice repeated gesture to the cross is appropriate
for the question. There follow three more gestures to the cross, to point
out the thieves, the crown of thorns, and the pierced side of Christ. The
latter object of her pointing was visible to the audience in the original
production, which apparently used a still extant crucifix with a full-sized
effigy of Christ, and the thieves were probably imagined as being to left
and right of that crucifix.[8] These three objects were sufficiently separated
to allow for differentiation in pointing. Between the two sets of gestures,
it is important that she move. The item ends with the same stage direction,
and the same melodic cadence and syllables, as in her two preceding
items (15 and 17), and suggests a similarly held gesture of breast-beating
as she continues to stare at the cross.

ITEM 20. John moves toward the cross. The stage directions for this item
are an imitation of those for Mary Major's appropriately longer question.
John gestures to the cross, and at the end of the item, after "nescia,"
beats his breast. If we disregard the breast-beating of Item 6 because the
item is not his, this is John's only instance of breast-beating. Its presence
here suggests not only that the gesture is suitable for men as well as for
women, as is the case in modern Italy, but also that its position at the
end of so many items is an intentional, formalizing element of the play.

ITEM 21. This concluding item is appropriately addressed to the audience,
upon whom Mary Major pours her indignation in a final burst of energy.
She has been near exhaustion, as Mary Magdalene tells us in Item 18,
but she rallies and moves center. The stage direction does not repeat it,
but one supposes that she is to use the same "cum manibus apertis" that
she had used in Items 15 and 17. Unlike the frequent directions for
gesture in her other items, there is only an initial direction here, that she
turn to the audience and stand as far as the words "ferre stipendium,"
only two words short of the finish. The word "stet" is, I think, an indication for an almost statuesque posture here, the gesture held throughout,
without pointing or breast-beating. Then, at the very end, she can sustain
this regal, morning-star posture no longer. The stage direction breaks off,
and cannot be interpolated as easily as can the words and music of the
missing page. "Et tunc se . . ." can be completed only by analogy either
with other plays at a similar moment or with earlier stage directions of
this play. Smoldon suggests that "she should droop in sorrow and finally

---

[8] See plate 18. This crucifix is without a crown of thorns, though there may originally
have been one that was removed when the figure was reworked, presumably in the
sixteenth century. The stage directions use "crucem" and "Christum" interchangeably, an
indication that a crucifix is called for.

fall to the ground unless supported by her companions."[9] Another possibility, combined with the drooping, is that she beat her breast one final time ("et tunc se percutiat"), and then gesture to the cross ("et tunc se vertat ad crucem"). Some kind of tableau of the three other characters around her is essential, and the evidence of her exhaustion may have motivated their moving to her, perhaps as early as "maioribus," to support her gently.[10] They look with her as she makes her final gesture to the cross, which has been at the center of the play and is now, appropriately, the focus of the final tableau.

COSTUMES

Costumes for the four characters in *The Lament of Mary* are identical in style with those of *The Visit to the Sepulcher*,[11] and need not be further described here, except as to their colors.[12]

For the Virgin Mary the traditional color is what is known as Mary blue. This is the color of the Cloisters statue (Italian, thirteenth-century) reproduced herein as plate 15, and of a Marian statue from Cividale.[13] Often her costume has two colors: her long tunic is a brownish red, largely covered by a Mary blue cape or mantle, and her hood is of the same blue.

Mary Magdalene, as in her costume for *The Visit to the Sepulcher*, is traditionally in a shade of red that will not clash with Mary blue, and like Mary Major she has a tunic of a complementary color. Mary Jacobi is less colorful, but also in two tones. John is usually in a blue-grey or lilac mantle over a rich brown tunic. Since he wears no hat, the colors of his costume should not clash with his traditional red hair.

A fifteenth-century reference to mourning clothes ("vestibus lamentabilibus") worn by students representing Mary and John is of doubtful relevance here.[14] It is contained in a semidramatic *ordo* from Regensburg

[9] Smoldon, *Planctus Mariae*, p. v. For the image of Mary swooning, see G. McN. Rushforth, *Medieval Christian Imagery* (Oxford, 1936), p. 194, note 4.

[10] In the Tours version of *The Visit to the Sepulcher* (Young, I, 444) Mary Magdalene apparently faints after an impassioned lament, whereupon Mary Jacobi and Mary Salome, one on each arm, raise her from the floor. With this precedent, the two women in *The Lament* would raise Mary Major.

[11] See above, pp. 78–79.

[12] See above, p. 294n, for some sources of color illustrations of costumes for all four characters in this play. Since most of the collections cited are fourteenth-century, the style of costume will do well enough for *The Lament of Mary*, itself probably a fourteenth-century play.

[13] See Santangelo, *Cividale*, p. 83, for the illustration. He does not mention the color, but I have observed it.

[14] Young, I, 505.

for the Adoration of the Cross. If special mourning vestments were used at Regensburg a century after the Cividale *Lament,* they can hardly constitute in reverse chronology a costume tradition about which *The Visit* plays with their more advanced dramaturgy and contemporary costuming are entirely silent. I surmise that the Regensburg reference is to ecclesiastical vestments used in offices for the burial of the dead.

The Pilgrim

(See above, pp. 99–116)

COSTUMES

JUDGING from the stage directions of the Roeun and Fleury versions of *The Pilgrim,* and from the many illustrations of the subject, the three disciples and the Christus usually appear dressed as pilgrims (peregrini"), wearing a costume which is distinguished by its accessories: wallets, staves, hats, and bare feet. The only exception is the Rouen version of the play, in which the direction for alb, amice, and cross may have been conditioned by the fact that in that version the Christus makes only one appearance, or by the possibility that the scribe of the Rouen version confused the pilgrim costume with that of the glorified Christ without including the later scene in his manuscript.

The dress is the usual long tunic and trimmed mantle, as all illustrations show (e.g., plates 13, 14, 19–25), and as described above in the Introduction and in the discussion of costumes for *The Visit to the Sepulcher.*

The wallet, specifically illustrated in plate 19, is hung by a strap over the shoulder. In depictions of Christ's wallet, there is a cruciform design on the flap, to identify him. The cross is also used on other articles associated with Christ in this narrative and others, notably on the wafers on the table at Emmaus (plate 21).

The staves are straight walking sticks, often nearly as tall as the bearer (plates 21 and 23), but occasionally shorter (plate 19). The top of the staff is unusually capped with a plain round knob (plates 21 and 23), but if the staff is shorter it may have more of a handle, like a cane (plate 19). In most of the illustrations which show the pilgrims in motion on the road, the staff is carried over the shoulder when not needed for support (plate 19), or rests upright on the ground.[1] Lest the wrong impression be given, I should note that none of the play versions

---

[1] For a better example of the carrying position, see The Pierpont Morgan Library, "Miniatures" 44, fol. 13 recto. The position of the staff in my plate 21 is conditioned by the fact that the disciple is pointing to the sun or the inn.

gives Christ as the pilgrim a staff. Rouen, already confused about his pilgrim's costume, inappropriately gives him a cross to carry, perhaps a holdover from *The Visit to the Sepulcher*. Fleury gives him a palm frond, like that of the Archangel in its version of *The Visit to the Sepulcher*. The medieval audience would have recognized the palm frond as one of the badges of a medieval pilgrim, who has been where palms grow. But the illustrations of this subject most frequently provide him with a staff (plates 19, 21, 23).

Hats are not *de rigeur* but appear frequently on the heads of Christ and one or more of the disciples. Fortunately for stage use, the period style of men's hats was not consistently wide-brimmed, although throughout the two centuries there was some variation in hat styles, and no one of these was particularly identified as pilgrim's style. Plates 21 and 23 show two styles of hat worn in the road-to-Emmaus scene, and plates 26, 43, and 60 represent other contemporary and appropriate styles.

Two production problems were created by the use of hats in *The Pilgrim*. One was that even the narrowest brim shaded the face of the actor. In this connection I do not understand Smoldon's recommendation of "hats with broad brims" for the pilgrims.[2] If these were used, the front of the brims would have to be pinned back with a badge, as in some representations of St. James. The other problem concerned the disposition of the hats in the second scene of the play, at the table. Even though one miniature shows the two disciples hatted at the table (plate 21), the others do not, and the effect of hats is not good in this parody of the Last Supper. Presumably they could be disposed of in the move from the road scene to the Emmaus inn and table, but this would have required a place to lay them and could have unnecessarily complicated the movement. If, however, a place to lay the hats were found in the Emmaus inn setting, there would have been some effectiveness in having the two disciples retrieve their hats after Christ's first disappearance, indicating that they were moving out of the inn to search "per ecclesiam" (all over the church) as the Beauvais version directs.

To judge from the evidence in art and occasionally from stage directions, shoes were not generally used, even for pilgrims on the road (plates 22, 23, 25). The kind of naturalism which reasons that the pilgrims' feet would be bloody if they were not shod is not typically medieval. The Rouen version specifies "nudus pedes" for the Christus, and Fleury also attests that as the Pilgrim he is to be barefoot. From the

[2] Smoldon, *Peregrinus*, p. vii.

point of view of the actor the prescription of bare feet on the usually cold stone floors of churches could not have been a happy one.

Thomas's costume may have been slightly different from those of the other pilgrim disciples and Christ. The Fleury stage direction for his costume distinguishes him by his silk cloak ("clamide serico"), but otherwise gives him the same staff and hat as the other disciples (but no wallet). The intention of the silk texture (and brighter color?) of Thomas's cloak may have been to suggest that his background is affluent, intellectual, and therefore skeptical, and that he is to be contrasted with the homespun forthrightness of the other two disciples. Silk costumes are elsewhere prescribed for the three Marys at the Sepulcher and for the three Kings in the Limoges version of the *Herod.* Whether or not the Fleury playwright had nobility in mind for Thomas, the distinction would have been worth making.

The two majestic costumes for the Christus in *The Pilgrim* are described in the Fleury stage directions. Beauvais requires only one costume change, vaguely stated as "in alia effigie" (in another outfit), but a second change may be introduced at the same point in the play as Fleury requires one, at the second rendition of the *Pax vobis.* A reading of Fleury's two descriptions indicates their practical relationships for costume changes that had to be done, as Beauvais says of the first one, "mox" (quickly):

". . . colobio candido vestitus, cappa rubea superindutus, ob signum Passionis crucem auream in manu gestans, infulatus candida infula cum aurifrisia . . ."
(. . . dressed in a white tunic, with a red cope over it, carrying in his hand a golden cross as the sign of the Passion, and on his head a white fillet embroidered in gold . . .)

"colobio candido et cappa rubea vestitus, coronam gestans in capite ex amicto et philacteriis compositam, crucem auream cum vexillo in dextra, textum Evangelii habens in sinistra . . ."
(. . . dressed in the white tunic and the red cope, wearing a fillet on his head made of embroidered wool, in his right hand a golden cross with a banner, in his left hand the Gospel Book . . .) [3]

The dress remains the same, but the headdress is radically changed; to the cross is added a banner, and in the left hand is now a Gospel Book. What the stage directions for both omit is mainly the lavish trim on cope and tunic. Illustrations show a wide, ornamented collar band and belt on the tunic, and wide, similarly ornamented trim on the hem of the tunic and all edges of the cope.[4] Fleury's description of the first headdress is so

[3] For the "Vexillum," see Young, I, plate XI.

[4] See above, pp. 78–80, for other details from the costuming for *The Visit to the Sepulcher.*

similar to its description of that of the glorified Christ in *The Visit to the Sepulcher* that the same article was almost certainly used in both Fleury plays.

A special feature of the white tunic in its second use is a temporary flap in the right side, long enough to allow the Christus to expose his right breast to Thomas in the manner shown in plates 21 and 25. This slit would show under the red cope only when needed for the exposure.

PROPERTIES AND FURNISHINGS

Other than the costume props discussed above, the only major properties and furnishings required for the play were the table, bench or stools, and the table setting at the Emmaus inn. The table is roughly waist high, long enough for the three characters to sit behind it, and covered with a white (usually linen) cloth which is wide enough to cover the table top and to hang down in front in pleats. This cloth must have been made in two pieces, one for the top, the other much longer so that it could be pleated at sides and front, and the two pieces sewn together at the front edge of the table. Probably the original production used an altar cloth. The Sicilian (Norman French) version of the play sets the scene "ad altare." The bench or stools did not show, since they were behind the table, and could have been plain articles. These matters, not mentioned in stage directions of versions of *The Pilgrim,* are amply illustrated in plates 20, 21, 24, and 25.

The food and drink on the table at the opening of the scene are variously described by stage directions and illustrations. The Saintes version says "hostiam" (a wafer); Sicily, "pane et vino" (bread and wine); Rouen, "panem"; *Carmina Burana,* "panis"; Beauvais, "panem"; Fleury, "pannis inscissus" (an uncut loaf), "tres nebulae" (three wafers), and "calix cum vino" (a chalice of wine). Four of the six versions agree on "panem," which they derived from Luke's narrative; Fleury specifies that the bread shall be in the form of an uncut loaf, so that Christ has to break it. Two versions specify wafers (unleavened discs of considerable size), and two versions require wine. The pictorial arts of the period, as exemplified in plates 20, 24, and 25, usually require more articles, and all have the chalice of wine centered on the table. There may also be round wafers left and right of the chalice, and whole fish in two ewers beyond the wafers. The fish are the chief addition to the stage directions. There was every reason to set a good table for this scene; in fact the Fleury direction requires it to be "bene parata" (well set). The inn at Emmaus offered first-class accommodations. Luke calls it a "castellum," and this is followed by all stage directions and by the artists, who picture the inn as a chateau. The table was therefore properly set with sumptuous elegance.

Even the chalice would have been of silver or copper-gilt, reminiscent of that utensil (or perhaps the same one) used in the Mass, which intentionally suggested the Last Supper. The Sicilian version, in locating the table "ad altare" and thus apparently reflecting an earlier way of handling the scene (before the day of the reliquary and reredos), perhaps encouraged later playwrights in a more secular setting to keep the table and its cloth and settings elegant.

During the scene on the Road to Emmaus, Luke and some stage directions call for the disguised Christus to sit during his "Haec Moyses" item, probably on some small non-naturalistic object, like the medieval faldstooi (a folding stool like a campstool) with a good pillow on top of it. Plate 19, while not illustrating it, suggests that such a stool, placed on set before the play begins, is first used by one of the disciples after their long walk, and later by Christ after he appears to them and the disciple rises to converse. This repeated use would have made the stool less an obvious expedient and more an integrated property of the play.

MAKEUP: BEARDS AND HAIRSTYLES

The silence of the stage directions of all versions does not mean that the men of this play were not bearded. Analysis of illustrations in art shows that between the early twelfth and the middle thirteenth century, all three characters in this story were bearded, the only exception being the Hildesheim portrait showing Cleopas clean-shaven (plate 24). By the fourteenth century none of the three men is bearded (plate 23). The chances therefore are that in the original Beauvais performance in the twelfth century the actors wore beards, but were not necessarily characterized by them.

The sampling of beard characterizations reported in the Introduction shows that of thirteen portraits of the Christus in play subjects, the artists bearded him in ten. The audience's expectation must therefore have been to see Christ in a beard. The evidence from the adjacent play, *The Visit to the Sepulcher,* as reported above, is that the Christus is always bearded and that his hair is shoulder length. In *The Pilgrim* his hair is that length, somewhat longer than that of the disciples.

From the producer's point of view, then and now, wig and beard for the Christus are helpful in disguising the head and personality of the actor of this difficult role. For the disciples there seems little advantage unless their short beards balance the necessarily long haircuts as achieved by wigs. If the suggestion made above in the section on characterization, that the "Other Disciple" be interpreted to mean Peter rather than Luke, the type of beard proposed for Peter in *The Visit to the Sepulcher* would again have been used here. When these plays are performed today in a single bill, the actor of clean-shaven John in *The Visit to the Sepulcher* can be bearded for the role of Thomas in *The Pilgrim*. An illustration possibly to be identified as Thomas in the *Lazarus* resurrection scene shows him beardless (plate 41, right).

LIGHTING

In *The Pilgrim* there is little opportunity for medieval lighting techniques. The crown light could have been used in the Emmaus chateau set, but illustrations of this scene show no lighting fixtures.

If the audience-procession technique of the Rouen version were attempted, as suggested above, candles and torches in the hands of those processing would have been effective. After they became the audience, they could have snuffed the candles as the scene moved to the platform set, but the torches would have remained lighted and held in locations near that set to augment its lighting. The type of torch lamp shown in some illustrations of the Wise and Foolish Maidens (as in plates 46 and 47), with a long handle so that the torch may be raised and held aloft, would have been appropriate for this purpose.

SOUND EFFECTS

In the Rouen version the procession is to sing the antiphon, *In exitu*, to lead into the appearance of the disciples singing the *Jesu, nostra redemptio*. The short phrase of chime bells suggested by Smoldon as an introduction to the *Jesu, nostra redemptio* (Item 1) may be a good bridge between these two musical items. Smoldon uses the chime bells effectively at several other points: after Item 1c, before Item 2, in Item 16c as a part of the communion ceremony, in Item 24 during Thomas's "O Jesu

Domine," and at the close of the last item of the play. These six entries of the chime bells would have sufficiently enlivened the performance.

Drums and cymbals, if handled lightly, may have been effective at the two moments when Christ suddenly disappears. The use of these instruments was probably limited to occasions not already covered by harp, organ, and bell passages, as in the Smoldon edition.

The Shepherds

(See above, pp. 117–127)

COSTUMES

THE Archangel in *The Shepherds* is the same splendidly white apparition we have already encountered in *The Visit to the Sepulcher*. His cohorts, the Multitude of the Heavenly Host, are only one degree less splendid, but were not like him adorned with wings or they would never have been able to cluster as a multitude in the gallery.

The Shepherds' costumes are so well portrayed in contemporary illustrations that a detailed verbal description is superfluous. One may note, however, that the hats or cowls of those who have them are various, never all the same style (plates 26–28). Cowls and hoods were worn on or off the head; in fact one Shepherd may, for humorous effect, have worn a hood off the head and a hat on it, the latter borrowed from the hatless third Shepherd of plate 27. They usually have short cloaks and always wear much shorter tunics than the disciples, belted and sometimes tattered at the bottom hem. Unlike the disciples, they have soft shoes, like those of royalty and soldiers. All shepherds carry staves as a badge of office, and these seldom have crooked handles; they look more like shillelaghs, with heavy knobs at the top or bottom.

Mary in plate 29 wears a long-sleeved green tunic with a Mary-blue coverlet. The nimbus in this plaque looks almost like a hat, and nearly obscures her long hair.

MAKEUP: BEARDS AND HAIRSTYLES

The older Shepherd always has a beard (e.g., plates 26–28, 30). If one of the younger Shepherds has a cowl, he can hardly use any more beard than the soldiers in theirs. The third Shepherd is really only a boy, and in the medieval scheme of things would not have a beard. A rough beard for the older Shepherd would therefore seem to be all that was required.

The hairstyle of the Midwives is distinctive of their lower class, to judge from contemporary illustrations. Usually the top of their heads is covered by a snood, as in plate 29; less often, it is bound by a headband. In either event, the long hair down their backs is usually braided, not hanging loose. One wonders whether this hairstyle and covering are occupational. Mary is without snood, her hair long and parted in the middle (plate 28).

LIGHTING

The *sedes* for scene two required very careful lighting. The artists of the period tried to emphasize the Christ Child in his upstage position by height and gilt. Given enough height to see him beyond the Virgin, neither is so effective as warm lighting on the Child and somewhat less warm light on the pondering Virgin. Candelabra flanking the Child would have helped, but these do not often appear in contemporary illustrations, possibly because of conflict with the curtains of the tableau and the dangers of the candles either being blown out at the drawing of the front curtains, or setting fire to them. The medieval artist achieved something of the effect of modern spotlighting by the golden nimbus that encompasses the face of every sacred character, even that of the newborn Babe.

In an illustration of the birth of the Virgin Mary (plate 29) there are shown, hanging from the Romanesque arches that frame the tableau, two ampulla-type oil lamps. These, rather than crown lights, would be appropriate for Christ's nativity in a manger, and in fact somewhat resemble the barn lanterns of not so long ago.

SOUND EFFECTS

The arrival of the Archangel may have been accompanied by drum and cymbal, or by bells. Either seems possible as an introduction to the play, to focus the attention of the audience, as well as to motivate the initial antics of the Shepherds. A single, sustained belltone may accompany the two kneeling adorations of the Shepherds in scene two.

While it involves more than a sound effect, this is a good place to suggest a possible conclusion to the play. Though somewhat outside the strict liturgical context, the cast of the play—the Archangel, the Heavenly Host, the Midwives, and the Shepherds—could have made their departure up the nave to the singing of an appropriate hymn. Two pages later in the Rouen playscript is a direction that the Shepherds are to signalize the end of Mass by leading the singing of a *Benedicamus,* a famous and beautiful hymn. It is of sufficient length to permit the entire cast to process up the nave and out. Actually the Rouen cast did not process, because the Shepherds stayed and eventually sang the appropriate but undramatic antiphon, *Ecce completa sunt,* from the pulpit.

The Play of Herod
with The Slaughter of the Innocents

(See above, pp. 129–142)

COSTUMES

K INGLY costumes in these plays are extravagant and necessary. My only objection to the Ter-Arutunian royal costumes concerns their head gear, which as crowns are so top-heavy and dehumanizing that no playwright of the Middle Ages would have tolerated them. The dress itself has many varieties, to be distinguished not so much by style as by the great quantity of material used. Even among kings, Herod's costume is more voluminous than those of the Magi (plates 32–33 and 35–36) though they are splendidly outfitted for their kingly mission.[1] The tenth-eleventh-century Echternach illustrations (plates 32 and 34) are atypical in not providing as long a tunic and mantle as were customary in the twelfth and thirteenth centuries; the length of these is more correctly shown in plates 33 and 36. These regal characters are never barefoot, nor are their attendants.

Crowns for such kings, without being top-heavy, may be as spectacular as that of Darius in plate 67, and as modest and "classical" as those of the kings in the other plates referred to above. The crowns for the three Magi should be individualized; there are many styles, as the examples herein show. The Magi in northern French illustrations of the period generally wear crowns in the same design as those of contemporary Norman kings. Four or five crosses are mounted on the top of the rim.

The Courtiers are described in a Fleury stage direction as "in habitu iuvenili" (in the dress of young men). The best one can do with this obscure direction, aided by references to other versions of the play, is to reason that Herod's is a military court, that the Courtiers are therefore military officers, only slightly superior to the Armiger who is sent to interview the Magi. The Courtiers may be furnished with swords and shields (plate 32), the Armiger with a banner (plate 36).

[1] Plate 33 shows Herod "in a red mantle and blue robe," from M. R. James, *A Descriptive Catalogue of the McClean Collection of Manuscripts in the Fitzwilliam Museum* (Cambridge, 1912), p. 61.

The Scribes are apparently not military attendants, but priests. Their costumes may be derived from plate 32, but should be lengthened. Fleury specifies only that the Scribes should be bearded. The Midwives are dressed as in *The Shepherds,* and wear snoods.

In the Fleury version of the play the stage directions are concerned only with costumes for the Courtiers, and otherwise deal chiefly with basic movement. Though the twelfth-century Bilsen version of the Magi play even writes its stage directions in hexameters, it is as reticent about costume as the other mature versions of the play.[2] From semidramatic ceremonies recorded at Limoges, Besançon, and Rouen, more costume data may be gathered, substantiating the illustrations.[3] The Magi are dressed in differently colored silk costumes, with gold crowns. They either carry pyxes (plate 8) in their own hands or have page boys ("famuli") to carry them, and possibly other attendants to bear their silver staves or scepters.

PROPERTIES AND FURNISHINGS

The pyxes (plate 8) carried by the Marys to the Sepulcher seem from the illustrations to have been purposely re-used as the containers for the Magi's gifts to the infant Christ. This parallelism goes with the intentional similarity of the crib to the sepulcher in its altar position, and of the Midwives to the Angels at the sepulcher. The swords of Herod's soldiers, to judge from the art of the period, were broadswords, not fencing rapiers or the like (plates 32, 35, 36).

The Fleury script emphasizes the "libris prophetarum" (Book of the Prophets) as an important "practical" property. The Scribes must turn the pages a while until they appear to discover the prophecy, at which moment they say "Vidimus, Domine," point out the passage to the un-learned Herod, and translate it for him. ("Tunc Scribe diu revolvant librum, et tandem, inventa quasi prophetia, dicant 'Vidimus, Domine,' et ostendentes cum digito, Regi incredulo tradant librum.") The dimensions of this book may be derived from the Echternach illustration (plate 32), held in the hands of the leading Scribe.

MAKEUP: BEARD AND HAIRSTYLES

To judge from the survey of the beards prescribed by repertory stage directions and shown in illustrations, the Angel is not bearded. Joseph,

[2] Young, II, 75–80.   [3] Young, II, 34, 37, 43.

an old man, has a long beard, probably gray (plate 71), which the *Carmina Burana* version calls a "prolixa barba." Herod and the First Magi have relatively short beards (as in plates 32, 36), and the Second Magi may also have had a beard (plate 34). Mâle's evidence, quoted above, is somewhat different.[4] However, these regal beards were trimmed (as also in plates 33–36); they would not have been the flowing beards of the Pro Musica production, which obscured the actors' faces. The Scribes are directed by Fleury to be bearded, no doubt because they are priests. The Courtiers and the Armiger, wearing the usual military helmets and chain-mail (plates 32, 35, 36), have no place for beards, though a leader of the Courtiers in plate 36 (top) has his chain mail cowl open in front and could have a short, scraggly beard. Archelaus is represented in the illustrations of his coronation as a very young, clean-shaven man.

The hairstyles for the Virgin and the Midwives have been discussed in connection with *The Shepherds,* above. Rachel and the Mothers and Consolers, being out in public, wear veils similar to those of the Marys in *The Visit to the Sepulcher* and *The Lament of Mary,* as described above.

LIGHTING

The crown light shown in the Echternach illustration of Herod's court (plate 32) seems highly desirable for that set, though no mention of it is made in any Fleury stage directions. The Fleury version, by its repeated directions for the Magi and the star to move, suggests that the crown light was manipulated from some position in the nave, possibly by the rope specified by the Limoges version and with pulleys at each end. It could thus be moved until it arrived over or just outside the Manger set, where it would remain for the duration of the play.[5]

The two major sets, the Manger and Herod's Court, were likely to have been similarly decorated with a crown light, the "crown" for the Manger being presumably somewhat larger and therefore brighter than the lighting for the more sinister court of Herod. If the latter crown light proved to be too competitive with that of the Manger, Herod could have

---

[4] See above, p. 137.

[5] Greenberg and Smoldon, *Herod,* p. 77, convey the impression that the Star was "apparently a candelabrum," but the problem of keeping a flame alive while moving over such a distance is much greater with candles than with the fueled and shielded crown light.

got along without it, but as a further means of balancing the two sets the crown light would have been retained for both locations if at all possible.

SOUND EFFECTS

Since Greenberg and Smoldon have provided so excellent a score for *The Play of Herod,* with copious use of bells and drums, there is no need to suggest further uses of nonvocal sound in this play.

The Procession of the Prophets

(See above, pp. 143–149)

COSTUMES

THE Laon and Rouen versions of *The Procession of the Prophets* describe the costumes in vestment terms, but we have seen that this terminology may apply equally well to the secular tunic, mantle, cape, and hood. Considerable latitude was probably allowed in adjusting the style of the costume, as described in the stage directions, to those depicted in the arts of the period.

Costumes, properties, and makeup are listed below in translation for each character, the first character being unique to the Limoges version. These descriptions form a composite of the Laon, Rouen, and *Carmina Burana* stage directions.

ISRAEL is pictured in art as "a son of Jacob representing Israel."

MOSES wears a long mantle and short cape over a tunic, with horns on his head ("cornuta facie"); see plate 37. The horns could be gold, red, blue, or green.[1] He is bearded, carries his tablets of the Law and a staff.

ISAIAH wears a red stole crossed in front, over a long mantle; he is bearded and bold ("discrinitus"). (plate 38)

JEREMIAH is dressed in the ornamented vestments of a priest, but without a stole. He holds a scroll and is bearded. (plate 38)

DANIEL is youthful, and dressed in a splendid green tunic of below-knee length. See plate 65 for his portrait. Usually he holds a spear, as in plate 65, but he appears in plate 38 without this property.

[1] For documentation of these colors in pictorial art, and for a refutation of Mâle's theory that the Rouen version of the play originated the idea of horns for Moses, see Arthur Watson, *The Tree of Jesse*, pp. 26–27. The horns were applied to Moses in the Vulgate translation of Exodus 34:29.

HABAKKUK is a lame old man, stooped and hunchbacked, bearded, and wearing a long mantle. He enters eating radishes from a wallet, and brandishing a long palm branch—longer than that in plate 11—with which he beats people (the audience or the choir). Plate 38, however, shows him as a "straight" character.

DAVID wears an ornate King's robes, as in plates 33 and 36.

SIMEON is a bearded old man in a silk cope. See his portrait in plate 70. He holds a palm branch of ordinary length, as in plate 11.

ELIZABETH wears a woman's white mantle; she is obviously pregnant (plate 69).

JOHN THE BAPTIST is barefoot and bearded, in long hair and a hairshirt. He holds a palm branch like the one in plate 11, or a book, as in plate 38.

VIRGIL is ornately dressed as a young man, in a costume similar to Daniel's but probably in another color; he wears a crown of ivy and carries his reed pen, ink horn, and writing board.

NEBUCHADNEZZAR is attired in an elaborate regal outfit, like that of Darius in plate 67. His walk and posture are haughty.

SIBYL wears an ornate woman's dress, her stringy hair ("decapillata") crowned with ivy, like Virgil's. She has an "expression of mad inspiration" ("insanienti simillima"),[2] and gesticulates wildly in the direction of the heavens (plate 38).

CANTORS are identified either as "cantores" (song leaders), "vocatores" (callers), "appellatores" (summoners), or chorus. While the Cantor is not described, or even named, in the Limoges version, I prefer a single interlocutor, who may be costumed as St. Augustine, whose sermon is here dramatized, versified, and set to music. The *Carmina Burana* version has Augustine on stage. The illustrations of St. Nicholas may serve as guides for his costume, showing the dress of a bishop (plates 51, 52). The Cantor may, however, merely have been dressed as the soloist of the church choir. He would have to be vocally talented to sing thirteen

---

[2] Young's translation, II, 151.

stanzas. The Laon and Rouen versions, perhaps for this reason, have this role sung jointly by "vocatores" or "appellatores," respectively. The single Cantor, suggested by Young, seems a more dramatic solution.[3] Earlier scholars, with what Young describes as "undue editorial certainty," suggested "praecentor" (the presenter, as in a masque), and "sacerdos" (priest).

LIGHTING

Crown lights above each of the arches, as are illustrated in at least two art works of the period (plates 10, 32), might have been effective. Three such lights would not have provoked comparison with the necessarily single crown light for *The Visit to the Sepulcher* and one or two for *The Play of Herod*.

SOUND EFFCTS

Chime bells may have been used during the opening stanzas ("Omnes gentes . . . natus hodie"), and a single tolling bell before the Cantor summons the first prophet, as well as after the last stanza. Thereafter, a chime bell (C pitch) might have been used as a preliminary to each summons, and technically as a concealed method of re-establishing that pitch with which the manuscript begins each summons.

The melodic variation for the Simeon episode, for which the notation is lacking in the manuscript, must be reconstructed. Since the Laon and Rouen versions are preserved only in manuscripts without musical notation, nothing can be borrowed from them.

[3] Young, II, 138, note 2.

The Raising of Lazarus

(See above, pp. 151–169)

COSTUMES

ILLUSTRATIONS from the period (plates 39–41) and earlier show Jesus and the Disciples in the usual tunics and mantles, with no special distinction for Jesus' costume. The lower half of plate 40 illustrates this point, and is helpful concerning the costumes of the Pharisees. None of the men wears a hat.

Mary Magdalene's dress is the traditional red of the prostitute and may be of tattered silk.[1] Martha's costume is of heavy cotton, and less colorful. In the first scene, Mary Magdalene would wear no veil, again to indicate her profession. At home in their Bethany house the heads of neither Martha nor Mary Magdalene would be covered, but as each in turn rushes out to meet Jesus on the road, or after Lazarus's body has been removed from the Bethany house, Martha would put on a heavy veil identical with those worn by the three Marys in *The Visit to the Sepulcher*. Compare plates 4 and 10 with 40 for the identity of the veil in the two plays. Black mourning mantles (as in plate 41) would be donned by Martha and Mary Magdalene before their last re-entrances, and would be effectively discarded and left on the chancel floor, after Lazarus rises.

Lazarus has a complete change of costume during the play. In his first scene he is dressed like any other man in plate 40. His grave costume is rather more special, as plates 39 through 41 indicate in one way or another. The consistent pattern in all illustrations of the Lazarus graveclothes is that diagonal bands or ropes wrap the *lintheamina* tightly around the body. The *sudarium* is wrapped around his head but not over his face, mummy-style, and there are no bands over the *sudarium*. For the dimensions and materials of graveclothes, see their description in discussion of properties for *The Visit to the Sepulcher* (p. 288).

The artists did not have to concern themselves with the problem of how

---

[1] Chambers, II, 76, points out that, in the *Carmina Burana* version of the incident at Simon's house, Mary Magdalene wears black as a sign of her conversion and penitence. The contexts, however, are too different for relevant comparison.

Lazarus, bound hand and foot, could walk from the sepulcher to the front archway of the tomb and thence down the nave in procession, but the producer did. Presumably the Disciples recover from their stupefaction in time to carry out Jesus' order to loosen the bands of his *lintheamina,* while Lazarus is sitting up in the sarcophagus. Lazarus had to walk in the recessional, possibly with his bands entirely shed and left at the entrance to the tomb. The audience, and the characters in the play, needed this demonstration that Lazarus was not just a momentary apparition but was really returning to life with his friends and sisters.

PROPERTIES AND FURNISHINGS

Peter has the same key or keys (plate 40 shows only one) that he carried in *The Visit to the Sepulcher.* He may also carry a short sword, with which he will later cut off an enemy's ear. Jesus in many illustrations has a cross-staff with which he seems to be touching Lazarus. In the Biblical account, which the playwright follows, he uses only his voice to resuscitate Lazarus, and a staff-cross would probably be awkward in relation to the archway and interior of the tomb. The requirements of the playwright are not always identical with those of the visual artist.

Another hand property is the large ring worn by Mary Magdalene. She instructs the Messengers to present this token to Jesus in order to authenticate the message ("Et praesenti praesentes dicite/ Hoc mandatum"). The nature of the token is made clear by the Messengers' subsequent line to Jesus, "Anularum dolorem respice" (Gaze upon this sad ring). Although this line mentions only one ring, one may interpret Mary Magdalene's use of the plural "praesentes" to mean that Martha also gives a ring to the Messengers.

Mary Magdalene had to have another hand property when she appeared at Simon's house: a pyx containing the ointment with which she was to anoint Jesus' head. This property would be identical with those carried by the three Marys in *The Visit to the Sepulcher* and by the Magi in the *Herod.*

The furnishings for the first scene, supper at Simon's house, would have been kept to about the same minimum as those for the supper at Emmaus in *The Pilgrim.* Nearly the same arrangement of food and drink on the table would have been sufficient, except that the wafers would not be crossed, and there would probably be several chalices for use by the actors during the scene. There would have been no hand utensils for eating. The table would have been long, narrow, light enough to strike at the conclusion of the scene, and not so large as to take valuable space from the cast of eleven in this scene. Presumably only Jesus and his four Disciples would be seated at the table. The sumptuous table setting and table-cloth should be enough to indicate that this is the house of a prosperous Pharisee, and to contrast it easily with the humble house of Mary Magdalene and Martha in the next scene. For other table settings, see those of *Daniel, The Wise and Foolish Maidens,* and *The Son of Getron* (plates 66, 48, and 64).

For the house at Bethany, after Simon's supper table was removed through the back curtains, the pallet or cot for Lazarus would have been brought in, with two coverlets over it, one masking the construction of the cot, as in the illustrations of the Magi's beds in the *Herod* (plate 34) but less elaborate. The other coverlet or blanket would cover Lazarus after he lay down to die. It should have been long enough to cover him, head and foot, after he died. In addition to the cot, only a small plain bench or table was needed for the transformation.

MAKEUP: BEARDS AND HAIRSTYLES

Christ is bearded in most illustrations, as we have observed before. One illustration of the Lazarus scene (plate 40, eleventh century) shows him clean-shaven. Peter, as in *The Visit to the Sepulcher,* is represented in a square-cut beard (plates 40, 41). The Disciples either may or may not be bearded. An illustration in which I think Thomas can be identified (plate 41, right) shows him beardless. A group portrait of the Pharisees as they witness Lazarus' resurrection (plate 40, bottom) shows some of them bearded, others not. One would surmise that Simon had a well-trimmed beard. Lazarus would be clean shaven, if for no other reason than that his *sudarium,* like the soldiers' helmets in *The Visit to the Sepulcher* and *The Herod,* would make a beard superfluous because largely invisible.

The length of Mary Magdalene's hair is variously portrayed. One extreme illustration of the foot-washing scene shows her with wavy hair to her knees; others merely make it long enough to be convenient to use in washing Jesus' feet. This practical necessity would probably result in her hair being longer than Martha's. Because both are bare-headed when at home in the Bethany scenes, medieval boy actors would probably have worn wigs for both roles.

322

LIGHTING

Since in this play the crown light would have no symbolic use as a star or as the rising sun, it was no doubt avoided. Providing adequate lighting for the simultaneous illumination of the three sets must have been a considerable medieval task, made only slightly less onerous by the fact that the tomb does not require interior lighting. Only the front archway need be lit, at the moment of Lazarus's appearance in the last scene.

SOUND EFFECTS

The tolling of a small bell to announce the death of a parishioner, a common medieval practice, would apply to Lazarus's death, after he has been carried off. The great tower bells were customarily sounded at the conclusion of the *Te Deum* procession. Such parallel uses of bells, earlier as mourning for his death and later as rejoicing in his resurrection, might have been effective and within the theatrical usage of the times.

The Wise and Foolish Maidens

(See above, pp. 183–195)

MOVEMENT AND GESTURE

OVEMENT in *The Wise and Foolish Maidens* play must be predicated on the precise assignment of lines and items to the various members of the cast. The manuscript of the play being diffident at many staging points, and scholarly opinion being of small help because it does not fully project an actual production, I offer below an estimate of probable line assignments and movements.

Line number in Young edition	Singer	Movement
1	First Wise and Foolish	Leading the others in.
2	Second Wise and Foolish	To audience.
3–4	Third Wise and Foolish	Indicating Hellmouth.
5–6	Fourth Wise and Foolish	Still at Hellmouth.
7–8	Fifth Wise and Foolish	To a crucifix.
9–10	All Wise and Foolish	To audience, but keeping gesture to crucifix.
11		Foolish Maidens begin to drowse.[1] Enter Gabriel.
11–30	Gabriel	To all Maidens.
30		Gabriel leaves. First, Second, and Third Foolish Maidens awaken.
31–34	First Foolish Maiden	To Wise Maidens.
35	First Three Foolish Maidens	To each other.
36–39	Second Foolish Maiden	To Wise Maidens.
40	First *four* Foolish Maidens	To each other (Fourth F. M. has awakened.)
41–44	Third Foolish Maiden	To Wise Maidens.

[1] London, British Museum, MS Harley 1526–1527, fol. 46 recto (first half of the thirteenth century), shows some Foolish Maidens asleep.

Line number in Young edition	Singer	Movement
45	All Foolish Maidens	To Wise Maidens (Fifth F. M. has awakened.)
46–49	First and Second Wise Maidens	To Foolish Maidens.
50	All Foolish Maidens	To Wise Maidens (usual refrain.)
51–54	Third, Fourth, and Fifth Wise Maidens	To Foolish Maidens.
55	All Foolish Maidens	To Wise Maidens.
56	First Foolish Maiden	To Foolish Maidens.
57	Second Foolish Maiden	To Foolish Maidens.
58	Third Foolish Maiden	To Foolish Maidens.
59	Fourth Foolish Maiden	To Foolish Maidens.
60	All Foolish Maidens	To Wise Maidens.
66	First Wise Maiden	To Foolish Maidens.
67	Second Wise Maiden	To Foolish Maidens.
68	Third Wise Maiden	To Foolish Maidens.
69	First Foolish Maiden	To Merchants at booth.[2]
70	All Foolish Maidens	To Merchants.
61–62	First and Second Foolish Maidens	To Wise Maidens.
63–64	Third, Fourth, Fifth Foolish Maidens	To Wise Maidens.
65	All Foolish Maidens	To Wise Maidens.
71–72	First Merchant	To Foolish Maidens.
73–74	Second Merchant	To Foolish Maidens.
75–77	First Merchant	To Foolish Maidens.
78	Second Merchant	To Foolish Maidens.
79	First Foolish Maiden	To Foolish Maidens, at booth.
80	Second Foolish Maiden	To Foolish Maidens.
81	Third Foolish Maiden	To Foolish Maidens.
82	Fourth Foolish Maiden	To Foolish Maidens.
83	All Foolish Maidens	To each other, leaving booth. Merchants withdraw from booth. Enter Bridegroom.
84	First Foolish Maiden	To Bridegroom.
85	Second Foolish Maiden	To Bridegroom.
86	Third Foolish Maiden	To Bridegroom.

[2] For line 69 a conjectural restoration, "Vos marchaan, nos poet coseler," was supplied by Thomas, *Sponsus,* p. 184, note 1. This line may be sung to the melody of line 54.

Line number in Young edition	Singer	Movement
87	Fourth Foolish Maiden	To Bridegroom. (ll. 84–87 are to melody of ll. 79–82)
88	All Foolish Maidens	To Bridegroom.
89–90	Bridegroom	To Foolish Maidens. (To melody of ll. 1–2)
91–93	Bridegroom	To Foolish Maidens (to melody of ll. 46–48). Demons appear from Hellmouth.
93	Bridegroom	Repeated, to Demons. They surround the Foolish Maidens, thrust the first four Foolish Maidens into Hellmouth, and follow out.

The Bridegroom escorts the entering Ecclesia to the banquet table, and returns to beckon the Wise Maidens to come in. They pass through the door of the banquet room, and he closes it after them. The Fifth Foolish Maiden has evaded the Demons, rushes to the banquet room door, and tries to open it.[3] Demons reappear and drag her into Hellmouth. The Bridegroom, the Wise Maidens, and Ecclesia form a tableau at the table, perhaps a free-standing altar (plate 48).

The Maidens' gestures with their torches, upright and topsy-turvy, are traditional for the subject (e.g., plates 46–47), and may be assumed to have been the major gesture in the play.

COSTUMES

To judge from illustrations of the period, the costumes of the Maidens were to be individualized (e.g., plates 46–47), and were of course within the style of the period. The illustrations suggest that the Maidens were richly attired, as befitting young ladies (or bridesmaids) at a wedding.

In most illustrations, except those which show the Wise Maidens at the banquet crowned (plates 47, 48), the heads of the Maidens are not veiled.

[3] At Modena Cathedral, sculpture on the portal of St. Gall illustrates the moment at which a Foolish Maiden tries the door. The Bridegroom and the Wise Maidens are on the other side of a "practical" door. This sculpture is reproduced in Francovich, *Benedetto Antelami*, plates 325 and 327.

They are depicted with caps in a Strasbourg Cathedral sculpture (plate 46). How a lack of headdress is to be reconciled with the action at the Merchants' booth, which must be a public place, is a question which would bother a medieval more than a modern producer. Unlike the situation in the *Lazarus,* where Mary Magdalene's lack of veil characterizes her in relation to her sister Martha, all the women in *The Wise and Foolish Maidens* may have been bare-headed and no invidious distinctions made. In a modern wedding party, which may reflect a long tradition, the bride is veiled but not the bridesmaids. Flat-soled soft shoes on the Maidens are shown wherever the pose requires it. Generally their long, full tunics and mantles obviated the need to show their shoes.

The costume of the Bridegroom varies considerably in the illustrations. While the costume of the glorified Christ is entirely appropriate, some illustrations show an elaborate secular costume of a nobleman, with cruciform accessories as the only symbolic connection with the Christus and his second coming. This deliberately anachronistic costume is comparable to the treatment of Christ as a medieval pilgrim in *The Pilgrim.*

Demon costumes varied considerably in the Middle Ages, but most require a skin-tight tunic and tights, a black cloak, and an animal-like full mask, with pointed ears (plate 50).[4]

The Oil Merchants may simply have had the same costume as the Spice Merchants of the St. Quentin version of *The Visit to the Sepulcher.* The only distinctive item of the Oil Merchants' costume may have been a knee-length apron, like that of the Innkeeper in *The Three Clerks* (plate 57), to keep their tunics from being soiled by their merchandise. The headdress and costuming for Ecclesia are illustrated in plates 27 (top right medallion), 47, and 48.

PROPERTIES AND FURNISHINGS

The chief properties, as mentioned in discussing gesture in this play, are the ten torches or lamps. After considering this matter, M. Thomas concludes from his study of portrayals in art that we do not know whether the Maidens carried torches, as shown in plate 47, or a vase-type lamp which resembles ancient and modern cathedral lamps (plates 29, 46).[5] Since both styles are illustrated in the period, we are at liberty to choose whichever is more effective and more practical for the repeated gesturing during

[4] Nicoll, p. 190, has other illustrations.   [5] Thomas, *Sponsus,* p. 67.

the play. When torches are shown, those of the Wise Maidens have solid flames coming from them, rising as much as three inches above the rim of the torch basin. In performance these flames would probably have had to be painted cutouts, like the conventional flames of Hellmouth. The flame of the vase-type lamp, on the other hand, is sufficiently protected by its long throat to permit broad gestures without spilling. The presence of live flames in the five lamps of the Wise Maidens has a symbolic sense as well as a theatrical effect, and this type of lamp may have been what was used in the medieval theater. In lines 41 and 53 the lights are referred to as "lampadibus"; had torches been intended the word would more likely have been "torchiis," as in the Besançon *Visit to the Sepulcher*,[6] for the medieval scribe is usually careful to distinguish between candles, lamps, and torches. Internal and circumstantial evidence, then, point to stage use of lamps rather than the attractive but impractical torches; in this case the theatrical gesture of the Foolish Maidens turning their empty lamps upside down, so abundantly illustrated in the period, would still have been practical.

The set-piece for Hellmouth is generally drawn as a large, three-dimensional cutout, placed so that its back end leads to an area out of sight lines, as in plate 49. The visible portion was often painted in flame reds and yellows.

A staff-cross or crosier for the Bridegroom would have had rather too blatant a symbolic attachment, suggesting that he intends to harrow Hell, and would in any event be in the way of his handling the door and beckoning the Wise Maidens to enter.

If the Oil Merchants used as a counter one or two oil barrels, no other merchandizing equipment needed to show, since no more is used. The Oil Merchants stand, and hence require no bench or stools like those of the Spice Merchants.

No clubs or pitchforks are suggested for the Demons. Their clawlike hands are more effective in seizing and thrusting the Foolish Maidens, and any implement would probably interfere with movements by the group of Demons.

Gabriel may have used a palm branch to aid his gestures during his four stanzas of annunciation to the Maidens, but a long straight trumpet would have been even better. The stagecoach horn of the last century is surprisingly like the type of horn shown in Gabriel's hands in twelfth century illustrations.

[6] Young, I, 290.

STAGING AND DEFINITION OF
ACTING AREAS

The considerable variety of portrayals of the three main episodes forestalls a precise definition of their staging from this source. There are, moreover, no indications whatever in the only two stage directions. I posit three locations for the action of the play, each of which may have required a *sedes* or set-piece: Hellmouth, the Merchants' counter, and the door to the banquet room.

The offstage areas for Hellmouth and for the banquet room had to be of sufficient size to accommodate eight and seven persons respectively. These locations are probably at opposite ends of the staging area, with their contrast between the celestial and the hellish. The door to the banquet room may have been an existing architectural element of the church, such as the door to the sacristy or to the cloister, rather than one constructed for the play. A similar size of opening beyond the Hellmouth set-piece was a necessity, in order to let some of the eight actors out the back end. Since action is generally considered from left to right, the door to the banquet room would have been stage right, and Hellmouth stage left. The Bridegroom enters right, moving toward center to the Wise Maidens, attracting the Foolish from left of center, where the Merchants' booth may have been. Another suggestion for the location of these set-pieces is seen in plate 48, in which the Merchants' booth is upstage left, the door to stage right of center and free-standing in profile as such stage doors seem often to have been.

Still another suggestion from the art of the period is that the door was the common towerlike "castellum" structure, with a practical *phlyakes* door therein (plates 21, 22, 27, 32, 34, 35, 48, 61, 66). This solution is more aesthetically satisfactory because it marks all three locations with scenery in the same theatrical style, and thus unifies the staging. Further, the imagination of the audience in regard to the door to the banquet room would have been somewhat frustrated if they knew full well that the presumed door to such uncommon delights was really just the old familiar sacristy or cloister door, which had no such ceremonial associations with the subject of the play as the Easter and Christmas plays often had with the altar. The door to Jerusalem in *Lazarus* is a different matter, for the audience knew that one would have to go outdoors to reach a Jerusalem, but not to reach the banquet room. In many illustrations the door to the banquet room is centered. With this focus, and it is the focus of the action of the play, Hellmouth would be extreme stage left, the Merchants' booth stage right. The Bridegroom would still enter from stage right, passing by the booth to accost the Foolish Maidens who have just departed from the booth and are moving left. The Wise Maidens would be to the left of the door at this point in the action.

I have mentioned the blocking here, rather than under the heading of movement, because the blocking tests the validity of the arrangement of the three *sedes* or set-pieces. All that is lost in this otherwise plausible and effective setting is the extreme opposition of banquet room and Hellmouth. Without this kind of contrast, enough space must have been available to keep the door and Hellmouth decently separated, though here too a juxtaposition—the doors to Heaven and Hell side by side—may have proved as dramatically effective as their opposition.

The mention of available staging space brings our attention to the proportions of space needed for this play. As in the first three St. Nicholas plays, the *sedes* are all in the same part of the world, and there are no such journeys as are required in *Lazarus, The Pilgrim, The Conversion of St. Paul,* and *The Visit to the Sepulcher.* The present play could have been played in the width of the chancel of St. Martial at Limoges, a large abbey. If the staging were overextended laterally, the play would lose its compact quality. On the other hand, a crowded stage, with ten Maidens and a booth and Hellmouth, would have had an equally unhappy effect on the choreography of the play. With these reflections, one becomes aware that the dimensions of the stage area are perhaps more crucial to the success of this play than they are in other plays of the repertory, the latter being rather more flexible and adjustable in this respect.

A further possible staging pattern would be created by mounting the door to the banquet room on a curtained platform, with Hellmouth under the platform, and with steps leading up to the room level from one or both sides. The Merchants' booth would then be on another lower platform or at floor level. This arrangement for Hellmouth is rather typical of the staging of the later, craft cycle plays, which may well have learned their staging techniques from plays of the Latin repertory. The width required for this pattern of staging *The Wise and Foolish Maidens* is even less than for that suggested above.

To make a more accurate inference as to how the medieval producer staged the play, one would need more information about the building in which it was staged. Unfortunately St. Martin's of Limoges was demolished in the eighteenth century. Presumably the play was performed somewhere in that monastic church, but there is nothing in the playscript or elsewhere to locate the performance in any particular area of that church. In this connection we should note that the requisite area of the adjoining script of *The Procession of the Prophets,* in the Limoges manuscript, requires no more space than the most compressed staging we can adduce for *The Wise and Foolish Maidens,* and there is therefore a possibility that both were played in the same section of the building and may have used the same platform or platforms, with the lower level of the tall platform covered for *The Procession of the Prophets.*

MAKEUP: BEARDS AND HAIRSTYLES

The Oil Merchants may have had beards, as in the St. Quentin version of *The Visit to the Sepulcher;* or the older Merchant could have been bearded, his younger apprentice clean shaven, as in the case of the Shepherds. The Bridegroom would have a trimmed short beard, much like those of Herod and of the Christus in other plays. See especially plate 49 for the beard of the Sponsus. Gabriel, as usual, is clean shaven. The Demons wore full masks, which took care of their makeup requirements. For a twelfth-century illustration of such masks, see plate 50.

The hairstyles of the maidens do not appear to reflect much individuality. In nearly every twelfth- and thirteenth-century illustration the Maidens' hair is at least shoulder-length and parted in the middle (e.g., plates 46, 47). The parting is apparently not restricted to maidens but was the fashion for all throughout the period, and even male angels and Christ are so depicted (see plate 19). If choirboys played the Maidens, wigs would have been necessary, the pictorial evidence being against the Maidens wearing veils.

LIGHTING

Strong warm lighting through the banquet room door, possibly by means of a candelabrum on the banquet table, and a fiery red light through Hellmouth would have been theatrically desirable, whether or not a twelfth-century producer would or could contrive them. The lighting for the area in front of the set-pieces would have been somewhat less brilliant, and would have allowed the lighted lamps of the Wise Maidens to make an interesting pattern as the Maidens moved and gestured. A crown light over the door of the banquet room would have been effective in inducing the feeling that a sumptuous room is within. The Merchants' booth could have been lighted merely with small oil lamps, unobtrusively lighted by the Merchants only a few moments before attention was called to them by the Wise Maidens.

SOUND EFFECTS

High pitched bells from off stage, or hand cymbals played by the Maidens, and the low drum-rumble of thunder inside Hellmouth for the entrance of the Demons and their departure with the Foolish Maidens, would have been desirable sound effects for this play. The entrances of Gabriel and of the Bridegroom may have been accompanied by short runs on a medieval horn, to take a suggestion from the later Tudor sounding of tuckets for royal entrances. Gabriel may himself have blown the horn at his entrance.

The Three Daughters

(See above, pp. 197–211)

COSTUMES

THERE are no particular problems with costumes for *The Three Daughters,* but attention is called to some features. The blanket over the Father should be considered a part of his costume. He holds it around himself as he rises from the bed, and the Daughter fastens it quickly around his waist. He is going to prostrate himself at the feet of St. Nicholas, and must not in this activity expose himself, even though he would properly have a loincloth underneath.

The design of the episcopal costume for St. Nicholas is best taken from the Winchester illustration (plate 55), in which the full regalia is specified. The mitre is not the later high-peaked model but is much flatter and worn with the points left and right. Except for the Father, all characters in this play wear shoes.

The Three Daughters wear either light veils or fillets, as has been remarked above; the trimming of their tunics is highly elaborate, and the sleeves are wide. One of the Daughters, presumably the Third, wears a large amulet. The costume designs of plates 51–53 are too thoroughly fourteenth-century to be useful in this twelfth-century play. The Winchester font (plate 55) is one of the few extant portrayals of this subject dating from the period of the plays.

The Suitors may have shared a single costume if the three actors had similar measurements. There is time after the exit of one Suitor for him to remove his tunic and mantle, and for the next Suitor to put them on before he is due on stage. The reverse in costuming is equally possible. If one actor played all three suitors, he may have worn a different colored mantle for each appearance. Either the actor or the costume, that is, would be varied for each appearance of a Suitor.

PROPERTIES AND FURNISHINGS

St. Nicholas's crosier is clearly illustrated on the Winchester font (plate 55), though the thickness of the staff is a little out of proportion to the man. This illustration also shows the construction and decoration of the crook of the crosier, as does plate 56. The bags of gold are the size of a large apple, and presumably are made of tooled leather or heavy, embroidered cloth. They have drawstrings at the top. The coins they contain are never visible in the play, but there should be a clinking sound as the bags hit the floor. At least thirty such bags, with drawstrings, appear to be illustrated in the frame of plate 52.

All three Suitors may be provided with falcons, though only one is necessary as a property since the Three Suitors appear separately. While there are some exquisite medieval sculptures of birds,[1] they were usually firmly attached to their bases, and the medieval producer would have found less difficulty and more realism in borrowing a falcon in the neighborhood. A modern temptation would be to substitute a pigeon, but this would socially downgrade the Suitors. Only a peasant would bring his intended such a plebian bird. The technique of carrying a falcon, tied to the wrist, is explained in the many books of falconry.

The proper style of bed is illustrated in plates 53 and 54, where it appears to be a kind of chaise-lounge. Details of other furnishings in the room may be identified from the miniature in the Carmelite Missal (plate 51), whose modern editor lists its contents: "a low wooden stand at the foot of the bed, containing an empty candlestick of blue-grey (pewter?); a shelf under the window contains a ewer (also of pewter?)."[2] Ambrogio Lorenzetti's pictorial narrative likewise shows a ewer on a shelf, as well as a table (plate 53). Both of these illustrations are fourteenth-century, when interest in genre detail developed. Earlier illustrations show no such interest, and one doubts that the original producer of *The Three Daughters* was more interested than they. In any event, the poverty of the Father would have been expressed in a comparatively bare room, with only a shelf, a ewer, an empty candlestick, and possibly a low wooden stand. If he has sold the shirt off his back, clothes being in a class with furniture for expense, he would have retained only such furnishings as were bare necessities.

STAGING AND THE DEFINITION OF ACTING AREAS

The type of staging the play requires was suggested in the discussion of characterizations and movements above. A main feature is the window.

[1] See, for example, Rorimer, *A Medieval Treasury,* plates 33 and 37.
[2] Margaret Rickert, *The Reconstructed Carmelite Missal: An English Manuscript of the Late XIV Century in the British Museum* (London, 1952), p. 113.

The house wall into which the window is built was slightly raked (as in plate 52) so that St. Nicholas would be visible to the audience through the window. The wall was probably a three-dimensional cross section, like the door-wall posited for *The Wise and Foolish Maidens.* The window is often portrayed as a kind of ticket window (plate 52), with a high sill which suggests that St. Nicholas ducked down below the sill to hide (plate 52). The audience was then able to see his approach to and departure from the window, and his exit upstage only a few feet away, as if the stage space outside were a narrow medieval alley (plate 53). The door, as remarked above, is imagined, and entrance to the room is gained around the downstage end of the wall. If the acting area were elevated, the one platform would be wide enough to contain the interior of the room but probably not the exterior alley. Wherever the stage platform was placed, a curtain across the back was probably used (as in plate 52).

In as many ways as possible, the decor of the set would have emphasized the number three, which seems to have been the design of the playwright. Whether by coincidence or influence, the artist of the "Prayer Book of Joanna of Naples" (plate 52) goes some distance in this direction, with intricate trefoils left and right, and three arches above. The latter are Gothic because the illustration is from the second half of the fourteenth century; less pointed Romanesque arches would be more consistent with the period of the play, in the style of the window arch, and in the style of the triple arch of the illustration of the scene in the "Queen Mary Psalter" (plate 54).

MAKEUP: BEARDS AND HAIRSTYLES

All men in this play are customarily bearded in illustrations of the subject. The Winchester font portrayal (plate 55) is of a variety of beards. The Suitor has a moustache and a neatly trimmed (and waxed?) short beard; Saint Nicholas has a beard only, it very slightly longer and curlier than the Suitor's; and the Father has both a moustache and a longer beard, which hangs in curls from his chin (plates 54, 55). In other illustrations (plates 52, 53) the Father and St. Nicholas are clean shaven, which may be an example of the flux of fashion in beards. The Winchester illustration is a more reliable guide because it is of the second half of the twelfth century, while the beardless characters are in illustrations from the fourteenth.

The same Winchester font is the best arbiter of hairstyle and headdress for the Three Daughters. It, as well as Lorenzetti's (plate 53), shows them with ornamented fillets. The fact that they are at home, and not visiting their ailing father, is better emphasized by their lack of veils, yet the fillets probably permitted them to go out into the alley with their fiancés. The hairstyle of the Winchester Daughters under their fillets is much longer than that of their descendants, and is elaborately waved, as is that of the Suitor. It would appear that the Winchester Father, as befitted his age, is bald from forehead to top knot, and has hair to his shoulders on the sides (and back?). The Suitor's full head of hair is shorter and more wavy.

LIGHTING

There are no special requirements for lighting this play. Candelabra in the interior would probably conflict with the intended impression of poverty. We have noted that the *Carmelite Missal* illustration appropriately shows an empty candlestick. A crown light would be entirely inappropriate for the same reason.

SOUND EFFECTS

One use for bells in this play would be to announce the arrivals of the Suitors. Realistically, the Suitors will not fail to ring before walking into the Father's private house. The Daughters would have more possibility of movement if each in turn answered the doorbell and pantomimed the letting in of her Suitor. A chime bell could be used to underline the sound of the bag of gold hitting the floor. This bell, followed by another of lower pitch for the doorbell, might make an amusing bit of sound effect, and keep the wit of the play in the foreground.

The Three Clerks

(See above, pp. 213–219)

MOVEMENT AND GESTURE

A STAGE DIRECTION is badly needed in *The Three Clerks* to time the murders at a point preceding St. Nicholas's entrance. As the script now reads, there is nothing between the plotting and his entrance. A considerable amount of miming is obviously required: the Innkeeper finds his ax; he and the Old Woman move stealthily off into the Students' cubicle to see if the intended victims are asleep; the Innkeeper is heard hacking away at them; The Old Woman reappears and fearfully answers the knock of St. Nicholas at the door of the other room; the Innkeeper is heard cutting up the corpses as St. Nicholas speaks to the Old Woman. No doubt the actors at the abbey knew what they would do and needed no prompting from the score; for the same reason *The Three Daughters,* from the same manuscript, is almost as reticent about stage action, though the other two St. Nicholas plays in the "Fleury Playbook" are quite explicit.

Gestures in this play require little comment, since they will easily be melodramatic. The Innkeeper's gesture in plate 57, upper section, seems properly theatrical. The *orant* gesture of St. Nicholas in his prayer at the end of the play is traditional, and has been described above in the discussion of gestures in the *Lazarus.*

COSTUMES

The Students, as in plate 57, upper section, wear tunics and cloaks; two of them have hoods, while the third wears a round cap. The First Student has his hood down. They appear to be without shoes. Wallets are slung over their shoulders. In bed they wear nightcaps. The Innkeeper, in the same stained-glass window at Rouen, has a shorter tunic, as befits his class, and an apron to his knees. He is apparently bareheaded in this illustration and in that from Zedelghem (plate 58). The Old Woman wears a tunic and a long mantle.

St. Nicholas is in the same bishop's costume as in the other St. Nicholas plays. In some illustrations he carries a crosier (plates 56, 59); in others, none. Since literal realism had little bearing on these plays, the audience was able to identify him by his episcopal vestments—mitre, crosier, and all—but the Innkeeper and the Old Woman were not. The illustrations make this convention clear. Without their information we might suppose that since St. Nicholas tells the Old Woman that he is a "peregrinus" (pilgrim) he should be disguised like the Christus in *The Pilgrim.* We have observed that even in *The Pilgrim* the identity of the strange pilgrim, obvious because of the cross-mark on his pilgrim's pouch, is lost on the Disciples but not on the audience.

PROPERTIES AND FURNISHINGS

The weapon wielded by the Innkeeper is called a sword ("gladium") in the text of the play, and without the advice of the illustrations we might not have known to avoid the inappropriate sword and to supply an ax.[1] The Old Woman's telling her husband "Evagines vero iam gladium" (Draw now in good sooth thy sword) seems therefore to have been intended by the playwright as a humorous parody of chivalric ideals, and at the same time shows the Old Woman's effort to embolden her weak old husband. The innkeeper's ax has a much longer handle than one would expect. The Rouen Cathedral illustration (plate 57, top) shows his ax hung through his belt like a sword. The minimum length, as in the Besançon *Psalter,*[2] is at least two feet. The ax head flares to the cutting edge, as in plates 57, 58.

The Students' wallets ("marsupia") are leather pouches, the size of those carried by the pilgrims in the play of that title (plate 19). The First Student carries a plain staff (plate 57, top).

The furnishings of the main room of the inn are not portrayed by artists of the period, but we know from St. Nicholas's request for supper that there is a table, and we may borrow one from the inn at Emmaus (plates 24, 25), covering it with less elegant material. The table is not

[1] Pictorial evidence similarly shows the Angel's "gladium" in the *Daniel* as a lion-tamer's instrument, not a sword. The word is probably best translated as "blade" and thus applies to any sharp instrument.

[2] Besançon, Bibliothèque Municipale, MS 54, fol. 10 recto.

set, though an empty bowl or flagon of wine could have been on the table to indicate its purpose and to prepare for St. Nicholas's request. A single rough bench would probably have been alongside the table, and perhaps another along the wall opposite the common partition between the main room and the cubicle. The basket or large bowl which the Old Woman takes to the cubicle may have been in a corner. A basket would have been better if she were also to carry a candle, as suggested below.

STAGING AND THE DEFINITION OF ACTING AREAS

The overall requirements for the stage are somewhat like those for *The Three Daughters,* with one full-sized room space and one adjoining narrow space. There was a doorway to the street that ran along beside or in front of the stage platform (as in plate 57, top), with a practical door. A faded drape over the archway to the cubicle would have been helpful to action in that area. The effect of these structures was certainly dark, dirty, and sinister, with perhaps more attention to naturalistic detail because of the documentary nature of the play.

MAKEUP: BEARDS AND HAIRSTYLES

Neither the Innkeeper nor the Students are bearded; St. Nicholas is the only one who wears a beard, and he may also have a moustache (plates 55, 59). The hair of the Innkeeper and of the Students is for some reason cut rather shorter than usual in the period (plates 57, 58). The Old Woman's hair, at least in the Zedelghem illustration, is plaited and almost waist length.

LIGHTING

A candlestick with a lighted candle would have been effective for the Innkeeper to carry to the door when the Students arrive, and to place at the table when they enter. He may also have given them a candle, in a stick, to light their way to bed in the cubicle. The Old Woman may later have picked up the candlestick from the table in the main room and held it for the Innkeeper while he murdered the Students. The conjectured use of candles in this fashion would contribute to the atmosphere of mystery and murder.

SOUND EFFECTS

There may well have been a bell on the post of the doorway from street to main room, for the Students and St. Nicholas to use, as the visitors do in *The Three Daughters*.

The Image of St. Nicholas

(See above, pp. 221–228)

COSTUMES

THE costume for the Jew in *The Image of St. Nicholas* is rather clearly and typically delineated in the Rouen example (plate 60). His conical hat is evident also in the Cologne picture of him sleeping.

The Robbers' costumes are less clearly exhibited in the Cologne fresco (plate 61). They are wearing below-knee-length tunics with long sleeves, waist-length sleeveless shirts over the tunics, and dark, pointed hoods, somewhat like the hoods of the Shepherds in the play of that title (plates 26, 27).

St. Nicholas's costume has been described before in discussion of costumes for *The Three Daughters* and *The Three Clerks*. The illustrations of his appearance in *The Image* do not add anything, though they confirm the general outlines, including the presence of the crosier (plates 56, 60, 61).

PROPERTIES AND FURNISHINGS

The treasure chest is large and heavy, so heavy that the Robbers decide to carry off its contents rather than to lift it and lug it. In part the weight is that of the contents, but the dimensions as depicted in plates 60 and 61 are sufficient to give the Robbers pause. In effect the chest is a secular reliquary, the lid often shown peaked like the roof of a house, and the whole structure being elaborately ornamented (plate 60). Perhaps the peaked lid was the idea of the monastic artist at Rouen, whose conception of a treasure chest was the kind to be seen in the cathedral treasury in the crypt. It is even possible that the medieval producer of the play actually borrowed a reliquary from the crypt, rather than constructing a theatrical chest. The artist of the Cologne fresco, on the other hand, shows a more secular but no less heavy chest, with panelling, legs, and a flat lid. In either case, the chest must have been handsomely decorated, to suggest the wealth within. The lid would undoubtedly have been hinged, not loose as the Cologne artist has it, perhaps influenced by illustrations of the Easter sarcophagus. It was essential that the chest show that the Jew was leaving it unlocked, which means that the hinges of the lid would have been upstage, the hasp and pin large and visible to the audience.

The contents of the chest are more than bags of gold; the Jew and St. Nicholas also mention silver and clothes (ll. 98, 124). The Cologne artist shows a large chalice, presumably of gold, and there may have been heavy gold chains, amulets, and the like. Mombritius's literary version of the legend mentions "aurum, argentum, vestes, et caetera" (gold, silver, clothes, and so forth).[1] The Robbers load the contents of the chest into large sacks, which are carried over the shoulder, as in plate 61. They are unloading their sacks when St. Nicholas catches up with them. It would appear that one of the Robbers in this illustration is, on request, giving over to St. Nicholas an apple-shaped bag of gold similar to those used in *The Three Daughters.*

The image in the Cologne fresco (plate 61) is of the size and shape of a nineteenth-century tombstone—Mombritius calls it a "tabula" (tablet)—probably made of wood and elaborately painted with a good likeness of the actor of St. Nicholas in his episcopal regalia and nimbus. This likeness is essential to the double image conjecturally produced in the last scene, and is in any case important for the audience to compare with the real St. Nicholas when he appears at the hide-out of the Robbers. The niche in which the image is customarily kept by the Jew must of course have been of the proper size, providing an architectural frame (plate 60).

If the Jew were to faint or to fall asleep exhausted by his rage, he would have been provided a couch to fall on. A person of his means would not sleep on the floor, and he is better seen by the audience if he is somewhat elevated, as in plates 34 and 61. He did not need a blanket over him, and the illustrations show none.

The furnishings of the remainder of the Jew's room were probably not portrayed on stage, as long as the draperies at back and sides of the *sedes* were rich and full, to contrast with the tawdry hangings of the Robbers' bleak room. Other than the hand properties described above, the Robbers' hideout needed only a plain bench to accomodate some of the Robbers or their loot.

[1] As reproduced by Young, II, 494.

MAKEUP: BEARDS AND HAIRSTYLES

The Jew would have had a beard, in accordance with Hilarius's name for him and with most illustrations (e.g., plates 60, 61). He is dark and swarthy, and his beard and moustache would be as luxuriant as Shylock's, of whom the Jew is a direct ancestor. In the Cologne illustration (plate 61) two of the Robbers are apparently bearded (their hoods do not cover their chins) and one is clean shaven. St. Nicholas's beard has been described in connection with *The Three Daughters* and *The Three Clerks*.

LIGHTING

At the end of the Jew's lament he says that night has literally come upon him. When the Robbers returned the loot, without a sound, they may have brought a lantern along and, in their haste to leave, forgotten to take it with them. This would have simulated a building up of the light level for the last scene, when the Jew awakens, sees the returned treasure, and rejoices.

SOUND EFFECTS

The only opportunity for bells is to back up the Jew's final "Gaudeamus" item.

The Son of Getron

(See above, pp. 229–239)

MAKEUP: BEARDS AND HAIRSTYLES

KING MARMORINUS in *The Son of Getron* is a type of King Herod, and may have had the same well-trimmed beard. Getron, as a parallel with Simon in the *Lazarus,* had a similar beard. There would have been some variation in beards, or no beards at all, for the three officers (see plate 64). The Soldiers would not need beards because of their chain mail helmets. St. Nicholas would be bearded as in the other miracle plays.

The four women in the play wear veils throughout, even Euphrosina in her own house, unless there she removed hers and hurriedly replaced it when she rushed out to the Gates to embrace her son at the end of the play. The hair of all women in the twelfth century was customarily long.

LIGHTING

If there was a crown light for the Court scene, in imitation of the *Herod* court scene, there might have been crown lights as well for the Church scene and for Getron's expensive house. King Marmorinus's throne is required by the stage directions to be elevated, as in plates 36 and 67, and may have been too high to permit a crown light in the proper relation to the Court area, though the Echternach illustration of the *Herod* scene contrives both (plate 32).

The stage direction for the first Church scene calls for a high service to be in progress there when King Marmorinus's Soldiers attack and carry off the Boy. Lighted candelabra, to be blown out during the attack, might have created this sense of religious celebration and would have served likewise to contrast the next church scene, Euphrosina's lament, which would properly have been less brilliantly lit.

SOUND EFFECTS

Drums may have been an accessory to the Soldiers' pantomimed march
on the Church (Melody A seems distinctly a marching song), and there
may have been a clash or two of cymbals during the attack and the
resultant confusion and flight of the Congregation, Clergy, and Choir.

Inasmuch as the entire score of the play is in verse and therefore mensuralized, a similar version of the *Copiosae Karitatis* antiphon seems more
appropriate than a plainchant alternative. The manuscript source for the
transcription that follows is a twelfth-century versified *Historia,* or liturgical office of St. Nicholas. The *incipit* given in the Fleury *Son of Getron*
is a variant of the opening of this piece.

Copiosae Karitatis

Bibliothèque Nationale MS Latin 12044, fol. 224 v.

CHOIR AND CAST: Transcribed by Fletcher Collins, Jr.

The Play of the Annunciation

(See above, pp. 257–269)

COSTUMES

GABRIEL'S costume has been described in connection with his appearance in *The Visit to the Sepulcher, The Shepherds,* and *The Wise and Foolish Maidens.* The Tuscan relief (plate 68) does not adequately show the details of his dress.

The priest Zacharias, though retired, probably still wore an ecclesiastical costume. It would, however, have been untrimmed, without amice or shoes.

Mary and Elizabeth wore the same costume as the Marys in *The Visit to the Sepulcher* and *The Lament of Mary,* except for the heavy veils. The Virgin would wear her Mary blue, and the colors in Elizabeth's costume would presumably have been darker than those in Mary's, for Elizabeth is "well-stricken in years."

Joseph, also much older than Mary, wears a dark tunic and no shoes in most contemporary illustrations of the Nativity.

MAKEUP: BEARDS AND HAIRSTYLES

Since the two women of the play are at home at the opening of the play, they would then have been bare headed, their hair styled as in other plays of the repertory. Elizabeth's hair would have been greyed to indicate her advanced age, and of course both actors of these roles would have had to be wigged. Mary would have thrown a veil over her head before she left her platform to go to Juda.

In the illustrations Joseph and Zacharias are usually bearded. The *Carmina Burana* has Joseph in a "prolixa barba." Zacharias's beard is a lighter grey than Elizabeth's hair, Joseph's beard a darker grey. Gabriel's hair is usually filleted and shoulder-length. The Tuscan relief (plate 68) shows his hair somewhat longer.

LIGHTING

The processions customarily involved lighted tapers. Gabriel's staff was probably not illuminated until he got inside the cathedral.

SOUND EFFECTS

Processions usually required hand bells. If Gabriel was to make a spectacular appearance to Mary, a strike of cymbals may have emphasized his entrance.

Appendix

Index

APPENDIX

The Practical Repertory of Medieval Church Music-Drama, with Manuscript Locations

English Title	Latin Title	Manuscript Location
The Visit to the Sepulcher	*Visitatio Sepulchri*	Orléans, Bibliothèque de la Ville, MS 201, pp. 220–25.
The Visit to the Sepulcher	*Visitatio Sepulchri*	St. Quentin, Bibliothèque de la Ville, MS 86, pp. 609–25.
The Visit to the Sepulcher	*Visitatio Sepulchri*	Tours, Bibliothèque de la Ville, MS 927, fols. 1^r–8^v.
The Lament of Mary	*Planctus Mariae*	Cividale, Museo Archeologico Nazionale, MS CI, fols. 74^r–76^v.
The Pilgrim	*Peregrinus*	Paris, Bibliothèque Nationale, Nouvelles Acquisitions, MS Latin 1064, fols. 8^r–11^v.
The Shepherds	*Officium Pastorum*	Paris, Bibliothèque Nationale, MS Latin 904, fols. 11^v–14^r.
The Play of Herod, *with* The Slaughter Of The Innocents	*Ordo ad Representandum Herodem, with Ad Interfectionem Puerorum*	Orléans, MS 201, pp. 205–20.
The Procession of The Prophets	*Ordo Prophetarum*	Paris, Bibliothèque Nationale, MS Latin 1139, fols. 55^v–58^r.

English Title	Latin Title	Manuscript Location
The Raising of Lazarus	*Resuscitatio Lazari*	Orléans, MS 201, pp. 233–43.
The Conversion of St. Paul	*Conversio Beati Pauli*	Orléans, MS 201, pp. 230–33.
The Wise and Foolish Maidens	*Sponsus*	Paris, Bibliothèque Nationale, MS Latin 1139, fols. 53^r–55^v.
The Three Daughters	*Tres Filiae*	Orléans, MS 201, pp. 176–82.
The Three Clerks	*Tres Clerici*	Orléans, MS 201, pp. 183–87.
The Image of St. Nicholas	*Iconia Sancti Nicolai*	Orléans, MS 201, pp. 188–96.
The Son of Getron	*Filius Getronis*	Orléans, MS 201, pp. 196–205.
The Play of Daniel	*Danielis Ludus*	London, British Museum, MS Edgerton 2615, fols. 95^r–108^r.
The Play of the Annunciation	*In Annunciatione Beatae Mariae Virginis Representatio*	Padua, Biblioteca Capitale, MS C. 56, fols. 35^v–38^r.
The Purification	*Purificatio*	Padua, MS C. 56, fols. 14^r–16^v.

Index

*The Production of
Medieval Church Music-Drama*

was composed, printed, and bound by
Kingsport Press, Inc., Kingsport, Tennessee.
The types are Garamond and Garamont,
and the paper is Mohawk Superfine.
Design is by Edward G. Foss.